Radical Realism, Autofictional Narratives and the Reinvention of the Novel

Fiona J. Doloughan

ANTHEM PRESS

Anthem Press
An imprint of Wimbledon Publishing Company
www.anthempress.com

This edition first published in UK and USA 2025
by ANTHEM PRESS
75–76 Blackfriars Road, London SE1 8HA, UK
or PO Box 9779, London SW19 7ZG, UK
and
244 Madison Ave #116, New York, NY 10016, USA

First published in the UK and USA by Anthem Press in 2023

© 2025 Fiona J. Doloughan

The author asserts the moral right to be identified as the author of this work.

All rights reserved. Without limiting the rights under copyright reserved above,
no part of this publication may be reproduced, stored or introduced
into a retrieval system, or transmitted, in any form or by any means
(electronic, mechanical, photocopying, recording or otherwise),
without the prior written permission of both the copyright
owner and the above publisher of this book.

British Library Cataloguing-in-Publication Data
A catalogue record for this book is available from the British Library.

Library of Congress Control Number: 2025937242

ISBN-13: 978-1-83999-637-5 (Pbk)
ISBN-10: 1-83999-637-4 (Pbk)

This title is also available as an e-book.

DEDICATION

This book is dedicated to the memory of my mother,
Phyllis Emmeline Doloughan (1931–2019).

CONTENTS

Preface		vii
Acknowledgements		xi
1.	Introduction	1
2.	Theoretical and Critical Concerns: Key Terms and Arguments	19
3.	The Anatomy of a Writer: Karl Ove Knausgaard's *My Struggle*	41
4.	Companion Pieces: Jeanette Winterson's *Why Be Happy When You Could Be Normal?* in Relation to *Oranges Are Not the Only Fruit*	71
5.	A Cross-Cultural Memoir: Xiaolu Guo's *Once Upon a Time in the East*	101
6.	Rachel Cusk's Search for New Forms: Self-Projection and Refraction in Fiction and Non-Fiction	125
7.	Conclusion	147
References		157
Index		167

PREFACE

The origins of this book are hybrid in that they reside both in my professional and personal history. As an academic of some thirty years standing, my interest in the development of the novel form has not waned, even if it has taken shape in different contexts. From a PhD thesis in 1989 on conceptions of realism in the nineteenth- and early twentieth-century French and English novels via two monographs on aspects of contemporary narrative in 2011 and 2016, it seems in some ways that I have come full circle in rethinking relationships between and among social context, writerly aims at a particular historical juncture, and readerly and critical responses to a body of literature selected as much for the questions posed and reactions elicited as for the tentative answers given. Yet there are notable differences between then (1989) and now (2022), not least my current focus on very recent literature and on emerging trends, rather than on an established set of canonical works and their critical contexts.

There are both positive and negative aspects to this change of emphasis: firstly, my background in Comparative Literature and prior engagement with literature in France and England from 1840–1940 means that I am not coming to late twentieth- and early twenty-first-century literature as a novice but with some knowledge of preceding texts and contexts; it has also permitted some critical reading in French as well as English. Arguably, the downside is that in focussing on recent contexts and trends, there is a risk that what is emergent and exciting in the present moment is already old news by the time my monograph reaches its audience and/or that writerly and readerly concerns have moved on. Yet, as I hope will become apparent, some of the key notions and terms in the book would seem, if anything, to be generating increasing interest. Indeed, in the time it has taken to write this book, there have been a number of publications focussed on autofiction and the autofictional, most recently an edited volume by Alexandra Effe and Hannie Lawlor entitled *The Autofictional: Approaches, Affordances, Forms* (2022) published by Palgrave Macmillan. While the conjunction of 'radical' and 'realism' is less frequent, there has nevertheless been acknowledgement of what Martina Wagner Egelhaaf (2022, 28) calls 'a new need for the real' and what David Shields (2011) famously called a 'reality hunger'.

Yet it would be fair to say that my interest in considering a cluster of questions around the value of literature today, the rise of the memoir and increased interrogation of the novel form in the twenty-first century, and particularly my selection of books for inclusion, has a personal as well as professional dimension. The personal dimension relates to the loss of my father in 2015 and a chance encounter with a paperback entitled *A Death in the Family*, a work which I quickly realized to be the first work in translation of a series called *My Struggle* written originally in Norwegian by author Karl Ove Knausgaard, about whom I began to hear and read more. The book gripped me and, like Zadie Smith, I felt I needed my Knausgaardian 'fix' on a regular basis. The questions raised in the course of *Min Kamp* (*My Struggle*) seemed particularly pertinent at a number of levels, since Knausgaard appeared to use a form of the novel, one he called a 'non-fictional novel', to pose serious questions about narrator Karl Ove's relationship to the world around him and specifically about his sense of self as it developed over time and in relation to his family circumstances. In focussing on what is involved in the construction of a self through writing and insisting on depicting the humdrum and quotidian alongside the dramas of family life, he seemed to have touched a nerve in terms of the potential of writing to be disruptive, even harmful, as well as creative and therapeutic; and in interrogating 'real' rather than 'fictional' lives in an apparently uncensored way, his work proved controversial with detractors as well as adherents debating the ethics of disclosure and where the boundaries and limits between art and life may lie.

Another writer who generated controversy around writing from life was Rachel Cusk but rather than dwell on reception of her trilogy of memoirs, I was drawn to the critical success of her 'Outline' trilogy and her experiments with a narrator who 'appears only in her interaction with others' (James 2022, 50), yet whose trajectory and phase of life is consistent with that of author Rachel Cusk. Cusk, like Knausgaard, has been vocal in her rejection of fabrication and conventional narrative arcs in fiction and has indicated her preference for the philosophical and poetical. While she has much in common with Knausgaard, in terms of her rejection of conventional forms of the novel, it was also the differences which interested me, particularly as Cusk's 'Outline' trilogy is as interested in self-construction, and constructions of the 'real' as is Knausgaard but she has greater focus, not surprisingly perhaps, on the female experience and the extent to which gender politics and structural and political realities circumscribe it.

This, then, was the start but by no means the end of a somewhat tricky journey, given the advent of Coronavirus which has hit everyone to a greater or lesser extent. The closure of libraries and the imposition of travel restrictions at the height of the pandemic meant long periods reading online, and few opportunities for face-to-face interactions at national and international conferences. All this to say that the monograph was written in circumstances that were far from ideal. Yet, I hope that despite this, it will prove of value and interest to colleagues, fellow academics, writers, critics, and anyone interested in the future of literature.

ACKNOWLEDGEMENTS

While a single-authored monograph may feel like an individual enterprise, there are inevitably people other than the author involved in its production. My sincere thanks go to the anonymous peer reviewers whose insightful comments gave me pause while I reflected on all, and acted on many, of their well-intentioned suggestions. Any remaining defects are of course my own.

As I was working on the monograph during a period of lockdown, I was unable to travel to the US to view Rachel Cusk's papers deposited at the Harry Ransom Center, University of Texas at Austin. However, during that period, the Harry Ransom Center generously waived fees in respect of researcher requests for digital access via an onsite librarian to some of the Cusk materials. In this regard, I wish to thank especially Kristen Wilson for her help in forwarding digital copies of materials of possible interest from the inventory that I scrutinized.

To Anthem Press for giving me the opportunity to develop my proposal and for their patience in awaiting the full draft of the revised manuscript, I also extend my thanks. Thanks are due, too, to the production and editorial teams for ensuring delivery of the book I wished to see.

I also owe a debt of gratitude to two Heads of Department, namely Prof. Suman Gupta and Prof. Delia da Sousa Correa, who understood both what I was trying to do and why it was taking me so long. I wish to acknowledge their patience and encouragement.

Finally, to my partner and fellow academic, Prof. Regine Hampel, thank you not only for reading my initial chapters and making some useful suggestions but also for your help with formatting of the manuscript. Most of all, thank you for accepting with grace the fact that until I had completed the manuscript, my mind would often be elsewhere!

Chapter 1

INTRODUCTION

1.1 Literary Context

While there have been periodic intimations of the death of the novel in the twentieth century, the first two decades of the twentieth-first century have seen an intensification of debates around the health, value and function of the novel. These debates have engaged erstwhile novelists as well as critics, reviewers and academics, as they discuss the novel's merits in terms of its ability to respond to changing times, adapt to competition from other media and representational forms and continue to respond meaningfully to aspects of the social world. Questions of both form and function arise in these discussions as writers and critics wrestle with the novel's potential for change in relation to what they see as its evolutionary and critical purposes at a time of crisis and transformation or what one academic calls 'a period of extreme media and technological change' (Hutton 2018, 193). Peter Boxall's *The Value of the Novel* (2015) represents an impassioned intervention in favour of the novel's continued purposefulness in times of uncertainty, 'a kind of mechanism for coping with change' (Jeffery 2017, 8), and a signal that while the death of the novel has oft been foretold, there does not yet appear to be a corpse in sight.

The question of why the novel matters (or fails to matter) underpins discussion of both its presumed survival and, indeed, its apparent demise. For some, it is the inherent flexibility and variety of works coexisting under the 'novel' label that is evidence not of generic vagueness or slipperiness but of the novel's essential multivalence, hybridity and vitality. For others, new technologies and social media risk calling into question a focus on an imagined or mimetic world realized through the medium of words, rather than images; they have the potential to shift ways of engaging with or reacting to reality that are seemingly more real or more immersive than the virtual representations of fiction. Consequently, the question of what the novel can do – what its affordances are – relative to other genres and media has come back into the frame, as have questions of credibility, relevance and truthfulness in relation to deployment of particular genres and modes of representation.

In what has been termed the post-truth age, questions are being asked even by novelists themselves about the legitimacy and effectiveness of invention and fictionalized narratives at a time when fakery, fabrication and lies seem to be ubiquitous and pose a potential threat to a search for knowledge, truth, enlightenment and self-understanding.

Equally, in terms of theorization of the novel, conventional assumptions about its function, status and modus operandi have come under renewed scrutiny, with increasing interrogation of the notion that narrative fiction is synonymous with the novel. Furthermore, there has been engagement on the part of some theorists of narrative with the idea of fictionality as a mode rather than as a constitutive property of the novel genre *per se* (Nielsen et al. 2015). This is in recognition of the fact that while novels may be designed to project possible worlds, some of which may aim to mirror aspects of the actual or real world, the same techniques of fictionalization can, and often are, applied to narratives that stem from a more 'factual' basis. In other words, narratives, in the sense of stories told by someone (a narrator) to someone else (a narratee), in which characters are set against a particular temporal and spatial backdrop, can be fictionally or factually orientated, at a global as well as local level. In many cases, these different narrative orientations deploy similar techniques to project their story and to create interest and investment in the storyworld. The idea, therefore, that there is an essential, rather than a pragmatic, rhetorical or contextually determined difference between fiction and non-fiction has been interrogated anew.

At the same time, the rise of the memoir and of auto/biographical narratives in the past few decades, alongside evidence of a 'non-fictional turn' (Nixon 2012, 30), considered 'part of a broader rise in the cultural industrialization of the real – or at least the real's aura' (30) is yet another indication of shifting preferences and changing evaluations of the affordances of different genres and modes and of a reinvestment, by many writers known for their novelistic invention, in matters and states of affairs closer to home and to their everyday reality. While the history of the novel may be read as tracing differing degrees of investment in representation of the worlds of actuality and of fantasy, of romance and reality, recent debates about the function and value not just of the novel in particular but indeed of literature in general must be set against the backdrop of a particular cultural climate, one in which a certain lassitude with the seeming ubiquity of fiction has emerged and with it a renewed desire to get to grips with the realities of human experience, however understood, in a language fit for the purpose. While such a quest might appear retrograde and naïve in the wake of poststructuralist insights about the role of language in constraining, if not directing thought, and of the challenges inherent in any commitment to reality or truth, it can also be viewed as a rejection of artifice and language games, a challenge to the narrativization of experience, and a desire to break through the fourth wall. In this sense, it is possible to speak not just of a reality hunger (Shields 2011) but, I would argue, of a radical realism.

As an artistic and literary project, realism has a long and complex history and one that I do not intend to rehearse in detail, given my focus on the work of four contemporary writers, each of whom, in different ways, and to varying extents, has produced work that crosses or extends generic boundaries, and is self-reflexive and philosophical, interrogating modes of literary production and what it means to write in the twenty-first century. For present, introductory purposes, it is sufficient to note that the writers on whom I concentrate – about whom more presently – are all conscious of the complexities and limitations of representation in writing and are the products of a broadly modernist sensibility attuned to the critical, linguistic and philosophical revolutions underpinning the late twentieth and early twenty-first centuries. In other words, in situating and discussing the work of Karl Ove Knausgaard, Rachel Cusk, Jeanette Winterson and Xiaolu Guo, it will be important to bear in mind the general literary and cultural contexts underpinning their work as well as understanding the extent to which their individual literary histories and works produced can be seen to contribute to or undercut more general trends in terms of novelistic renewal, rejection, reinvention and/or transformation.

The question of my selection of, and focus on, these four writers may seem somewhat arbitrary. There is, however, a logic to their inclusion. Knausgaard and Cusk have both been vocal in their comments rejecting 'conventional' narrative forms that place a premium on plotting and characterization and privilege 'showing' over 'telling'. Moreover, as writers engaging with aspects of the world around them and their place as interrogative subjects in it, they have turned away from the veil of fiction to explore moments from their own lives with a view to making sense of their experience against the backdrop of the cultures, institutions and systems with which they inevitably interact. While their trajectories are not the same, they overlap and complement one another in terms of a desire to get closer to the so-called reality of things and to create a literature that engages with material from real life and/or points to the limitations and illusions that necessarily permeate pursuit of the real. While very much of the same generation, Knausgaard and Cusk do of course come from different cultures and write in different languages. Yet in terms of their literary preoccupations, as will be seen, they have quite a bit in common and are both internationally recognized big hitters on the world literary scene. In this sense, they constitute a useful pairing both for what they have in common and for the differences between them, differences that arguably pertain as much to questions of gender as of genre.

As a writer formed at a slightly earlier and different cultural moment – almost a decade separates Winterson from Knausgaard and Cusk – Winterson's inclusion might be seen to represent a challenge both to scepticism in relation to the novel and to a seeming rejection of narrative invention and fabrication. It must also be remembered that while Winterson is now part of the British literary establishment, it was not always so. In fact, her first semi-autobiographical novel caused a stir as did Winterson's early projection of herself as following in the footsteps of Virginia Woolf (Winterson 1995, 164). In many ways, Winterson, as a novelist who incorporated in her work both social critique and postmodernist experimentation, is a figure who spearheaded an interrogation of the possibilities and constraints of the novel form in relation to a postmodern generic blend of fact and fantasy, critique and speculation. Moreover, treatment of Winterson's memoir in relation to her first novel permits scrutiny of the conventions of generic form, both novel and memoir, and their persistent interrogation, as well as changing patterns of reception, over time. Like Cusk, Winterson is a writer conscious of the interplay of genre and gender.

While Knausgaard, Cusk and Winterson all write in a first or primary language, Guo is a translingual writer and film-maker, working predominantly now through the medium of English, though an English conscious of its translational genesis and movement and its comparative cultural interactions. Guo, like Winterson, though largely a writer of fiction, has also produced a memoir, reception of which has raised questions about cross-cultural writing, as well as reading, practices. In this sense, treatment of Guo's work permits consideration of translingual writing and extends the focus to an interrogation of cross-cultural deployment and reception of different genres in relation to issues of mode and media. This is important in terms of ensuring that ideas about trends in literature are formed, not simply relative to what is prevalent in English alone and/or in Anglophone cultures, but that issues of literary production and reception are interrogated via a broader set of linguistic and cultural contours.

If Guo's literary reach may not appear to extend as far as that of Knausgaard, Cusk or Winterson, it must be remembered that she is slightly younger as well as hailing from a different culture. (Guo was born in 1973 in China and was just 12 years old when Winterson was already publishing her first novel in the UK.) Yet while her English-language writing only began with publication of *A Concise Chinese-English Dictionary for Lovers* in 2007, her international reputation has developed and been consolidated very quickly with widespread recognition of her literary and intellectual talents in terms of literary prizes (e.g. Winner of the National Book Critics Circle Award for Autobiography, 2017) and prestigious international research fellowships (e.g. Columbia University). Indeed, a recent article proposes Guo as 'a world author' in recognition of her contribution to world literature (Shi 2021), an attribution that seems to me entirely merited.

With justification, then, it can be said that all four writers included in the present study are writers of international standing who have worked across genres, expanding their own repertoires in the process as well as stretching and enabling the realm of the possible more generally in genre terms. As a platform for signalling changes in the literary landscape in relation to modes of fictionality and their generic apprehension and exploitation, as well as in terms of a study of writing in the late twentieth and early twenty-first centuries, these writers both individually and collectively represent a kind of literary barometer that may tell us something about shifting patterns in, and perceptions of, literary culture today.

1.2 Motivations: Academic, Critical and Writerly

One of the motivations for writing this book was a sense that literature in the late twentieth and early twenty-first centuries has been assuming a new shape or, more precisely, that many writers have been rethinking their engagement with established literary forms and genres, and, in some cases, searching for an alternative to the so-called conventional novel. Arguably, of course, there is nothing conventional about the novel form as it emerged and developed over time: from Daniel Defoe's *Robinson Crusoe* (1719) or Miguel de Cervantes's *Don Quixote* (1605) to the present, via what many consider the novel's heyday in the long nineteenth century, its history and shape reflect transition and change in the wake of social, economic and technological developments, as well as responding to the aspirations and innovations of particular writers. Yet alongside the broader tendencies identified in histories of the novel, as it moved from the world of romance and adventure towards ever greater realism in its presentation of individualized protagonists, some more recent literary production can be seen to represent a reaction to the creation of a 'purely' fictional world and/or a motivated attempt to produce an illusion of reality in fictionalized form. While claims of the death of the novel are perhaps overstated, and in any case such claims tend to be cyclical (Boxall and Cheyette 2016), there is some evidence of a reality hunger (Shields 2011) and a desire on the part of many writers to bring into closer alignment life experiences and their depiction in a form that gets closer to the truth of that reality.

Such writerly dissatisfaction with prevailing novelistic norms and conventions reveals not only elements of the *Zeitgeist* in terms of perceived uses and abuses of 'fact' and 'fiction' more generally in the social, political and literary worlds, but also speaks to a feeling shared by some contemporary writers concerned that fiction has become a screen behind which writers (and readers) can hide, thus preventing them from getting to the truth and reality of experience (see, e.g., Zadie Smith's 2008 discussion of lyrical realism in 'Two Paths for the Novel'). So when successful novelists with an international reputation and readership, such as Rachel Cusk and Karl Ove Knausgaard, among others, seemingly turn their backs on invention and fabrication in favour of narrative forms more consonant with their real-life preoccupations, existential concerns and personal dilemmas, they give weight to a series of questions. These questions concern the status of fiction today, the value and shape of the novel, and the motivations of writers intent on reworking it, hybridizing it with other forms or jettisoning it altogether in favour of a more radically personal and/or seemingly documentary account of a life. To ask questions about what the novel can and cannot do, what it means to write a life, one's own or that of another, and to consider where the frontier between truth and fiction might lie (Lavocat 2016), are all issues with which writers like Knausgaard and Cusk, among others, have grappled and continue to do so.

Without some definition and contextualization, the terms of the title of the monograph might seem mere provocations rather than navigational parameters. They are intended as a kind of shorthand to encapsulate what are, in effect, quite complex, high-level and potentially shifting notions, fuller understanding of which it is my aim to explore in relation to the work and trajectory of specific authors, as well as in more general terms. What I do not intend to do is to rehearse a history of the novel, given the plethora of books that sketch this out in interesting and informative ways (see, e.g., Auerbach 2003 [1953], Lukács 1989 [1920], Watt 1963, Mazzoni 2017 [2011], among others). Rather I wish to focus on some of the parameters guiding recent debates about genre, and the distinguishing features of particular genres (novel, auto/biography, memoir, autofiction), their mode of existence (fictional, factual, referential, self-referential), purpose/s (aesthetic, ethical, critical, creative) and perceived status as truthful, fabular and realistic. In so doing, I wish to take account of the intentions and aspirations of the writers themselves, as producers of text, as well as of the commentaries and evaluations of the critics and reviewers who act as mediators and brokers of a work's textual reception.

The term 'radical realism' in the title of this book is one that I use to capture aspects of what appears to be motivating attempts on the part of some writers – Knausgaard is a prime example – to create work that engages with the 'stuff' of reality and the complex relationship between and among modes of perception, structures of feeling, writing and representation.

Without wishing to rehearse a whole history of realism in the novel, I will introduce the term in a subsequent section and flesh out my usage of the term in reference to Knausgaard's work in particular, in his determination to pursue a project across the six volumes of the *My Struggle* series that would allow him to treat with the same degree of writerly attention the apparent trivia of everyday life and the higher-order problems and vicissitudes of existence. In attempting to account for his struggle to become a writer, in the face of the challenges and constraints posed by everyday life and the strictures of family life, Knausgaard came into conflict with the views and perspectives of others, particularly around presentation of his father in his work *Min Kamp* (*My Struggle*). This resulted, as will be discussed later, in proposed legal challenges as well as ethical dilemmas. In this respect, radical realism points to the method adopted by Knausgaard in his determination to record life as he experienced it, regardless of the possible consequences, in a book originally published in Norway as a novel. This work has also been received and read differently (as memoir and as autofiction) across languages and cultures, and it is with its designation and reception that I will be primarily concerned, given that I am reading the work in English translation.

In Chapter 3, I will address more fully Knausgaard's avowed aims in writing the *My Struggle* series and examine them in relation both to the finished work in English translation and to its cross-cultural reception. But for the purposes of this introductory chapter, radical realism is an expression intended to capture Knausgaard's search for meaning in the world he inhabited and speaks to his desire to represent his experience of reality in all its complexity and in a way that remains truthful to aspects of his experience, even as he acknowledges the unreliability of memory and the challenges posed by the very act of writing, given the necessary gap between and among living, experiencing, reflecting and writing. Rather than continuing to explore through the veil of fiction his conflicted relationship with his father, Knausgaard decided just to write blindly, leaving behind his inner critic, 'to write without an audience, without readers, in a room on my own' (Knausgaard 2016b), and to try to recreate in all its particularity and concreteness his experience of life. Writer Ben Lerner (2014) also speaks of Knausgaard's 'radical inclusiveness' in terms of the degree of detail he incorporates in his account and characterizes *My Struggle* as making 'a bid to be co-extensive with a life'. What for some readers may simply be manic self-confession is for Knausgaard a sustained attempt to explore the factors shaping his identity, as he moves from childhood through adolescence to adulthood, reflect on the mediating role of memory in presentation of self and other, and consider what it means to write. The *My Struggle* series, as will be seen, is not a wholly linear narrative but rather a recursive and extremely detailed account of character-narrator Karl Ove's experience of the world he inhabits alongside reflections, speculations and commentaries on a range of political, social, personal and existential matters. It is neither a conventional work of fiction in terms of structure and plot nor is it self-evidently non-fictional in the sense that narrator Karl Ove, while bearing the same name as author Knausgaard, resembles an autofictional character, insofar as it is through a process of speedy and seemingly unreflective and unconsciously structured writing that he attempts to evade familiar narrative prescriptions and allow the writing about self to flow as freely as possible.

In discussing *My Struggle*, Knausgaard himself describes it as a 'an experiment in realistic prose' and a 'non-fiction novel' (Knausgaard 2016b). The latter, seemingly contradictory, epithet is in many ways in line with Knausgaard's consciousness of the effects of the writing process that cannot simply reproduce lived experience even as it attempts to narrow the gap between life as it is experienced and its representation. Even as he tries to evade the imposition of narrative structure and simply write, Knausgaard is aware of the difficulty in escaping narrative modes of organization and of avoiding the pull of specific scenes and dramas which, in their exposition, are inevitably layered and composite, rather than singular and discrete. As fellow writer Hari Kunzru (2014) puts it in a review of the first three volumes of *My Struggle*:

> The book is the record of someone trying and failing (failing better, as Beckett has it) to make an accurate representation of himself; the gap between the world and that representation, between the world and itself, is the space where all sorts of questions about truth and personal identity arise.

Knausgaard's malaise and sense of crisis – 'Just the thought of a fabricated character in a fabricated plot made me nauseous' (Knausgaard 2014b, 568) – took him away from the thinly veiled disguises adopted in fictional form in previous novels towards 'a first-person narrative about his life' (Kunzru 2014); he also moved away from reading fiction to reading dairies and essays, which he found more valuable in his quest for truth and authenticity. Abandoning what he saw as the ornate vestments of literature for writing about the banality of everyday life, he sought to 'make the world step out from the world', as Kunzru (2014) puts it, by which I understand him to be referring to Knausgaard's investment in a search for meaning as he sets down in writing memories from his childhood, youth and adulthood and lays out in inordinate detail scenes from his life, creating thereby a kind of thick description such that readers either become immersed in his world, identifying with his plight, or find it tedious and dull.

Knausgaard's work tends to draw strong reactions: while writers such as Zadie Smith and reviewers like James Wood were drawn into Knausgaard's world and could not wait to get more of it, others were less convinced of Knausgaard's literary genius, seeing *My Struggle* as monotonous, overly long and self-indulgent, 'a giant selfie, a 3,600-page blogologue', as writer and reviewer William Deresiewicz (2014) puts it. Another reviewer admits that 'Knausgaard has a knack for locating the drama that lurks within tedium' (Camp 2018), while for writer Ben Lerner (2014), Knausgaard's 'extremely – at times almost absurdly – detailed description' can be read as a kind of failure to differentiate between things or as a rejection of a hierarchy of value. Yet ultimately, Lerner (2014) sees *My Struggle* as 'the chronicle of Knausgaard turning his back on the genre of the novel', while Danish academic and critic, Claus Elholm Andersen (2018, 35) argues that Knausgaard is in fact simply 'taking to an extreme the biographical elements many novelists have included' in their work, thereby giving 'the genre of the novel a new relevance, a new vitality'.

Like Knausgaard, Canadian-born British writer, Rachel Cusk, has been vocal in her criticism of novels that are plot- and character-driven and invoke in readers a need to find out what happens next. As she puts it in an interview with Jennie McPhee at the New York Public Library (2 April 2019) on publication in the United States of *Kudos*, volume 3 of the 'Outline' Trilogy, she is struggling always to find the right form in which to construct aspects of the female experience and wanted on this occasion to turn the knowledge basis of narrative inside out. To understand what Cusk might mean by this, in terms of her rejection of a display of knowledge without apparent justification and her preference for attribution to an individual perspective, it is important to set her trilogy and so-called reinvention of the novel form in context. Cusk's trajectory and motivations as a writer, while, in some ways, similar to those of Knausgaard, nevertheless have some pertinent differences. Like Knausgaard, she was a well-regarded novelist who sought to be 'free of inventing stuff' (NYPL 2019) and went on to write a series of memoirs, some of which generated so much criticism and debate that she fell silent for a period following the publication of *Aftermath* (2012). This searingly honest and finely structured book about the effects of the break-up of her marriage and the fallout from it in terms of family life antagonized many and left its author publicly scarred and feeling that she needed to find an alternative way of voicing her concerns than through adversarial discourses. Interesting to note then that while Knausgaard's *My Struggle* provoked controversy and ethical dilemmas, the fact that it was originally published in Norway as a novel, rather than a memoir, may have softened the impact of its reception. For Cusk, the memoir label on works such as *A Life's Work* (2008) that speaks of her experience of motherhood and *Aftermath* (2012) on separation and divorce had the effect of drawing attention to the female voice and its owning of personal experience. Yet following this period of silence, Cusk, described by McPhee, applying words from Calvino, as a genreless writer, returned to the literary field with an almost universally admired novelistic trilogy, consisting of *Outline* (2014), *Transit* (2016) and *Kudos* (2018), a work whose female narrator is largely invisible, even as she recounts the stories of others.

Given the 'condemnation Cusk endured before the publication of her acclaimed trilogy', which 'had the hallmarks of scapegoating' (Maris 2019), the relationship between memoir series and novelistic trilogy in terms of visibility and voice is all the more interesting. Like Knausgaard, Cusk has been vocal in interview about her rejection of the conventional novel and the production of blatant fictions. She prefers these days, she says (Louisiana Channel 2019), to read works of philosophy and sometimes poetry, rather than fiction. In both cases, even if they have taken slightly different routes, as will be explored in later chapters, Knausgaard and Cusk are essentially writers who might be said to privilege forms of truth-telling over fabrication, to have rejected a view of creative writing that privileges showing over telling, and for whom life, particularly the life of the artist, provides an impetus to their work. In the Introduction to the 2008 edition of *A Life's Work: On Becoming a Mother,* Cusk writes: 'The relationship between literature and life is not fundamentally altered for the writer by the removal of the term 'fiction'' (Cusk 2008, 1), a statement that would seem to blur the distinctions between fiction and non-fiction, placing the emphasis on the writer's task in shaping the work. What is important is 'to impose a form' and use the writer's tools to chisel and sculpt the 'block of stone', which is the raw material presented to the writer. For Cusk, then, it is the relationship between form and matter that are of primary importance to the writer, not the fact of whether 'a thing is called fiction or fact' (1).

Cusk's remarks also suggest a high degree of both art and artifice in writing, regardless of how it is labelled in terms of fiction and non-fiction. What is of particular interest in her case is the almost universal acclaim heaped on her novelistic trilogy described in the *New Yorker* as 'a radical experiment in passivity' (Schwartz 2018), given narrator Faye's seeming lack of 'personal agency and narrative authority'. I say seeming because, in fact, Faye does become more visible across the series, and it must not be forgotten that in relaying and foregrounding the stories of others, narrator Faye, a kind of Cuskian alter ego, selects and shapes what she hears by putting it into language/writing it down. In addition, as Cusk has indicated in different terms across a number of interviews: 'I've always stayed very close to the line of my own life and I've never sort of made things up or been particularly interested in narrative arcs or fantasy of any kind' (Schwartz 2018).

So, while the 'Outline' Trilogy is in some ways an antidote to her memoir writing, given that Cusk is not writing in her own person but has created a character from whose perspective and in whose voice the reader sees and hears the world around her, Cusk's comment above helps align the novelistic trilogy with her series of memoirs insofar as she acknowledges that her work, regardless of generic categorization, does not stray very far from the outline of her own life. She also makes clear her preference for what is close to life or life-like, in a sense using her own experience as both subject and object. While Faye may not be Cusk, nevertheless their trajectories in terms of life stages and experiences across the trilogy are rather similar: Faye is, according to Cusk, 'indexed to my own experience but not me' (Maris 2019). Cusk sees Faye as a woman whose concept of reality has failed, something that might have been said of Cusk's own situation as narrated in *Aftermath* in particular. And to the extent that criticism of *A Life's Work* and *Aftermath* was linked to what some perceived as Cusk's self-absorption, heightened sense of injury and extreme honesty, Faye's passivity, lack of agency and deflection of attention away from herself may well be read as an equal and opposite reaction.

Indeed, both Knausgaard and Cusk have been accused of narcissism and both have questioned the value of fiction that fails to delve deep into the problems and vicissitudes of existence. Yet, as will be seen, their responses, while complementary and to an extent, overlapping, also depart in some details, not least in the question of length and the manner in which they have approached writing, with Knausgaard's *My Struggle* series a mammoth affair (approximately 3,600 pages) written quickly and apparently without much regard for structure and selection, though this is indeed debatable (see, e.g., Andersen 2018); Cusk's output, on the other hand, is more minimalist in terms of length and highly controlled in terms of style, whether this relates to her memoirs or to her novelistic trilogy. What both writers share is a deep commitment to their writing and to the kinds of truth about human existence literature can relay when it engages with equal earnestness with the routines of daily life and domesticity as well as with reflections on more philosophical matters. A review in the *New York Times* on publication of volume 2 of Cusk's 'Outline' Trilogy, for example, sees the books as 'a serious achievement: dense, aphoristic, philosophically acute novels that read like Iris Murdoch thrice distilled' (Garner 2018). Life, for both Knausgaard and Cusk, provides the material these authors need not so much to stretch their imaginations but to make sense of the realities around them and their place in the world. Individual life histories, then, provide substance for exposition and reflection and link the material of individual experience to more general questions of import to a wider audience. Certainly the international success enjoyed by *My Struggle* and by the 'Outline' Trilogy would seem to suggest that this is the case. Cusk's trajectory as a novelist turned memoirist who subsequently makes a return to a reinvented novel form provides an interesting counterpoint to the question of how far it is possible to stretch particular forms (the novel, life histories, narratives of a life) and the extent to which readers are willing to license or condone works that push the boundaries in terms of generic expectations, writerly scope and/or ambition and methods employed.

1.3 Aims and Scope

As a disciplinary field consisting of a large body of work, literature, even when narrowed down to contemporary literature or twenty-first century literature, is a vast and very broad field, and of necessity, I must delimit the phenomena examined and accounted for. It is important, therefore, to specify more precisely the locus of my interest and set out the questions and issues with which the book aims to engage. Broadly speaking, my interest relates to both what contemporary writers do in the context of their writing – and how they position the texts they construct – and how readers, including critics and reviewers, engage with and categorize the texts produced. In this sense, it relates to questions of genre, from the perspective of both writer and reader – what kind of text has been presented to us or do we imagine it to be, and how do we know? Is it on the basis of the constitutive properties of the text in question (narrative, non-narrative; fictional, non-fictional) and/or with the kind of world projected (realistic, speculative, fictional, fabular)? Or has it more to do with the contexts (historical, societal, cultural) circumscribing production and reception of specific works at a given moment? More specifically, my interest lies in looking closely at the output of several writers – Karl Ove Knausgaard, Jeanette Winterson, Xiaolu Guo and Rachel Cusk – whose work has attracted attention precisely because it has posed categorial problems and/or has elicited a variety of conflicting critical responses.

Of the writers on whom I focus, inclusion of Winterson might appear at odds with the other three insofar as, unlike Knausgaard and Cusk, Winterson is committed to and has not expressed doubts about the potential of the novel for getting at the truth of experience, though what truth means in this context is subject to debate. For Winterson, imagination and experience are not mutually exclusive and the self is a product of both, just as she sees life as part fact, part fiction (see Winterson on World Book Club, 1 August 2015). Of course, across her literary trajectory, Winterson has produced lots of novels, many of which are less obviously based on her own biography than *Oranges Are Not the Only Fruit* (henceforth, *Oranges*) would appear to be, even as she contends that 'we write from who we are' and that all of her works are 'just one continuous stretch of narrative' (World Book Club 2015). Her latest novel, *Frankissstein* (2020), for example, is both a rewriting and an updating of Mary Shelley's *Frankenstein*, and can be viewed as a creative intervention into the debates around Artificial Intelligence (AI), its potentials as well as its challenges. These are also explored in her latest volume of essays, *12 Bytes* (2021). Yet Winterson's entry into the world of novel writing as an ambitious young working-class, lesbian woman drawing on her own experience in semi-fictional form was not an easy one, even though *Oranges* won the Whitbread Award for first novel and remains one of the books said to have shaped the 1980s (Blake 2020). As Winterson writes on her website in relation to her use of the name Jeanette in her first fiction: 'So *Oranges* uses myself as a fictional character. It's me and it's not me. It's early autofiction, and it's a way of experimenting with truth, not to distort it but to distill it' (https://www.jeanettewinterson.com/authorabout Oranges).

In focusing on both *Oranges* and Winterson's memoir, *Why Be Happy When You Could Be Normal?*, a work that revisits the territory she trod in her first fictional work from the perspective of a, by now, highly successful writer and in relation to more recent events and revelations in her autobiography, my interest lies in determining the extent to which each evidences distinctive generic characteristics and/or is a recognizable Wintersonian work. Given that Winterson began writing in the 1980s, perceived as the period when postmodernism came to the fore, and when there was a conscious blurring of boundaries between fact and fiction, looking back at Winterson's debut novel from a different cultural moment, as well as in the light of her memoir, will allow me to put into perspective more recent general dissatisfaction with fabrication and invention on the part of writers who have come to prominence in the early decades of the twentieth century.

All the writers on whom I focus, regardless of age or critical longevity, have a presence on the national and international literary stages and have gained academic and media attention. Their views on writing and the experiments they have undertaken in their literary works are indicative of, and feed into, broader issues and directions in terms of the future of the novel, modes of fictionality and the value of what they understand truth and authenticity in writing to mean. All have produced work published under different labels (fiction and non-fiction), some of which is based on their own biographies presented in auto/biographical and/or novelistic terms. This allows for discussion of the specifics of their work and their individual trajectories in relation to its generic categorization and critical reception. Broader questions about the value of the novel in the late twentieth and early twenty-first centuries and attendant issues of truth, both documentary and emotional, in relation to auto/biographical and autofictional narratives, will be examined in relation to specific texts produced by these writers with a view to determining the extent to which their narratives conform to or subvert normative generic classifications and are understood by critics and reviewers to be consciously interrogating these generic conventions and/or employing modes of fictionality in their work more generally.

To be clear, all the writers whose work I am reviewing have written successful and well-received novels. They have also written works that engage closely with aspects of their own lives and biographies; some of these have been designated memoirs or autobiographies, others have had the label novel attached to them, or been read as fictions or autofictions. So, the question of categorization in relation to reader expectation is clearly pertinent, as are issues of the status and value of fiction today compared with accounts of a life deemed truthful and factual. While not denying the 'historical variability of novelistic form' (Dawson 2016, 149), and attentive to current debates around fictionality as a mode rather than a constitutive property of certain text types, my interest lies in the historical and cultural contexts that shape how we read as well as in the literary output of writers who openly interrogate aspects of the novel – its focus on invention and fabrication, for example, which might appear quintessential to it as a form, while at the same time exploiting its affordances as a vehicle for constructing an immersive and/or credible reality that reflects or refracts truths and self-knowledge. At the same time, against the backdrop of a rise in the production of memoirs since the 1980s and an increase in the number of contemporary narratives read as or deemed autofictional, the question arises of the extent to which it is possible to distinguish accounts of self along a fact–fiction continuum.

In Chapter 2, there will be more in-depth discussion of autofiction and the autofictional but for now, it is sufficient to indicate that use of these terms has become more prevalent in the critical literature in recent decades (Burgelin et al. 2010; Bloom 2019; Effe and Lawlor 2022) and that they are often employed to acknowledge the, sometimes ambivalent, status of a character-narrator in relation to the authorial persona. In reviewing the history of the term, first applied to particular kinds of autobiographical works in France from the late 1970s onwards and its more recent, somewhat broader, application to a range of English-language works, I show that the autofictional is a kind of catch-all term that accommodates a range of relations between and among character-narrator and author on the fact–fiction spectrum and serves to reflect the consciousness of some writers that they become characters in their work through the process of writing and retrospective analysis; they may also be attentive to the fact that since it is never possible to close the (temporal and spatial) gap between the person experiencing life and the one writing about or representing that experience, it is through language itself – what it reveals and/or conceals – that any kind of truthful insight will emerge. What, if anything, separates the autofictional from the autobiographical will also be discussed.

I interrogate the extent to which terms like fiction and non-fiction are helpful in framing ways of reading a published work and in determining the kinds of truth claims that the work in question might be expected to make. I suggest that the factual and the fictive might more usefully be considered as modes that characterize and underpin, to differing extents perhaps, a variety of narratives of self and life stories along a kind of fact–fiction continuum. This is not to suggest that there is no difference between an autobiography intended to translate and illuminate a writer's lived experience and a work where fabrication and invention, in short, storytelling, are given free rein in novelistic form. It is, however, to acknowledge the fact that much literary production today is situated at the confluence of fact and fiction, history and story, and that its structural and thematic features invite reflection on perception and knowing in relation to modes of narration, and discussion of the differential values attributed to narrativity, exposition and commentary in texts deemed factual or fictional. Many writers today are also aware of the fact that discussions of terms such as truth, authenticity and sincerity seem to have made a comeback (cf. the new sincerity) and are often framed and applied to works of both fiction and non-fiction, suggesting the need to reconsider whether the deployment of particular modes of fictionality underpins or undermines certain generic labels, and whether the presence or absence of identity between and among author, character and narrator (cf. Lejeune) is sufficient to warrant a positive determination of the truth claims of a work in terms of its mode of existence as non-fiction. Indeed, many writers deploy a range of narrative tools in such a way as to complicate a dualistic understanding of fact and fiction, true history and credible story.

To be clear, I am not arguing for the continuation of a kind of panfictionalism nor am I suggesting that the writers I discuss are unaware of the extent to which language mediates perceptions and helps construct a view of reality. On the contrary, all the authors whose works I treat are profoundly conscious of the constitutive role of language in constructing perceptions of reality and of the material ways in which language impinges upon ways of seeing and structures of feeling. Indeed, as a second-language writer of English, Guo is extremely conscious of this and thematizes both the embeddedness of language in culture and the kinds of knowledge and insights gleaned in moving across languages and cultures. At the same time, all the writers I treat are also conscious of the fact that in changing the language, you may be able to change the narrative. And in creating new forms and/or reinvigorating or repurposing existing forms, such as the novel, writers use their agency as producers of literature and as social beings to set new critical and creative agendas. To what extent, for example, can it be said that Knausgaard has helped create a new genre – the non-fictional novel – or subverted or interrogated an existing one? And what of Cusk's creation in her 'Outline' Trilogy of what she herself has termed the annihilated perspective? Is this a structural innovation in fiction and, if so, what might it say about genre and gender? And to what extent do Guo's texts translate a perspective informed by her literary translingualism, thereby creating new genres through a process of cross-cultural contact? In the case of Winterson, what a focus on *Why Be Happy?* in relation to *Oranges* brings to the fore is the extent to which life and literature are closely intertwined and the autofictional a mode that Winterson continues to draw on in her work.

If, as reception of Winterson's *Oranges* seemed to suggest back in the mid-1980s, male authors were indulging in metafiction in lending their names to a character, while the presumption for women writers was that their work was confessional or autobiographical in doing likewise, the question arises of the extent to which patterns of reading, as well as expectations of writing, are still to an extent gendered. And what of the role of fantasy or the imagination, of invention in storytelling, at a moment when many writers have expressed dissatisfaction with the conventional novel form and have turned towards alternative ways of expressing themselves that cut across or interrogate existing genres and/or attempt to create new or hybrid forms? In the new millennium, is this turn away from narrative fabrication and the creation of fictional façades to employing forms of life-writing a means of getting closer to the reality of individual experience? And to what extent have the fictional and the factual, the speculative and the documentary, become modes of writing that coexist across a range of genres in a different mix or blend, depending perhaps on the aims and intentions of the writer in dialogue with normative cultural conventions and reader expectations? These are all questions considered in the course of this monograph.

Reading a writer's work in relation to their trajectory as well as through the prism of its cross-cultural reception is a way of grounding perceptions in the specifics of a time and place. So, for example, what motivates an award-winning young novelist from Norway, Karl Ove Knausgaard, to devote his time to writing a work of epic proportions – the six-volume *Min Kamp* series (*My Struggle* in English translation) – that seems to detail aspects of his own life, including the mundane, rather than continuing to create or fabricate stories relating to apparently invented characters? And how has his work been received both at home and abroad by readers, critics and other writers? And what motivates Chinese-born writer Xiaolu Guo to write an autobiographical work with a UK title that is clearly signalling the genre of the fairy tale, *Once Upon a Time in the East?* As an, by now, accomplished novelist in English, whose work has come to be identified by its cross-cultural thematic treatment and its preference for philosophical and intellectual discourse over conventional narrative, its employment of new forms (e.g. a dictionary novel in *A Concise Chinese-English Dictionary for Lovers*; a satiric story told through police case notes in *UFO in Her Eyes*), often incorporating a mix of languages (e.g. predominantly English and Chinese with some use of French and German) and modes (e.g. photographic and visual as well as graphic and verbal), the substance of Guo's life together with her experience as a documentary film-maker has already underpinned and provided raw material for her narrative production. Indeed, her fictional output, both short stories and novels, can be seen to draw in outline on aspects and phases of her life in a way similar to that in which Cusk sees herself as indexing a character's experience to her own.

In this respect, Guo's novelistic output already evidences close parallels between her lived experience and the kind of characters (and their histories) that she depicts. As will be seen, her books represent attempts to render the experience of a mostly young, Chinese woman who has left her place of origin and migrated to another 'foreign' location, whether that be from rural to urban China or from China to England and beyond; they focus on what it means to live in translation. It might be said that these fictional workings out of the problematics of cross-cultural and interpersonal communication and of the constitutive roles of language and culture in underpinning or effecting a sense of identity are preliminary sketches for, or multiple versions of, the story of her life. Alternatively, translating a life might be said to involve similar processes of selection, storying and organizational principles as those already activated by Guo in the course of her career as a writer of semi-autobiographical fiction. Be that as it may, Guo's translingualism, alongside her access to cross-cultural, cross-generic and cross-media avenues for realizing her ambitions as a writer and film-maker, complicates her literary trajectory as much as it does its international reception.

While consideration of the work of particular writers constitutes the substance of this book, it is also alert to more general trends, such as a questioning of the value and purpose of the novel at a cultural moment when the pressure to address societal challenges and find solutions to problems puts pressure on those in the 'business' of literature – its production, dissemination and consumption – to project and frame it in particular ways as a social good, for example, and to justify its existence in instrumental and practical, rather than in purely aesthetic or philosophical, terms. Critics of the novel and of the directions it has taken or seems to be taking include many writers themselves whose disaffection is often expressed in terms of the novel's complicity with the status quo and the unwillingness of writers to take artistic risks or experiment stylistically. Such writer-critics (e.g. Zadie Smith, Will Self and Jeffrey Eugenides, among others) point to a variety of ways in which the novel risks failing, be it in terms of offering consolation, rather than critique, to readers; its focus on beautifully wrought sentences, rather than on disquieting or challenging realities; its seeming inability to address the complexities of a post-truth era, and/or compete with the immersive worlds generated by computer technologies and the distractions of social media. Yet even these critics wish the novel to survive in a form fit for the twenty-first century and continue to write fiction themselves, albeit fiction aimed to disrupt the tempo of modern life and create spaces for reflective action.

What the writers on whom I focus here have in common is their fearlessness when it comes to pushing literary and generic boundaries in whatever direction seems appropriate to them at the time. This means that even since writing this book all four authors have continued to produce new work, not all of which I will be able to treat in detail, though it will be important to refer to it in the concluding chapter, where I have not already drawn on it in constructing a view of the interests and motivations of individual authors and sought to align their work with current literary debates. These relate to the notion of truth in fiction, the need to get closer to the realities of life as it is lived and experienced, rather than imagined, and the desire to reinvent the novel form for a new era.

Having introduced in broad brush form the writers whose work will form the focus of this monograph and the kind of issues to be discussed, I wish to turn more sustained attention in Chapter 2 to some of the key critical terms and assumptions that underpin later analysis and interrogation of the work of the individual authors treated. This will involve reflecting on understandings of the affordances and constraints of fiction, of considering in brief recent trends in writing in relation to conceptions of genre and setting out in more detail the navigational parameters underpinning this book in terms of key concepts such as realism, radical or otherwise, autofiction and autofictional narratives, and the extent to which they dovetail with or challenge a desire to reinvent the novel.

Chapter 2

THEORETICAL AND CRITICAL CONCERNS: KEY TERMS AND ARGUMENTS

2.1 Purpose and Scope

The introductory chapter set the scene in terms of the scope and substance of the monograph, sketching out the literary contexts in relation to which analysis and discussion of the work of the four writers selected will proceed. Against this contextual backdrop, it drew attention to the fact that some of their works have raised classificatory and generic questions and garnered strong critical reactions, both positive and negative, as they push against narrative conventions and seek forms of expression and literary modes which they deem to be more attuned to their creative and critical purposes. While the chapters which follow will be devoted to detailed discussion of the work of each of the writers selected, namely Karl Ove Knausgaard, Jeanette Winterson, Xiaolu Guo and Rachel Cusk, the purpose of the current chapter is to put flesh on the bones of the theoretical and critical concerns of the book and to provide some further definition of the key terms and elements of what is a complex and nuanced argument as it relates to the specifics of the production of the different writers under consideration.

It will do this, not in a vacuum, but by grounding terminology in the literary and critical contexts that give rise to it and will preview key elements of the argument through reference to the work of the writers under scrutiny. This performs two key functions: to ensure that statements made are illustrated with reference to actual literary production and to the contexts out of which that production emerges; it will also provide validation of the views of writers as well as those of theorists and critics, since often it is writers, rather than critics, who are in the vanguard of what might be considered 'theoretical' developments by virtue of disrupting the status quo in their work.

The monograph is essentially concerned with a twenty-first century literary context in which questions are being asked by many writers about the value of the novel and of the role and extent of fiction and fabrication in writing. Why invent stories with conventionalized narrative arcs about fictional others, they ask, rather than seek as writers to mine one's own lived experience and create in writing a complex and multi-layered sense of what it is like to be 'me' (or someone very like me) and to raise questions about the 'real', while, at the same time, understanding that writing is always an act of mediation and of translation. It is as if the pendulum has swung from Barthes' contention of the death of the author to a sense that the author is alive and interested in breaking through the conventionalized fictive walls which seek to separate off author and narrator-protagonist and to 'get real' in the sense of trying to tease out possible answers to existential questions and dilemmas.

So, in slightly different ways and coming from slightly different directions, all four writers are interrogating assumptions about genre (the novel, the memoir, the auto/biography) and extending the fact-fiction continuum in line with their interests at a given time. Both Knausgaard and Cusk are interested in the status of the 'I' in fiction and non-fiction and in using their writing as a mode of interrogation to ask questions about 'truth', and the kind of relationship that pertains between the presented world and the 'real' experience of living. Winterson and Guo are writers who have consistently drawn on aspects of their own experiences in the creation of their fictions and their 'memoirs' are an extension of this autofictional impulse.

2.2 Realisms, Radical and Otherwise, and the Reality Effect in Literature

At the level of theories and histories of the novel, it can be said that realism, of various kinds, has enjoyed a privileged position in accounts of the novel's literary development, even if understandings of the term have been many and various. From the formal realism located in the work of eighteenth-century English writers like Defoe, Richardson and Fielding by critics such as Ian Watt, to presentation of the social realism that Georg Lukács attributes to much nineteenth-century fiction, via Roland Barthes' designation of 'l'effet de réel' (the reality effect) in the work of a writer such as Flaubert, to more recent usage of terms such as hyperrealism applied, for example, to the work of Knausgaard, myriad types of realism have been identified as pertinent to the development of the novel form across the centuries. These different types of realism reflect specific views of the novel's rise and are indicative of its thematic preoccupations, formal innovations, and variable focus on referentiality and artfulness in fiction.

For while the poles or antinomies may be weighted more in one direction than another – a greater or lesser emphasis on actuality and contemporary society or on the self-referential and literary qualities of an aesthetic realism – it is the very tension that holds these forces in apparent opposition that may be one of the defining properties of the novel: that literature is not life, nor life literature would seem to be an unproblematic truth until a series of questions raise their heads about the nature of reality, the real, and the links that obtain between experience of life and its representation. As Joseph Frank, writing of Lilian Furst's contribution to understanding of literary realism, puts it:

> The notion of realism as applied to literary and pictorial art is one that everybody uses, and whose meaning seems to be self-evident; but the moment questions are asked, it turns out to be extremely slippery and difficult to pin down. (Frank 2012, 215)

Trying to get a handle on the terms of the debates on realism and the novel form is certainly challenging; consideration of the epithet radical in conjunction with realism only adds to the challenge, since radical may be interpreted in different ways, depending on the context in which it is used and the assumptions that it challenges. So, for example, if realism is primarily viewed as a conservative or reactionary force in literature and art, then the addition of radical may suggest a more revolutionary force or one that affects its fundamental nature. In addition, disciplinary norms and critical frames do not easily map onto one another, and consequently there may be subtle differences in cross-disciplinary conceptualizations of terms like realism and indeed narrative, all of which can add to the slipperiness of terminology. Yet, it seems to me that the term radical realism, as expounded below, captures something of the dynamics of features of the work of some contemporary authors, who, like Knausgaard, are seeking methods that allow them to combine a focus on the everyday with a self-conscious understanding that the experiential, as lived, is not the same as its grounding in language and its narration.

To begin with, it is important to note that the term radical realism is not my coinage since it has already been applied in the context of papers on politics, philosophy and art, as well as in relation to the work of some writers. For example, in 'Visual Labour: Ruskin's Radical Realism', Caroline Levine (2000) discusses Victorian realism as a quintessentially revolutionary project and reads Ruskin's work, not as diffuse and in opposition to realism, but as a spur to the notion that to really see things, it is necessary to throw off habit and look again at nature. It is this conscious attentiveness to the world around one that characterizes the hard work of realism. Resisting habitual and taken-for-granted ideas and practices and overturning conventions are, therefore, radical acts. In speaking of Ruskin's radical realism, Levine writes:

> Conventional ways of seeing dangerously cloud and corrupt our vision, and thus Ruskin exhorts us to work assiduously to counteract their influence. We must seek to cast off the weight of established traditions and received judgments in favor of a more faithful relationship to the world. (Levine 2000, 78)

This casting off 'the weight of established [novelistic] traditions [...] in favor of a more faithful relationship to the world' might be applied to the work of Knausgaard, insofar as he labours to produce a work that projects not a predominantly fictionalized account of the behaviours and actions of imagined others but rather one that grapples with the remembered and retraced contours of his own existence and seeks to delineate and interrogate the relationship he constructs to the world around him. This world is both given and made, given insofar as the author is brought into a particular part of the world – Norway in the late 1960s – with its language, culture and norms of social behaviour; made insofar as the narrator-protagonist Karl Ove commits to paper his recollections of and reflections on the worlds of his childhood, youth and manhood. By inserting into a novel, not (more or less) credible fictional characters but real people implicated in, and contributors to, the patterning and development of his life, and in rejecting conventionalized notions of what constitutes plot and a plausible narrative arc, Knausgaard tries to counteract the influence of novelistic habit and custom. His 'non-fiction novel', with its excessive detail, recursive rather than linear patterning, essayistic digressions and existential musings, far from being a contradiction in terms, constitutes a radical act.

Closer to home, in a disciplinary sense, the term radical realism is also to be found in a 2001 article by Philip Tew on the work of B. S. Johnson. Tew's argument relates to the need to reassess B. S. Johnson's writing upon republication of *The Unfortunates* which he sees as an example of Johnson's seriousness, rather than playfulness, in terms of his experimentation with novelistic form, as he grapples with loss – the death of a friend – and attempts to resolve conflict and synthesize complexity through the act of writing. Like Knausgaard, though of a different era, class and country, Johnson distrusted fiction and invention, seeking instead to create 'a radical, dialectically-aware realism that reaffirms, interrogates and problematises the novel in a complex and often unacknowledged manner' (Tew 2001). For Tew, Johnson's experimentalism was not a kind of postmodernism *avant la lettre* but rather an inquiry into modes of perception, the nature of experience and the role of language in conveying a kind of critical consciousness.

Tew (2001) continues: 'The synthesis of observation and the experiential is key to placing Johnson'. The same might be said of Knausgaard insofar as his seemingly radical attention to detail and to the minutiae, some would say trivia, of everyday life, are also played back and reflected on through language. Autobiography in the form of a novel is what Johnson is said to have been writing and, in relation to Knausgaard, we might think in this regard of Schmitt and Kjerkegaard's 2016 article on *My Struggle*, subtitled 'A Real Life in a Novel', which considers Knausgaard's work as 'a literary experiment [which] by far exceeds the words on the page and includes elements of reality – not least Knausgaard himself' (Schmitt and Kjerkegaard 2016, 554). By this they mean to point to the fact that in reading and interacting with a work of apparently uncertain or ambivalent designation – Is it a memoir? Is it a novel? Is it a piece of autofiction? – paratextual markers play an enhanced role in guiding the ways in which a work is reviewed and discussed. As they see it, the gossip around both the book and the man – his aims, intentions and values – are all brought into the web underpinning the book's critical reception. And just as Johnson was not interested in writing fiction, which he saw as close to telling lies, since from his perspective the process of the selection of events and their transformation into a coherent narrative is a means of falsification of the randomness and flux of life, so Knausgaard is concerned about the way in which narrative fiction conventionally structures story, thereby falsifying the actual experience of life and depriving it of the richness, the randomness and the complexity it merits, in the name of narrative coherence.

At the same time, Knausgaard is conscious that it is not the novel *per se* but novelistic conventions and the premium placed on fiction that he wishes to disrupt in order to return to the reality of experience which is grounded in the mundane details of everyday life but also permits access to a variety of dispersed and not always fully formed thoughts, feelings, and reactions. Opening the novel up to the fluidity and randomness of life, seeking to represent complexity as a natural part of that process, and trying to unsettle or 'unfix' assumed boundaries between established categories (including those of fact and fiction) is part and parcel of what Knausgaard is trying to do. In this sense, the novel becomes a site for the coexistence of discourses of fictionality and factuality as it strives to get closer to the real and to the reality of selfhood. Of course, in many respects, modernist novelists such as Virginia Woolf had done exactly this in rejecting forms of realism that seemed outmoded for the twentieth century and, indeed, Woolf played with biographical, as well as novelistic, conventions in works like *Orlando*.

In looking more closely at the work of Jeanette Winterson, I shall return to parallels with aspects of the modernist project, its interrogation of notions of reality and a search for new novelistic methods for new times. Suffice to say, for now, that Knausgaard, too, is an inheritor of a modernist tradition, and has acknowledged in interview interest in both Joyce and Woolf. Yet, interestingly, in a *London Review of Books* interview on publication in English translation of his latest book, *The Morning Star* (2021), Knausgaard nominates as his perfect book, in terms of depth and intensity, *The Rings of Saturn* by W. G. Sebald, a work described by critics as 'part travelogue, part memoir, part essay-meditation and part fiction' (Burns 2015). As a writer who crosses generic boundaries and blends fact and fiction, it is perhaps not surprising that Sebald's work appeals to Knausgaard, since in many ways they are both interested in unfixing taken-for-granted categories, in complexity, in cultural formations and history, the limits of rationalism, subjectivity and agency, modes of perception, and the interplay of the visual and the verbal. Both incorporate into their writing a mix of narrative and essay; auto/biography and philosophical enquiry; the descriptive and documentary alongside the speculative and the fictional.

2.3 Fiction and the Novel

The assumption of fiction as exclusive to, and a defining property of, the novel form is challenged not only by the history of the novel but by its inclusion in other supposedly non-fictional genres such as memoir or autobiography. The 'a priori assumption of the novel as fiction' (Zetterberg Gjerlevsen 2016, 175) has more recently been recast as a broader investigation into modes of fictionality and how they operate in different contexts. Zetterberg Gjerlevsen (2016, 186), for example, proposes a historical investigation into 'how fictionality is deployed, negotiated, and developed within all works that display, negotiate or challenge the status of fiction'. This uncoupling of fictionality and fiction suggests the possibility of works challenging the status of fiction using modes of fictionality. In reviewing the differential role of authorial digressions and intrusions in Fielding, Walpole and Austen, Zetterberg Gjerlevsen (2016, 185) shows the extent to which each writer uses the space of the novel to discuss 'the discourse of what constitutes the novel genre'. She maintains, through her analysis, that 'fictionality is one of the most important constitutive features of the novel' (185) and posits realism as a 'set of constraints that novelistic invention works within' (177).

While Zetterberg Gjerlevsen is clear about the importance of paratext in helping to determine genre, she does not discuss the full range of paratexts that might come into play, simply noting that the cover designation of the work and possibly an author's preface may act as points of orientation in reading the work in question. In the case of the latter, actual readers may in fact read the preface following, rather than before, their encounter with a work. However, the general point stands: that there are signals presented to the reader as to how the work is intended to be read. Again, this is fine, as far as it goes, but in the case of some writers, such as some of those I discuss in this monograph, the question of how to read the work is in many ways fundamental and not as straightforward as such principled argumentation might suggest. To take Knausgaard as a case in point: is *My Struggle* a real life in a novel (Schmitt and Kjerkegaard 2016), a literary centaur (Andersen 2018), a piece of autobiographical writing (Sala 2018), an autofiction (Gibbons, Vermeulen and van den Akker 2019; Finch 2019), a hyperrealist text (Semeiks 2012; Franklin 2018), a novel *tout court*, or the equivalent of a modern-day selfie (Bloom 2019)? Even allowing for the fact that realism can be seen as a set of novelistic conventions that came to dominate critical and literary accounts of the development of the novel form, and that the form itself is subject to change, the fact that *My Struggle* has been read in so many different ways would suggest that the parameters for approaching it are not clear and that perceived intratextual features and paratextual frames can combine in different ways not only for different readers but also across cultures. While presented as a novel in Norway, the US edition of the work in translation, published by Archipelago, was deliberately left unlabelled, as the publisher felt that Knausgaard's project 'dwells comfortably between (and embraces) both fiction and memoir' (Rohter 2012).

Separating out fictionality from fiction is a useful move in acknowledging the ways in which fictional techniques and rhetorical devices can be used in other, non-fictional, contexts. Another useful move is contesting the implied opposition between realism and fictionality. However, the terms of the debate remain tricky to navigate insofar as the differences between mode, genre and discourse are not always clear. For example, in an endnote Zetterberg Gjerlevsen (2016) writes: 'I take fiction to be a genre in which the rhetorical act of fictionality determines the global frame. In that sense, fiction and fictionality are intimately connected, yet not synonymous' (187), while earlier the novel has been discussed as a genre, albeit one whose conventions are subject to change. From all of this, some issues arise: firstly, if fiction is a particular genre, then presumably non-fiction is another such kind, distinguished perhaps by predominant use of factual material and/or more local uses of fictionality rather than by a global fictional frame. Yet if the space of the novel genre gives rise to particular sets of discourses on which writers draw in signposting their contributions to new ways of writing and in situating their work in relation to neighbouring genres and discourses, might the concept of the 'non-fictional novel', to return to

Knausgaard's characterization of the *My Struggle* series, not begin to look like a possible way station on this historic route? Rather than being oppositional to the novel genre, it might be read as a particular instantiation of it, along a fact-fiction continuum.

What remains problematic perhaps in such an interpretation is the issue of the overall frame or standpoint from which the reader views the world created by the writer: as a globally fictional universe or as one intending to refer to actuality, and if the latter, at what point does novelistic deployment of modes of fictionality undermine or interrogate the autobiographical thrust? Is a hybrid mix of narrative and essay, diary-like entries and philosophical discussion, of necessity a borderline case? And is scepticism about storytelling and fictionality sufficient to warrant a more documentary reading? Gísli Magnússon (2020, 366), for example, sees Knausgaard as 'not only a writer belonging to the current of autofiction; he is also a highly reflective author and essayist', the intellectual side of whose writing 'is at least as important as the autobiographical'. And if the idea of non-fiction is itself simply a fiction, on what basis might critical readers determine whether a writer has expanded literary horizons or simply remained within the confines of blurred lines (Dewey 2013)? In other words, is *My Struggle* 'disruptive of contemporary fiction', with Knausgaard seeking to break the novel form or is it, ultimately a 'hybrid of autobiography, the essay and novel' (Franklin 2018, 109). In posing all these questions, I am seeking at present not to answer them but, through multiple characterizations and sources, to evidence the complexities of autobiographical writing, whether factual or fictional, and to point to the ways in which the novel form itself is being expanded through dialogue with autofictional narratives.

2.4 Autofiction and Autofictional Narratives

Autofiction is a term that entered the English language via the French *autofiction*, said to have been coined in 1977 by Serge Doubrovsky, in the context of his self-designated autofictional novel, *Fils*. Yet the very origin of the term is contested, with Myra Bloom (2019, 4) drawing attention to the fact that autofiction was 'coined by the British-American novelist and critic Paul West five years prior [to Doubrovsky], a point of origin that scholars have, strangely, neglected to note'. Be that as it may, the genealogy of autofiction is generally attributed to a French literary tradition and until recently was often seen as a peculiarly French phenomenon. As a literary critic, Professor of French literature, and writer of autofictional texts, Doubrovsky attempted over the years since *Fils* to define and refine what he meant by autofiction and to give examples of autofictional writers other than himself (such as Annie

Ernaux and Marguerite Duras) but the term remained contentious and ill-defined with different schools of thought both in France and beyond. Writer Philippe Vilain (2010), for example, sees these different schools as essentially falling into two camps: 'l'une privilégiant la fidélité d'un rapport historique à soi, l'autre revendiquant la recréation romanesque de soi' (one privileging accurate representation of the link between self and actual biography, the other asserting the right to novelistic self-invention – the translation is mine). Yet despite its troubled history and terminological inexactitude – is it a genre in its own right or a sub-genre of autobiography? Is it a theoretical approach, or cluster of approaches, to writing about self, and/or a practice or set of practices? – the term, though 'under-conceptualized and under-researched' (Dix 2017, 69), would seem to have made something of a comeback in the past decade or so. This is evidenced both by special issues of journals devoted to the topic (e.g. *L'Esprit Créateur* Fall 2009) and publication of conference proceedings and articles on the topic (see, e.g., *Autofiction(s)*, a collection of papers from a colloquium organized by Burgelin, Grell, and Roche 2010). Indeed, this 'critical interrogation' (Dix 2017, 74) may have much to do with current interest in modes of fictionality and concern with the prescriptions and laws of genre/s in relation to notions of truth.

This contention would seem to be borne out by recent publication of *The Autofictional* (2022), a volume of essays recognising the rise of autofiction as a 'term, concept and literary practice' (Effe and Lawlor 2022, 2). It discusses the affordances of what it ultimately sees as a mode, rather than a genre, of writing. Rather like this monograph, the volume seeks to understand why autofiction and the autofictional have become such seemingly relevant terms and practices favoured by so many writers at this particular cultural and literary juncture.

In the same way as theses about Fictionality have been driven by the need to understand whether fiction is a genre or a mode or both, Wagner-Egelhaaf (2022), one of the contributors to *The Autofictional*, draws up a set of five theses that attempt to characterize the autofictional. Starting with acknowledgement of the perceptible need (23) for such a term, she begins by positioning the autofictional as 'an intrinsic mode within the autobiographical' (28), one which draws on formal innovation and 'the constructive role of imagination and invention' (26) while recognizing a need for the real. Autofiction, she asserts, acknowledges that it 'produces real-world effects' (30) and has a performative dimension. Like a Möbius strip, it 'oscillates between fictionality and factuality' (32).

When referring to the autobiographical, however, Wagner-Egelhaaf (2022) does not distinguish between 'real' autobiographies and 'fictional' autobiographies, although the assumption in context is that she is referring to the former. It is unclear whether the autobiographical in Wagner-Egelhaaf's view is a mode or a genre – I have to assume the former – and this lack of clarity makes it difficult to decide whether the autofictional is a sub-mode of an autobiographical impulse which can veer in the direction of real, more 'factually-oriented' autobiography or towards autobiographical fiction, or whether autobiography is a genre which has different instantiations of which autofiction or better, the autofictional, is one type. In some ways, then, this typology begs as many questions as it seems to answer.

My own view is that it is preferable to position increased critical interest in autofiction in relation to the rise of Fictionality Studies and, paradoxically perhaps, the turn to the real or what Wagner-Egelhaaf (2022) calls 'a new need for the real' (28). This reality hunger, to use Shields's term, comes in the wake of a ludic postmodernism which I see many proponents of autofiction today as reacting against. These writers are aware that the very act of writing about self and/or about one's experience of reality is a complex rather than a simple process and one which, of necessity or by default, draws on memory, which is intrinsically deficient. Moreover, given that language itself performs a kind of mediation on an attempt to relate experience as authentically and transparently as possible, the resultant text is the product of a shaping consciousness perceptible via linguistic and aesthetic choices or 'moves', which themselves relate not only to a particular author's aims and intentions but are also imbued with traces of culturally available narrative discourses, and designs.

In interview with Roger Célestin on the topic of autobiography, Doubrovsky tries to situate his understanding of what autofiction is, and what it does/how it functions, in the context of a thumbnail sketch of theoretical developments and new writing practices since the 1980s, pointing to the fact that it is no longer possible to write conventional literary autobiographies, given the end of the *grand récit* (grand narrative). For Doubrovsky, it is important to acknowledge the contexts and circumstances in which ideas emerge and the fact that 'knowledge of man is always linked to a certain extent to the subject' (Célestin 1997, 398), a comment suggestive of the fact that knowledge, including self-knowledge, is a factor of perception, vision and subject position. In the wake of structuralism, there is post-structuralist acknowledgement not just of the role of subjectivity in perceiving the world but also greater emphasis on the role of language, and of memory, in negotiating and constituting personal history. 'The meaning of one's life', contends Doubrovsky, 'in certain ways escapes us, so we have to reinvent it in our writing, and that is what I personally call autofiction' (Célestin 1997, 400). In so doing, he points to the difference between experiencing, and writing, a life, both in the sense of the gap between the present of living and the moment of writing, and that between the writing 'I' and the 'I' that is written and comes to appearance through language. He goes on to talk about 'that new awareness of self as a story you tell yourself about yourself and so to a large extent fictitious' (401), positing both a narrative and a metafictional or reflexive dimension to literary writing about self, even as he wonders if this is the same for memoirs relating to public figures. For Doubrovsky, it was imperative to find a way of writing that would permit him to stay true to the basic referential facts of his life, or a part thereof, while acknowledging the fictive elements in a text, such as *Fils*, which is 'a forced totalization' (400), given that it cannot recapture his whole life in the artful representation of a day. And as Philippe Gasparini points out, *Fils* differentiates itself from autobiography at two levels, the level of language and the level of structure (Gasparini 2011).

It is indeed in relation to autobiography, both fictional and non-fictional, that *autofiction* as a supposed genre runs into difficulties, in addition to the fact that it has generally been seen as a peculiarly French invention (Burgelin 2010). In locating Proust's monumental *A la recherche du temps perdu* as an example of an earlier text (prior to 1977) which ploughed an autofictional furrow (Burgelin 2010), the potential complexities and specificities of autofiction as a distinct genre begin to surface. Categorized as a novel (or series of novels), the first-person character-narrator Marcel in Proust's *A la recherche* both is and is not Proust. For as Elisheva Rosen (1995, 65) points out, specific identity markers that would equate Proust with narrator Marcel, such as being half-Jewish and homosexual, are absent in *A la recherche* in the figure of the narrator, though these identity markers are re-distributed in the text in different ways, to Marcel's friend Swann and the baron de Charlus, for example. In this sense, Marcel has his doubles, often seen as a feature of some contemporary autofiction.

For Proustian critic Roger Shattuck (2001), *A la recherche* 'embodies and manifests the principle of intermittence: to live means to perceive different and often conflicting aspects of reality'. One might add, not just different and conflicting aspects of reality but different and conflicting aspects of self, insofar as the notion of self for modern-day writers of autofiction, far from being stable and unified, is at least double, if not multiple, and discontinuous, given the distance between past and present, lived experience and its representation. (One might, for example, think of Brett Easton Ellis's *Lunar Park* in this regard). For Shattuck what holds Proust's novel together is a 'lost and found' structure, one that brings together beginning and ending: across the novel Marcel moves from the routines and security of childhood out into the world, is disabused over time of his illusions, and, in his resolve to become a writer and write his life story, has regained a sense of his place in time. Marcel's quest to become a writer has been realized in the production of the book the reader has just finished; the end takes us back to the beginning.

If I have brought Proust's monumental work into the discussion, it is not by chance, since in the critical literature parallels have been drawn between Karl Ove Knausgaard's *My Struggle* series and Proust's *A la recherche* and this is something to which I will return in the Knausgaard chapter. For now, it is important to note that while Knausgaard is a fan of Proust as a writer – *A la recherche* is one of his top three books (Sullivan 2017) – in many ways his endeavour can be seen as anti-Proustian in the sense that his aim in writing quickly and at length was partly to avoid the imposition of narrative structure and a consciously motivated aesthetic which might colour with stylistic effects his search for a kind of raw truth. Admittedly, there is in Knausgaard's desire just to write without consciously considering structure and style a degree of wish fulfilment, if not bad faith, insofar as the work can indeed be said to have a discernible structure. In addition, in not paying much attention to style, he is in fact creating a new style which emerges across the various volumes. What Knausgaard is getting at, though, is the fact that there is what he recognizes as bad writing in *My Struggle* and he introduces volume 1, *A Death in the Family*, with a passage about what happens to the body upon death as bodily systems shut down, in a more self-conscious way in order to demonstrate that, if required, he can write in a carefully crafted way but that his aim was to move away from a focus on novelistic craft and stylistic effects in order to grasp through writing a more vital connection to the world around him. Indeed, he has been called 'one of the great realists of the twenty-first century' (Johnston 2018, 378). The question of generic categorization and how to read *My Struggle* is one to which I shall return but, as has already been noted, it has been received in a variety of ways: primarily a novel, albeit one based on the 'real life' of Karl Ove Knausgaard; a hyper-realist text; and a piece of autofiction.

In terms of autobiography, it may seem self-evident that there exists a difference between fictional and non-fictional autobiography or what we might call autobiography proper. Yet the narrative construction of an account of a life, or a part thereof, and of a self which claims in all essentials to be factually true and one that openly declares itself as fiction turns out to be more porous and trickier to determine than conventional categorizations (fiction vs. non-fiction) and notions of the autobiographical pact (Lejeune) might lead us to believe. What can be said to distinguish fictional autobiography from autobiography proper in terms of textual features? And in what does the difference lie between a work claiming to relate a person's real-life story (autobiography) and one that treats vicariously a life that shares aspects of the biography of the author (autobiographical fiction)? And to what extent does application of the term autofiction simply muddy the autobiographical waters rather than relay an interrogatory note to what might best be described as a fictional to non-fictional continuum, rather than a set of identifiable binaries? By the same token, one might wonder on what basis it is possible or even desirable to determine the degree of fictionality (or otherwise) of a text. What is at stake in the maintenance or dissolution of a fact/fiction boundary and why do so many writers seem to want to test the limits of the possible? Indeed, it has been argued (Lavocat 2016) that it is precisely the maintenance or at least invocation of a fact/fiction border that allows that border to be transgressed and permits readers to recognize the challenge of transgression.

2.5 The Liberties and Liabilities of Literature: The Status of the Narratorial 'I'

In a 2005 chapter in *A Companion to Narrative Theory* entitled 'The "I" of the Beholder: Equivocal Attachments and the Limits of Structuralist Narratology', Susan S. Lanser examines the status of the 'I' in a range of works which she sees as offering potential challenges to structuralist narrative orthodoxies. Drawing on the work of Bakhtin, Lanser (2005, 210–11) sees literary discourse as equivocal in terms of voice: 'The "I" that characterizes literary discourse […] is always potentially severed from and potentially tethered to the author's "I."' Reviewing examples from critical work, including essays, as well as narrative texts, she suggests that 'the liberties and liabilities of literature' (211) derive from such equivocation and engender 'some of the interpretive dilemmas that underlie our scholarly debates' (211). Conscious of the fact that the status of a text as unadulterated fiction or non-fiction cannot easily be determined on the basis of textual descriptors alone, she proposes a number of criteria, namely singularity, anonymity, identity, reliability and nonnarrativity or atemporality, whose application may help determination of the status of the 'I' in particular cases. She sets about defining them as legitimate parameters for considering the kind of relations that may be in force between character-narrator and (implied) author, though she notes that we do not generally talk about an implied author except in the case of texts deemed fictional.

At the same time, she points to the role of the reader in constructing or projecting a particular kind of narrative world. Lanser's interest in how readers navigate contextual as well as textual signals in making determinations of the status of an 'I' arose because of an act of reading in her own case which, had it not been for the explicit fiction marker in the pages of *The New Yorker*, she would have read as autobiography, and she goes on to cite examples of texts, such as Maxine Hong Kingston's *The Woman Warrior: Memoirs of a Girlhood Among Ghosts*, which was apparently written as a novel but marketed as autobiography, and whose reception by readers was guided as much by marketing and publicity, as by any inherent textual properties or generic prescriptions.

In talking about 'a literary text's potential' (213) for either attachment or detachment of the views of the narratorial 'I' to those of the (implied) author, Lanser considers what is at stake in terms of the pretended or potentially nonpretended nature of some of the speech acts. She reviews the default position for different genres including lyric poetry, drama and epistolary fiction, concluding that '[h]omodiegetic fiction emerges as the most equivocal of the equivocal genres, always technically detached and yet sometimes readily attachable' (214). In other words, she is pointing to the received idea in narrative studies that the implied author and character-narrator operate within a constructed world or imagined universe separate from that of the everyday reality of a particular author, even where there may be similarities in terms of type of universe and/ or attribution of views held. She also refers to the idea, following Henry Louis Gates, that writers are 'cultural impersonators' (Gates 1991, 26, cited in Lanser 2005, 209) and that they employ sets of discourses within their work to give substance and credibility to particular characters deployed within an otherwise fictional universe. However, she also acknowledges the important role of context and not just of form in making particular determinations (210ff).

That both context and the horizon of expectations that any reader brings to deciphering what s/he reads and/or is presented with are important in determining genre should not be surprising. Indeed, the signals and codes by which meanings are conventionally made and what happens when a different lens is brought to bear on the same material is thematized in Marina Warner's 2021 memoir, *Inventory of a Life Mislaid*, in which she looks back at, recreates, and speculates on, some scenes from and memories of her parents' lives with particular reference to the period from 1947 to 1952 in which they lived in Cairo where her father managed a bookshop on behalf of W. H. Smith. While the subtitle of the work, *An Unreliable Memoir*, signals the fact that some of what the memoir contains is not to be trusted, what is potentially unusual about Warner's book is the particular blend of so-called fact and fiction insofar as there is a 'Cast of characters' list at the back of the book (404–408), which includes three 'imaginary personae' in italics, two of whom are represented as being close to the author's mother. This is in addition to a timeline, 'Chronology', 'Notes' and a 'Bibliography', more conventionally associated with the kind of research that is involved in biography. In addition, a review of Warner's book in *The Guardian* refers to the fact that she originally planned to write a novel and was keen to use fictional techniques but was persuaded that this slice of history was important enough to warrant a more factual basis (Higgins 2021). In discussing the mix, Warner tells Higgins:

> With nonfiction you really need to make up your mind about your line of argument [...]. You need to go in a clear direction and I tried to do that, say, in my book on the Virgin Mary, or in my book *Monuments and Maidens*. But the great freedom of fiction is that you can admit the complexity and the ambiguity and search out the emotional textures and the feeling of it happening rather than the line you should take. It's not a comfortable place to be writing from, but it's reflective and it's emotionally sincere, it echoes the turbulence inside one.

This reference to the kind of freedom fiction offers a writer, enabling complexity, ambiguity, and a search for the 'emotional textures' which resonate both with reader and writer in different ways, is an important acknowledgement of the choices that present themselves to writers in constructing a work and in tending to aspects such as the feel of the work as a whole. Warner's remarks about the 'reflective and emotionally sincere' nature of the writing are also note-worthy at a time of concern with what is often called the new sincerity. Without wishing at this point to review notions of sincerity, never mind the new sincerity in literature, it is useful simply to note Warner's interest in both reflexivity and emotional sincerity, terms which might be glossed in this context as having to do with awareness of the constructed nature of text, even as the writing attends to the creation of a world of emotional power and integrity by drawing on the artifice of fiction. It is not that non-fiction has to be devoid of speculation nor that facts of necessity speak for themselves and require a minimum of contextual framing and interpretation. It is rather that the resources and techniques of fiction may be drawn upon to project a sensibility or vicariously inhabit a point of view seemingly at odds with biographical and temporal specificities. How, for example, can a child know what her mother was feeling at a particular moment except through an act of retrospective and empathetic imagination? The turbulence of which the authorial narrator speaks is at once both hers and her mother's, created and uncovered in the process of writing.

For example, the authorial narrator spends time representing a visit that her mother makes with a man she has been encouraged by her husband to spend time with. (It is only later that the reader learns that this character is in fact an invented one). As he lavishes attention on her, and gives her a present, she represents her mother as beginning to feel a certain attraction to him at the same time as she is concerned about what his attentiveness to her might mean. After presenting these fears, anxieties and anticipation on her mother's part, the narrator comments:

> But anyway, Dimitrino wasn't the kind of man who's interested in women ... however much he lavished gifts on a young new arrival like Ilia.
> Later, when she came to know him better, she realized why, but during that outing she was assailed by something improper, something terrible.
> (Warner 2021, 302)

Representation of a life, or a part thereof, begins to accrue lots of layers, as well as returning the reader to the question of how we read, how we come to know what we think we know and how meanings are constructed. Decoding of signs depends on knowledge of conventions and on prior experience, as well as on an interpretive frame for making judgements and evaluations. In this sense both life and narrative depend on the accretions of time and a retrospective as well as a prospective view. In principle, the present is as much shaped by future horizons, as it is by past events and experiences, even if forms of narrative limit a character's perspective on the present to understanding of the self and of others drawn from past experience and current knowledge. Characters, like narrators, may be wise after the event, as new information comes to light and/or with the accretion of experience. In turn, their reflections and review prompted by what has been newly discovered or uncovered may inform their behaviour and mode of thinking on future occasions.

Another example in Warner's memoir which reflects on the ways in which new knowledge is uncovered, helping to reshape the manner in which life history is storied, relates to her father's potential pre-marital relationship with a cabaret singer called Hildegarde (179–181). On finding an obituary published in *The Guardian* among her mother's papers with passages marked, Warner realizes that the 'family romance' (179) may well have been a credible story with a strong whiff of verisimilitude, rather than an actual fact, as new evidence comes to light not only about Hildegarde's real sexual history but also about her mother's discovery of the likely truth of the situation (180), given Hildegarde's sexual preference and love for another woman.

Warner's 'mix of fact and fiction, observation and speculation' is 'carefully constructed from the things that remain, the inventory of the title' (Sattin 2021, 1). In a chapter written in 2012 entitled 'Report to the Memoir Club: Scenes from a Colonial Childhood', Warner talks about some of the things that she and Virginia Woolf have in common in terms of conflicted views of their fathers and their assumptions about power and privilege, 'the blanket sense of otherness that issued from the vantage point of imperial London to demarcate most of the rest of the world' (Warner 2012, 59). She reads from and discusses aspects of her work-in-progress, originally conceived as a novel, because, she writes, 'I need the freedom to enter characters' thoughts and feelings, and I want to write dialogue; besides I was a small child at the time and so my memories, though vivid, are fragments' (61). Between then and its eventual publication, the work became what Frances Wilson (2021, 30) characterizes as 'high risk and multidimensional'.

In looking closely at the status of the 'I' in a range of works, variously labelled by critics, reviewers and the writers themselves, sometimes at different moments in their career, what can be gleaned from the role of textual and/or contextual factors in impacting upon a work's designation? For example, in terms of the relationship between and among author, narrator and protagonist, what does 'identity' or 'homonymy' actually mean and what is the burden of proof? Given that the heroine of Jeanette Winterson's *Oranges Are Not the Only Fruit* is called Jeanette and that it is a first-person narrative, which reflects aspects of the 'real' Winterson biography, albeit written in a playful manner with intertextual and storytelling interludes, and has been published as a novel, one might well wonder if the fact of sharing a name across these different domains is a sufficient condition to distinguish autobiography from autobiographical fiction or indeed autofiction. At the time of publication, the semi-autobiographical aspects of *Oranges* were frequently commented on to the point that Winterson herself explicitly asked why male authors who planted in their fiction alter egos bearing the authorial name were read as metafictions, while female writers who did something similar were read as confessional. In bringing the question of gender both in the production and reception of text to the surface Winterson was clearly drawing attention to apparent critical double standards. Yet in the light of publication of Winterson's *Why Be Happy When You Could Be Normal?*, ostensibly a memoir, produced over twenty-five years after *Oranges*, might there be grounds for seeing *Oranges* as a piece of autofiction? Or is it the memoir that is closer to autofiction insofar as Winterson refuses many of the conventions of writing about life, including passing over in silence much of her biography between publication of *Oranges* and her quest to find her biological mother, following a breakdown? For if trauma is often the motor of autofiction, it could be argued that it is only in the memoir that the trauma of adoption, of separation and of rupture, is finally confronted. These are questions to which I shall return in reviewing Winterson's 'Companion Pieces' in Chapter 4.

But apart from the fact that there are competing views of autofiction, there is also disagreement about the extent to which fictional and non-fictional texts can be determined on the basis of their textual characteristics alone rather than in conjunction with extra-textual or paratextual features such as cover designation and/or library categorization. In making the case for autofiction as a distinct genre, Siddharth Srikanth (2019) examines two works, V. S. Naipaul's *The Enigma of Arrival* and J. M. Coetzee's *Summertime*, both in relation to their paratextual, as well as their textual features, arguing that in different ways they invite an autofictional, rather than an autobiographical, pact on the part of their reader. Srikanth sees fictionality as a mode on which writers can draw locally as well as globally and suggests that continued uncertainty around definitions of autofiction is testimony not to inherent definitional vagueness but to autofiction's distinctive, hybrid nature as a genre. The autofictional impulse can be realized in the direction of 'the actual shot through with invention' (354) or 'to write an autobiography through the form of the novel' (356) in Naipaul's case; Srikanth sees Coetzee as using 'fictive discourse at length to reveal more accurately his sense of self' (362) in a volume trailed as the third part of his autobiography, in the first two parts of which he had used a third-person narrator. In the final volume, *Summertime*, Coetzee employs the more radical tactic of 'kill[ing] off the Nobel Prize winning author, "John Coetzee" (the death of the "author-ity") and bestow[ing] the responsibility of biographical testimony onto five fictional witnesses known to the homonymous author at various stages of his life' (Hughes 2011).

It is, then, the status of the 'I' in autofiction that has generated so much debate. Where the character-narrator bears the same name as the author, thereby suggesting a degree of equivalence or at least overlap or complementarity, in what does this reside and how far does it or can it go? Writer Catherine Cusset, for example, follows Doubrovsky, rather than Vincent Colonna or Philippe Vilain, in presenting her understanding of *autofiction* as non-fiction but with the recognition that insofar as it is, like any kind of writing, a work created through language, there are of necessity fictional elements. This would seem to suggest that language both conceals and reveals, indeed perhaps more than one intends. For Cusset, it's also a risky enterprise, since invariably it touches on the lives of others. 'Rien n'y est inventé, le but étant au contraire de cerner au plus près le réel – pas la réalité, mais le réel, qui est d'un autre ordre, qui relève de l'expérience intérieure' (Cusset 2010, 36). (Nothing is invented, the aim being to get as close to the real as possible – not reality but the real which is of a different order and relates to one's inner life, my translation.) As Cusset's remarks suggest, any venture in writing or adventure in language, as Doubrovsky would have it, is likely to surface revelations about self and the self's relation to others that may not be fully conscious. In addition, particularly where it turns to the lives of others, as they impact on self, ethical considerations are likely to arise for those not prepared to sacrifice their lives for art, and in this sense Cusset contends that the novel may have advantages for some journeys of self-discovery and attempts to get close to the real.

We might think here, once again, by way of example, of the controversies provoked by Karl Ove Knausgaard's *My Struggle* series. A threatened legal challenge by his uncle on his father's side meant that some names in the work had to be changed and there was a rift in the family as a result of narrator Karl Ove's revelations about his father's alcoholism and the supposed accuracy with which he depicted certain scenes. Self-described as a 'non-fictional novel', and often seen as riding the autofictional wave (Power 2018), Knausgaard engages across the various volumes of the series with issues of truth, reality, memory and the effects of writing and representation. That there is a cost to writing from life is apparent in this case. Indeed, volume 6, *The End*, in English translation, treats, among other things, the aftermath of publication of volumes one and two, as well as the cost to Knausgaard's second wife of his determination to complete the project. In an article that examines Knausgaard's reception in the US, following its initial *succès de scandale* in his native Norway, Günter Leypoldt (2017) posits the view that in addition to the charismatic value bestowed on the *My Struggle* series, Knausgaard's literary success owes much to a feature of the *Zeitgeist*, that is to say, a hunger for reality, and a certain fatigue with a kind of panfictionalism.

In this sense, Knausgaard's apparent rejection of fictionality and his brutal honesty in seemingly opening up his life and by extension that of his immediate family to public scrutiny in the published pages of *My Struggle* found a public welcoming of his attempts to press everyday life into the service of existential and autobiographical enquiry in a blend of narrative and essay. What became the Knausgaard phenomenon would seem to relate to international reception of, and reader response to, even identification with, the kind of immersive everyday reality rendered in *My Struggle*. Knausgaard's obsession with recording in great detail the rhythms and routines of his life, however banal, in conjunction with his method of writing fast so as to try to circumvent the imposition of a fake narrative order, becomes a kind of artistic credo as well as a search for freedom from the constraints and impositions of conventional narrative form.

This is something that despite other differences, Knausgaard would seem to share with fellow writer Rachel Cusk. In an article in *The New Statesman* reviewing Knausgaard and Cusk's parallel projects on publication of their final volumes, Chris Power (2018) points to their commonality of purpose while acknowledging the differences between them. Both Knausgaard and Cusk felt that fiction had become fake; Cusk famously indicated that it was no longer possible to return to writing the kind of fiction she had previously written before turning her attention to memoir. Following a breakdown and period of writer's block, her return to writing in the form of the critically acclaimed 'Outline' Trilogy has potentially put Cusk into the autofictional frame, despite her own denials. Whether the 'Outline' Trilogy be categorized as 'pure' fiction or as autofiction may depend on a reader's knowledge of Cusk's own biography as well as on the extent to which Cusk's reversioning of aspects of the novel form is acknowledged in the critical literature. For while it might be said that the difference between author Cusk and character-narrator Faye is marked in nominal terms and in terms of their exact trajectories or life course, the parallels are sufficiently intriguing to draw attention to the relationship between life and art; and to invite discussion of the means by which the novel, rather than the memoir, is able to create the conditions of possibility for an interrogation of modes of truth-telling as well as flagging up, through comparative analysis, gendered reading and writing practices.

2.6 Concluding Remarks

In this sense, it might appear that the 'novel' is being pulled in different directions at the same time, one factual or non-fictional, drawing it closer to everyday reality, and away from imagined and/or invented possibilities, the other anti-narrative, depleting it of events and returning it to a structure of telling, rather than showing. There are those, like Knausgaard, who want literature to get closer to the 'truth' of reality, and who invest in an accretion of detail as a kind of warrant of the real with recursivity and non-linearity a means of approaching experience from different perspectives and over time. In Knausgaard's case, length is essential to the project, as is speed, the former in order to flesh out the multidimensional nature of experience as it is recreated and reviewed, the latter to try to short circuit the imposition of a 'fake' narrative order and free up the unconscious. The focus on self in Knausgaard's case and the strong narrative presence is less evidence of narcissism and more a rejection of evasionary tactics, whereby someone else, a fictional or semi-fictional character 'stands in' for or represents the authorial stance.

Then there are writers like Cusk whose return to the novel form following a series of personally costly memoirs appears to be setting a new novelistic agenda whereby the narrative proceeds through a series of retellings with movement across the series from the apparently monologic to the increasingly dialogic whereby the female self is rendered as the product of an exercise in close listening as well as close reading. Unlike Knausgaard, Cusk's project is minimalistic, both in terms of length, and in terms of narrative presence, insofar as her narrator appears to stand at a distance from all she surveys and is more like a kind of listening device, though of course in reality transcription of what she hears and of what others choose to tell her is tightly controlled and organized. As a pairing coming at a reinvestment in the novel form from an autofictional standpoint, it might be said that in many ways Knausgaard and Cusk assume gendered positions, while at the same time contextualizing and interrogating them.

Indeed, a double issue of *English Studies in Canada* examines recent Anglophone interest in autofiction and includes an article on Cusk's 'Outline' Trilogy. Noting the disjuncture and differences between French *autofiction* and Anglophone understandings and applications of autofiction, it nevertheless considers autofiction to be 'an ascendant mode of production in the digital age' and 'a nascent lens within the field of English Studies' (Bloom 2019, 2). In introducing the double issue, Bloom acknowledges the fact that many female writers viewed by critics in autofictional terms reject the label, in some cases a reaction against previous attempts to categorize women's writing as confessional or concerned with the domestic and personal, rather than with larger issues of universal concern. While distinguishing autofiction as mode of reception as well as of production, she points to 'its overt play on the line between fact and fiction explicitly targeting these categories and, by extension, the hierarchy that subordinates (feminized) personal experience to the realm of (masculinized) high art' (Bloom 2019, 12). In so doing she reads this play as a deliberate contestation of taken-for-granted assumptions, based on gendered readings of text, that would align the confessional and the feminine.

The question of the extent to which Cusk may be said to engage with such an autofictional project is taken up by Karen Valihora (2019, 21), who sees Cusk's work as 'concerned with the border between art and life, as well as that between one person and another'. She points to the difference between the 'concentrated renditions and the reality of day-to-day conversation' (21) in Cusk's 'Outline' Trilogy which reflects the artfulness of the narrative method she employs in her use of reported speech and free indirect discourse, as narrator Faye both recounts and reflects on the stories told to her by others. Valihora (2019, 35) sees the 'form of the narratives' as creating 'an uncanny effect of reality', in incorporating in the novels a meditation on the blurring of the boundary between teller and hearer, writer and reader.

Where for some writers of autofiction, there must be a degree of referentiality in terms of the real, for other writers, such as Philippe

Vilain, the real is simply a point of departure for a fictionalization of self. In work such as *Faux-père* he considers what might have been, rather than what was, in relation to the outcome of a pregnancy on the part of a partner. In sum, he considers that the mechanism by which his stories function is by addition or subtraction, and so are partially true (Vilain 2010). The lived life of the writer and the proximity of his real-life preoccupations realized in fiction can be seen as a working through of psychic and material realities.

There are a couple of ways in which Vilain's understanding of the real as a point of departure for fictionalization through various translational processes, such as addition and subtraction, is of more general interest and import. Firstly, there is recognition of (necessary) translational difference in rendering aspects of a life in the move from lived experience to writing and documenting and/or recovering that experience. The translation of a life becomes an operation dependent on linguistic tools and psychological processes. Secondly, the notion of rendering the spirit or feel of a period by considering what might have happened rather than what actually happened is another translational move which affords the writer narrative techniques – what if? – to create dialogue between the actual and the might-have-been. As I have argued elsewhere (Doloughan 2019), in the case of a writer such as Xiaolu Guo, a creator of fictions, film documentaries, and a memoir, which she prefers to frame as a documentary novel, disentangling the documentary from the novelistic, across a series of interconnected projects, can be tricky. Rather, a line can be traced across Guo's *oeuvre* which links episodes and their narrative representation to thematic and aesthetic concerns, rather than in relation to notions of truth and fiction. As a writer and filmmaker who hails from China but whose education, professional and personal trajectory has placed her within a broadly European ambit, it is interesting to consider the extent to which different representational and narrative cultures may impact upon the generic shape of and response to her work.

Chapters 3–6 will review the writerly trajectories and ambitions of Knausgaard, Winterson, Guo, and Cusk in turn, focussing on analysis and reception of specific genre-challenging work in the case of each writer. The final chapter will return to the initial concerns of the monograph in the light of examination and discussion of the work of each writer and demonstrate the extent to which their interests, methods and philosophies dovetail with, or depart from, one another, as well as reflecting or refracting more general twenty-first century literary trends.

Chapter 3

THE ANATOMY OF A WRITER: KARL OVE KNAUSGAARD'S *MY STRUGGLE*

3.1 Introduction

This chapter will treat a work originally written in Norwegian and its critical reception in English translation. It will focus on debates relating to categorization of Knausgaard's work, taking account of the writer's stated aims and ambitions in producing his multivolume work, *Min Kamp* (2009–2011), published subsequently in English as *My Struggle* (2012–2018), as well as critical responses to it. In discussing a work in translation, analysis will inevitably remain at the structural and macro-level, rather than engaging in a detailed analysis of style at the micro-level. However, in navigating critical responses to the work's potentially controversial substance, its structural and thematic concerns, and in treating issues of genre in the light of authorial aims and ambitions, the chapter will set the scene for further discussion of trends in contemporary writing in terms of its autofictional tendencies and its apparent scepticism about the value of 'pure' fiction at a time when so-called real-world problems and issues are taking centre stage.

As the Introduction to the book has made clear, the choice of works under study has been motivated by a desire to understand an observable contemporary phenomenon which sees interrogation of generic conventions in relation to notions of so-called fact and fiction and a kind of 'deep dive' by a number of writers into the affordances and limitations of novelistic resources in facilitating exploration and articulation of the self and its manifestation in auto/biographically focussed narratives. Inclusion of Karl Ove Knausgaard with a focus on his *My Struggle* series has been motivated by a variety of factors, including the sheer scale of the work and the ambition of a writer who, having already enjoyed novelistic success at an early age, seemed to turn his back on fiction and move in the direction of writing from life. Indeed, much of the controversy relating to the work's reception has had to do with the very detailed account of the life, not just of narrator and central protagonist Karl Ove, but of the lives of other people close to him who might be said to have shaped and formed him (his father in particular; his brother) as well as those with whom he, in turn, created a home and family (his wife Linda and his children).

Min Kamp had already created quite a stir in Knausgaard's native country before it began to appear in English translation as *My Struggle*, with reviews and commentaries swift to follow. Given the work's length (approx. 3,600 pages in Norwegian), this vast translation project took time and energy on the part of its main translator Don Bartlett who produced volumes 1–5 of the *My Struggle* series in English translation, starting with volume 1, *A Death in the Family*, first published by Harvill Secker in hardback in 2012, with the paperback by Vintage following in 2014. The final volume, *The End*, appeared in 2018, having required the services of two translators, Don Bartlett and fellow translator Martin Aitken. As will be discussed, serial publication and the fact that the completed work was already available throughout Scandinavia to readers of Norwegian, Swedish and Danish impacted upon its reception by readers of English. This was particularly true in the case of the final volume whose inclusion of an essay on Hitler's *Mein Kampf* was much discussed and alluded to by critics and reviewers, well in advance of publication in English. And as most would not have had access to it except in translation, their pre-publication comments must inevitably have been formed by what had already been said about the work and its controversial content by others.

As well as the time lag in terms of access to the six volumes of *My Struggle* in English translation, the fact that the work has been differently presented and marketed across cultures has also impacted on its reception by readers, both general and specialist. At the level of generic categorization, for example, the work was originally published as a novel in Norway, despite, or perhaps because of, the controversies and proposed legal challenges surrounding publication. Knausgaard's uncle on his father's side is said to have taken exception to presentation of the author's father and threatened to sue. In the event the editor, Geir Gulliksen, of the Norwegian publishing house, Forlaget Oktober, required Knausgaard to circulate copies of the first two volumes to the main 'characters' featured in it, with the option of changing their names and/or removing parts from the final draft. In the case of presentation of his (dead) father, Knausgaard felt entitled, as his son, to present what he felt to be a truthful account of his father's demise and decided to go ahead with publication. While originally the idea was to have published the work in twelve monthly instalments, it was finally agreed that six volumes of *Min Kamp* would appear over a two-year period, with Knausgaard forced to produce the remaining four volumes at breakneck speed. Speed of production was, therefore, built into the project, not as a mere marketing ploy, but as part of Knausgaard's overall writing method.

In the context of the focus of this book on issues of genre and deployment of modes of fictionality in relation to the truthful presentation of aspects of reality and attempts by writers to get closer to the real, critical reception of Knausgaard's *Min Kamp/My Struggle* is clearly of relevance and of interest in several ways, including the overall conception and design of the project and Knausgaard's working methods in relation to his writerly aims and ambitions. The manner of publication and the work's subsequent release in translation to an international public, alongside the controversies it generated, both in terms of content and style and in relation to the ethical questions it raised, make it somewhat difficult to separate out the various factors likely to have underpinned the phenomenal success enjoyed by Knausgaard both at home and abroad. To understand the Knausgaard phenomenon, its mediation and consolidation through translation, publication and marketing strategies, and international critical reception, it is necessary to look not just to the books themselves but also to the figure of Knausgaard the author as he presented himself in interviews, reviews and podcasts.

With his so-called rock-star looks, international appeal, and considered responses to questions posed by interviewers and audience members, his appearances at literary festivals and publicity events in the US and the UK served to bolster sales and to further increase his profile. Many high-profile literary writers such as Zadie Smith, Rachel Cusk and Jeffrey Eugenides endorsed his work and sang his praises. Reviewers, like readers, were divided: for some he was a literary sensation (Kunzru 2014), for others the 'merciless specificity' (Faber 2012) he detailed in the work and the achingly dull prose he produced was a sign not of the depths of his commitment to reality but another example of the emperor's new clothes. Equally, he has been 'hailed as one of the foremost practitioners of the newly invigorated genre of autofiction' (Spaeth 2018) and as a disrupter of contemporary fiction who 'has sought nothing less than to break the form of the novel' (Franklin 2018). Even such a small range of comments is evidence of the different takes on Knausgaard's project and mirror the range of voices, some of whom were wildly enthusiastic, others of whom were unimpressed by what they saw as the dull reality of what Knausgaard had produced. It can be said that Knausgaard's international success is reflective of the extent to which his work seems to have chimed with a variety of readers, and indeed writers, at a particular cultural moment. Yet it can also be argued that Knausgaard's literary celebrity is evidence of the workings of the international publishing industry who invested in an already promising Norwegian writer, a recipient of literary prizes and awards, with cultural capital and prestige who posed minimal risk for the industry. As one reviewer put it: 'More than a "writer's writer" he was truly a publisher's writer' (Streeter 2018).

It may seem that such questions have little place in discussion of the merits of a work in terms of its contribution to an ongoing debate about the value and role of literature and the narrative strategies that best afford the writer a means of getting close to the reality of individual experience with a view to presenting it persuasively and with integrity to a reader whose own realities may differ. Yet understanding the cross-cultural reception of Knausgaard's work is part and parcel of getting to grips with its appeal and considering the extent to which it dovetails with, or departs from, the work of other contemporary writers such as Rachel Cusk who might be seen as mining similar autofictional terrain, albeit it in different ways.

3.2 Readerly Reception and Writerly Ambition

In a review of the first book in English translation of *Min Kamp*, James Wood writing in *The New Yorker* (13 August 2012) tries to characterize the work which he variously describes as an autobiography, a memoir and 'a kind of writing that accommodates variety – narrative and essay, the concrete and the theoretical, the general and the metaphoric' (88). Wood goes on to give a sense of the work's 'striking readability', despite, or perhaps because of, 'hundreds of pages of autopsied minutiae', noting Knausgaard's 'commitment to inexhaustibility'. He sees Knausgaard as a serious writer who reminds us of our mortality and notes the links with Proust's *A la recherche du temps perdu* in terms of Knausgaard's concern 'with the writing of a book that turns out to be the text we are reading'. Wood gives a sense of the power and strangeness of Knausgaard's world, as it is recreated in a blend of the 'sometimes visionary [...] sometimes banal [...] and sometimes momentous' course of a life. For Wood, *My Struggle* is a compelling read and even if at times he admits to having been bored, he assures the reader that he was never indifferent. Knausgaard's tendency to include everything means that while there are moments of banality, it is 'so extreme that it turns into its opposite, and becomes distinctive, curious in its radical transparency'.

Knausgaard himself describes his work in an article for *The Guardian* (26 February 2016) as 'a non-fictional novel' which draws on the confessional mode. Knausgaard's designation attends to the tension involved in writing from life: on the one hand, an expectation that 'you're dealing with something that actually happened' and therefore are presumed to be committed to telling the truth, however conceived; yet, on the other hand, and at the same time, there is awareness on Knausgaard's part that, of necessity, we try to impose patterns retrospectively on what has happened in order to make sense of it and thereby transform and re-arrange events and our (remembered) reactions to them. Elsewhere Knausgaard points to the irony of a book where there is 'a difference between the self who writes and the self who is written about' (Wood & Knausgaard 2014); one might add that there is always and necessarily a gap between the experiencing I and the writing I, as well as a difference between the author qua real person in the world and his, arguably, constructed, if not fictional, alter ego. In writing his multi-volume work so quickly (all six volumes were published in Norwegian between October 2009 and 2011), Knausgaard hoped to escape the effects of a consciously articulated and stylized way of writing and to inhabit as far as possible the immersive environment of his past, what Ben Lerner (2014) refers to in terms of the novel sequence as 'an artless infinity purchased at the cost of structure'. Yet, as will be discussed in what follows, the idea of this being an unstructured or incoherent novel sequence is not borne out by analysis nor does it conform to the reading experience of many for whom there is an emergent sense across the sequence of a deep engagement less with the so-called facts of a life but rather with both interiority – the life of the mind – and with the at times intangible connections made between aspects of existence and biography across a life through writing. This is a work that contests or at least interrogates the autobiographical pact (cf. Lejeune), while constructing a narrative of self, realized and brought into being through the act of writing.

For writer and critic Blake Morrison (2016), Knausgaard has written an 'autobiographical epic'. Morrison refers to its 'surprising narrative momentum', suggesting that as readers we might expect to be waylaid by the 'meticulous detail' at the expense of the plot or become absorbed by the 'Knausgaardian voice', such that we fail to appreciate the book's compelling (narrative) drive. Trying to pinpoint the appeal of Knausgaard's prose when descriptions of his work can make it sound unappealing (e.g. 'novelistic micro-realism' (Wood 2012); a world dominated by 'trifles and inconsequential detail' (Knausgaard 2016) is difficult but perhaps it has something to do both with the scale of the ambition – 'how to bring order to the undifferentiated mass of experience' (Lerner 2014) – and the manner of its realization – 'the elegant, large-scale formal symmetries Knausgaard's digressiveness often works to obscure' (Lerner 2014).

For me, as a reader, comparisons with Proust's *A la recherche du temps perdu* (henceforth *A la recherche*) are apposite both in terms of Knausgaard's 'dawning realisation that his talent lay in life writing' (Morrison 2016) – this is in many ways a *Künstlerroman* in which Knausgaard both discovers and realizes his vocation as a writer, and yet it is more complicated than that. For, as the title suggests, his struggle relates not just to writing but to his very relationship to the world and is existential in nature. Lerner (2014) suggests that this is 'a portrait of an artist who will turn his back on art' but perhaps the very motivation for the work is a tear in the fabric of existence – the very death in the family of volume one – consciousness of which spurs him on to find a means of creating or rather re-creating 'an ocean of quotidian existence', that diffuse but detailed universe which has enveloped him and will enfold the reader. Against this backdrop 'comes death with its unprecedented concentration of meaning' (Knausgaard 2016b). Meaning, for Knausgaard, seems to relate to loss and to language, while writing is 'drawing the essence of what we know out of the shadows' (Knausgaard 2014a, 212–213). Wood (2012) suggests that the 'insane attention to objects' in Knausgaard's work 'is an attempt to rescue them from loss, from the loss of meaning'. But it is not just objects to which Knausgaard directs his attention (e.g. books, paintings, guitars) but also behaviours, activities and reflections. In this sense, he might be considered a kind of ethnographer of the self. In describing it thus, I mean to suggest that Knausgaard's seeming self-absorption is less a kind of narcissism and more an exploration, through introspection and reflection, of the formation of self against the backdrop of cultural, social, and biographical norms and conventions, and a profound meditation on modes of perception and the nature of consciousness. Across the volumes of *My Struggle*, Knausgaard conducts a 'Me-Search', inserting a kind of 'thick' description within an autofictional narrative which reworks 'life-world experiences in lightly fictionalised form' (Brown and Patterson 2021, 13).

3.3 *A Death in the Family*: Narrative Themes and Structural Organization

Book 1, *A Death in the Family*, opens with reflections on death, both in the physical and the metaphysical sense. The narrator, who later identifies himself as 39-year-old Karl Ove Knausgaard, born in December 1968, married for the second time with three children (Knausgaard 2014a, 27), begins by contemplating the impact on the body of the heart stopping and outlines the subsequent changes to limbs, intestines, blood and skin of this ceasing of activity and of life. He goes on to reflect on the ways in which people in reality (rather than in fiction) react when confronted with a dead body and muses on the fact that in society there is a rush to cover and remove dead bodies, to keep them out of sight. For Knausgaard (2014a), this 'collective act of repression symbolized by the concealment of our dead' (5) is evidence of our inability to cope with too much reality. Rather we develop systems for dealing with death, for keeping death 'out of sight' (6) or alternatively we present death as something mysterious, something ethereal, something light, images with 'no weight, no depth, no time and no place' (7). Into these meditations on death, Knausgaard slips the narratorial 'I', almost unobserved, mid-paragraph (8) to relate an episode that will recur in the book where a young eight-year-old Karl Ove is watching news of the disappearance of a fishing boat off the coast of Northern Norway and, as he watches the waves, he sees the outline of a face. Frightened by what he sees, he has to tell someone and as his mother is out and his brother is playing football, he goes into the garden and tells his father. His relationship with his father, as the reader discovers, is vexed: later that night the young Karl Ove witnesses his father laughing when the news report comes on again and the father sees no face. Karl Ove, observing his father's reaction from a distance, feels such shame that he returns to his room and cries himself to sleep.

In relating the episode of this first mediated encounter with death, the narrator is careful to distinguish his relation of what happened at the time from his subsequent thoughts and feelings. Indeed, a double perspective is built into the narrative:

> My picture of my father on that evening in 1976 is, in other words, twofold: on the one hand I see him as I saw him at that time, through the eyes of an eight-year-old: unpredictable and frightening: on the other hand, I see him as a peer through whose life time is blowing and unremittingly sweeping large chunks of meaning along with it. (12)

Meaning (and loss of meaning) here seems to be connected with the passage of time. Knausgaard dramatizes the scene in which he tells his father what he has seen and records his father's reaction to it in dialogue as well as recounting the way in which the face that he has seen on television returns to his mind and now assumes his father's features, a sign to the reader, if it were needed, of the complexities of the father–son relationship and a foreshadowing of what is to come and what, in effect, constitutes the core of this volume, Karl Ove's father's death, detailed description of the circumstances of which will occupy the last two-fifths of the book.

Consideration of the opening of the book with its somewhat abstract focus on death and its air of meditation on meaning, knowledge and experience over time already gives a sense of the features of Knausgaard's work: its recursiveness, as scenes and images are revisited and mined for (sometimes shifting) meaning; its structure, as one section leads to another by virtue of thematic and associative, rather than linear or causal, connections; its density and texture as the reader moves from past to narrative present in a series of meditative loops, while engaging with a 'thick' description of aspects of a life remembered, reconstructed and reinvented. Already on p. 30, the narrative present disrupts the relation of past events to situate the writer's present conjunction of circumstances: sitting in his book-lined office, listening to music and thinking about what he has written and 'where it is leading' (30). He reflects, in his writing, on how he has got to this point in his life and how it would have been difficult to predict his present location in Stockholm, Sweden from his life just six years ago. A change of city and country, from one day to the next, initially for a short period, became his life (31). Serendipity plays a role, as does coincidence: he ends up marrying the woman he has known from a previous writing residential and whose name he comes across again when looking for a flat. The 'almost morbid amount of time' (32) he has spent thinking about the past and imbibing Proust's *A la recherche du temps perdu* has given way to his present life in which he is occupied by children and the art of daily life. Now his life is repetitive, enclosed and unchanging but it also serves to protect him from his doubts, vulnerabilities and self-destructive tendencies. What has kept the narrator going, he declares, is his life's ambition: 'to write something exceptional one day' (35), while acknowledging the struggle that is everyday life.

The birth of his children, particularly the first, has brought great joy; at the same time, however, the fact that time is slipping away, 'running through my fingers like sand' (35) frustrates Karl Ove who requires a great deal of solitude and time to write. He feels shame over his inability to cope with the demands of his children and daily life. He admits that the joys of family life are not his goal: 'I do everything I have to do for the family; that is my duty' (39). However, the happiness that family life produces 'is not sufficient to fulfil a whole life' (39). In playfully imagining his own epitaph, he indicates a need to use the time slipping through his fingers to good account in his writing. In effect, the whole multi-volume enterprise that is *My Struggle* is an attempt through writing to make sense of lived experience as it is remembered and transformed and to constitute a record of the trials of a compulsive need to write in the midst of a life that requires attendance to daily necessities. Knausgaard's story is at one level unique – the facts of his life are not those of another. Yet insofar as he is articulating the events and circumstances of his life and reflecting on his needs, desires and ambitions, particularly as they relate to his emerging vocation as a writer, this non-fictional novel fits a kind of pattern: that of the making of the artist. In this sense Knausgaard's work, as already indicated, can be seen to be yet another example of the *Künstlerroman* like Joyce's *A Portrait of the Artist as a Young Man*.

In conveying in volume 1 a kind of detailed exposé of his struggle to come to terms with the circumstances and aftermath of his father's death and in revisiting the strong sense of shame and humiliation attached to aspects of his life, including the somewhat abusive and certainly conflicted relationship with his father, Knausgaard begins a process that will extend over the duration of the work. Like Proust's *A la recherche*, Knausgaard's multi-volume work creates by virtue of its very extensiveness, recursivity and multi-layeredness an all-encompassing, all-absorbing textual universe. In *A Death in the Family*, the quest for meaning takes precedence over happiness which the narrator describes as 'banal' (Knausgaard 2014a, 39). He is concerned to understand what it is about art and about writing that compel his attention and cause him to react at a deep level: 'When I look at a beautiful painting I have tears in my eyes, but not when I look at my children' (39). This has nothing to do with the fact that he does not love his children. On the contrary, he indicates that he loves them with all his heart (39). What Knausgaard is trying to get at through a series of questions and answers about the exclusions and permissions of the writing life is the way in which it seems to entail certain choices or ways of living that put it at odds with the mainstream: he contrasts his messy, financially unstable family life with the kind of professional security and well-organized modes of living he sees around him. For Knausgaard, life is something to be endured and writing a way of 'burn[ing] up the longing generated by this' (39).

That writing is a kind of quest or a way of negotiating conflicts generated by competing realities or conflicting demands is not new. What is perhaps different about Knausgaard's work is the scale and ambition of the enterprise: a seriousness of purpose and a persistence in posing questions about meaning and about life. In addition, his ability to incorporate into the work all aspects of life from the seemingly banal – making coffee, having a shower, preparing something to eat, getting his children ready to go out – to the metaphysical and existential – how to make sense of experience, how to live life in a meaningful way – functions as a kind of refusal to filter out the everyday. This is a work at odds with prevailing orthodoxies in the Creative Writing classroom – to show, not tell. It is very much about telling, about musing and reflecting, about the battle between cognition and emotion and about the messiness and chaos of a life devoted to art. Knausgaard's espoused working method – writing at speed – is, he claims, an attempt to draw on the unconscious with a minimum of self-censorship in an effort to permit the unconscious free passage. Yet, arguably, *My Struggle* is also a work that bears scrutiny from a structural point of view.

Volume 1, *A Death in the Family*, is divided into two parts with no chapter divisions, just spaces separating out multiple sections or blocks of text. These blocks have no titles but can be seen upon reflection to have a certain coherence or at the very least an internal and associative logic that flows from their very contiguity. For example, early in part one, as Karl Ove moves from recollections of his eight-year-old self to an account of his thirty-nine year-old self – the one who is sitting writing (27–28) and looking at his reflection in the window – he muses on the gloominess of his face and how his features, furrowed brow and cheeks, serious and staring eyes, reflect aspects of his experience to date: a man for whom socializing comes at a cost and who would rather protect himself from the gaze of others. The following section moves from an assertion that while the ageing process engraves itself on the body, the eyes retain their brightness: 'the light in them never changes' (28). There is then an associative link to a late self-portrait by Rembrandt in the National Gallery in London which Knausgaard sees as emblematic of a work that both marks the passage of time in its rendering of the face and yet manages simultaneously to 'transcend the time that otherwise marks the face' (28) through the brightness with which the eyes are painted. He goes on:

> That which, in a human, time does not touch and whence the light in the eye springs. The difference between this painting and the others the late Rembrandt painted is the difference between seeing and being seen. That is, in this picture he sees himself seeing while also being seen, and no doubt it was only in the baroque period with its penchant for mirrors within mirrors, the play within the play, staged scenes and a belief in the interdependence of all things […] that such a painting was possible. But it exists in our age, it sees for us. (29)

If I have quoted this passage at length, it is because it is illustrative of Knausgaard's process, as he moves from consideration of his reflection in a window and of the features of his face, as they are marked by experience, to contemplation of what it is that remains through time of the essence of a person – his light – just as Rembrandt's late work might be seen to embody for us today this search for what remains after everything else has passed. Knausgaard's description in words of what he sees as he gazes at his reflection in the window, itself an act that leads to a meditation on the difference between early and late Rembrandt and what it means to see and be seen, is also a kind of figure of or for the writing life and the writing of a life. For in reviewing his life and committing to words a version of that life as it appears to him through writing, Knausgaard is both seeing and being seen. As the agent of the act (of seeing and of writing), Knausgaard is both initiator and object of the gaze of the reader, as well as being a subject to whom something is disclosed in the process of writing and made available thereafter to reflection. What, in effect, Knausgaard is describing are acts of consciousness and meaning-making; he is trying to articulate a link between perception and comprehension positioning both perceiving subject and object of perception within a space of mobility and simultaneity.

Knausgaard's father's death is a recurring and central event in volume 1 that culminates in a description of the lifeless body on a table in the funeral parlour.

> I saw his lifeless state. And that there was no longer any difference between what once had been my father and the table he was lying on, or the floor on which the table stood, or the wall socket beneath the window, or the cable running to the table lamp beside him. (490)

From the moment that Karl Ove learns of his father's death and sets out with his brother Yngve for Kristiansand by car, a good 200 pages are devoted, on and off, to the relation of a visit to the undertaker's; arrival at their grandmother's house where their father had been living and where his body had been found; and detailed descriptions of the clean-up operation on the house which they find in a terrible state. Their father's presence looms large over the narrative, even after his death, as his sons try to come to terms with what has happened to their estranged father, while dealing with the practicalities of death. It is almost like exorcizing a ghost who has pursued them relentlessly. The moment of 'letting go' comes for Karl Ove at the moment when he understands on seeing for a second time his father's body laid out on the table that his father's power has been extinguished and that death which he had always believed to be 'the greatest dimension of life, dark, compelling, was no more than a pipe that springs a leak, a branch that cracks in the wind, a jacket that slips off a clothes hanger and falls to the floor (490)'. The images, at least in English translation, suggest something ordinary, rather than extraordinary, an effect of chance or of pressure as much as an event consequent upon age or the passage of time. The image of the jacket slipping off a coat hanger makes death appear inconsequential, a mere trifle, and yet something over which you have no control.

In a Vintage podcast recorded on the occasion of publication of volume 2 of *My Struggle* entitled in English translation, *A Man in Love*, Knausgaard indicates that his interest lies in creating or evoking the space in between private things and big ideas. Volume 1 certainly shows evidence of this: from consideration of the 'moment life departs the body' (4) in a general meditation on death at the beginning of the book to an almost forensic account of the aftermath of the death of his father, a very particular death and set of circumstances, not all of which are explained or explainable. Death bookends the volume and casts a shadow over it but death is also connected to the passage of time and the Knausgaardian search for meaning. Knausgaard is at pains to understand the mechanisms by which meaning is produced and how to make sense of the flow and banality of life. He generalizes from his own experience inviting the reader to accept this 'universalizing' account. As with his initial observations of and commentary on the rituals and behaviours of death, Knausgaard's remarks are assertive and assume a common perspective on such phenomena.

> Throughout our childhood and teenage years we strive to attain the correct distance from objects and phenomena. We read, we learn, we experience, we make adjustments. Then one day we reach the point where all the necessary distances have been set, all the necessary systems have been put in place. That is when time begins to pick up speed. It no longer meets any obstacles, everything is set, time races through our lives, the days pass by in a flash and before we know what is happening we are forty, fifty, sixty [...]. Meaning requires content, content requires time, time requires resistance. Knowledge is distance, knowledge is stasis and the enemy of meaning. (12)

This passage precedes the one already quoted where Knausgaard acknowledges the double perspective embedded in his writing which allows him both to return to or conjure up the past while recognizing that time has altered the perspective from which the past is viewed. It talks about the role of knowledge and learning in mediating our perceptions of the past and the ways in which distance is critical in separating us from the immediacy and rawness of childhood feelings and reactions. It describes a quickening of time and conveys a sense of inevitability as we move towards death. That knowledge is stasis suggests that it stands in the way of movement and flux; it settles or determines meaning, the suggestion being that meanings are shifting and made in dynamic interaction between subject and object. With time, and a change in geography, Knausgaard's feelings about the patterning and purpose of life change. He indicates that having from one day to the next changed countries (from Norway to Sweden), his outlook also changed. He is cognizant of the impact of environment on eliciting memories: the 'small landslides of feeling' (224) triggered by certain landscapes and the people connected to them elude him here.

In the aforementioned podcast, Knausgaard talks about his desire to break free of form. What he means by form is not directly articulated but it might be assumed to relate to a mode of organization or recognizable textual design that helps shape reader reactions to the unfolding material. The extent to which a particular writer is conscious of creating or designing textual material in relation to formal requirements is of course itself a matter for debate or speculation but given that Knausgaard discusses form in relation to the production of literature in *A Death in the Family*, it is clearly a matter that preoccupies him as a writer. The context for this discussion of form is itself interesting insofar as it relates more generally to writing, what it entails and how it functions. Having found an office in the centre of Stockholm where he can come to write, the narrator describes his efforts to rework a draft novel he has written in line with the advice of a critical friend who indicates that he needs to tell a story and that, he indicates, is what he tries to do. Glancing at a poster in his office, a memory is triggered from his childhood and he is taken back to his parents' living room in the 1970s and to a moment in time that seems to have been preserved or re-awakened. The images which come to mind stir in him feelings, 'an almost uncontrollable longing' (Knausgaard 2014, 211) which he seeks to fathom. What follows next is a mix of description, reflection and commentary as Knausgaard attempts to get to the bottom of his reaction. 'Writing', he affirms, 'is drawing the essence of what we know out of the shadows' (212). In so doing, he acknowledges the role of the unconscious, the hidden or the forgotten in the creation of knowledge, attributing to writing the function of channelling this hidden or secret knowledge. A few pages further on, he reflects further on the quality of what he has produced and indicates what he is looking for. In terms of what he has produced, he reckons that it contains the 'germ of an idea' but 'in a form that was too compressed' (217) and describes how for several years he had tried to write about his father but hadn't succeeded in producing what he wanted, 'probably because the subject was too close to my life and thus not easy to force into another form, which of course is a prerequisite for literature' (217).

There are a number of observations to be made here. The compression of form that the narrator refers to seems to suggest that length and/or the oblique or elliptical nature of what he has written detract from the effect the work is intended to produce and is evidence of the fact that Knausgaard is conscious of there being something missing. The sense that a subject too close to life requires a different form, presumably from that of the draft novel Knausgaard has been working on, and that form is a prerequisite of literature, is indicative of a struggle to achieve in his writing a form appropriate to the material. In the discussion that follows, writing is characterized as being 'more about destroying than creating' (218). Extra-textual comments made by Knausgaard suggest that he saw what he was doing in *My Struggle* as a kind of literary suicide but that in some ways having broken the taboo of writing about his life and triggering a crisis of privacy, he ended up having the freedom he needed to continue. That Knausgaard exploits the tensions around genre in his work both intra-textually and extra-textually is reflected in the following quote by a critic: 'Knausgaard's stance, leveraged external to the book, but structurally echoed within it, cleverly skewers the line of attack that would seek to connect him too closely to the reality he portrays, even as he benefits – in often painstaking detail – from the grit of that reality' (Sala 2018,163). In other words, for Sala, there is a measure of narratorial performance at work here in the apparent spontaneity and honesty of Knausgaard's utterances which are belied in the work by strong evidence of structure and an associative logic; the public persona interacts with, and serves to frame, subsequent ways of reading the work. Sala (2018,166) continues:

> Knausgaard is less interested in literal truth as he is in the deeper representativeness that autobiographical detail can assume, if properly framed, arranged on the page and within the potential space of the text to create a degree of self-reflexive dissonance in the representation.

There are a number of points to be made here. Sala's reference to 'the deeper representativeness that autobiographical detail can assume' is suggestive perhaps of a truth or aura of authenticity that can be created through a telling detail, where verifiability or extra-textual correspondence is less important than 'self-reflexive dissonance' within the space/s of the text (Sala 2018, 166). Sala seems to be suggesting that awareness of things that don't quite stack up or which appear contradictory or out of keeping with the main tenor of the narrative are in fact markers of a self-aware agency. Perhaps he is alluding to a way of writing, and ultimately, of reading a text that allows for doubt, uncertainty and potential contradictions, even seeing these as guarantors of a sincerity and probity of purpose. In addition, it is difficult not to recall Barthes' notion of 'l'effet de réel' (Barthes 1968) or the reality effect, his characterization of the workings of Realist fiction whereby a text created an illusion of reality through an additive logic of description and/or by reference to a telling detail intended to 'stand in' for or connote aspects of a social reality. Insofar as Knausgaard's social and mental world is described in sometimes excessive detail, attention is drawn to the milieu (social and familial as well as psychological) he inhabits or, more accurately, is assumed by the reader to inhabit. Yet Knausgaard's role as narrator-protagonist is complemented and undercut by Knausgaard, the celebrity author who has engaged in readings, interviews and writing about his books and their construction. These media appearances and engagements with other writers, critics, reviewers and members of the audience, in person, in print and online, serve simultaneously to frame, contextualize, elaborate and comment on his own work, including its genesis, production and reception. In other words, there is a certain porosity at work here between interpretation and reception of the books themselves and the manner in which they are presented and discussed. Indeed, given their initial publication in Norwegian (2009–2011) and the time lag between their translation, across multiple volumes, into other languages including English (volumes 1–5 were published between 2012 and 2016; volume 6 did not appear in English translation until 2018), it is clear that their serial publication, international distribution and marketing across national and linguistic boundaries all created an interpretive frame for their reception and critical review.

3.4 Cultures of Reading and the Role of the Critic

Interestingly, towards the end of Lejeune's chapter on 'The autobiographical contract', in which he sets out parameters for distinguishing between autobiographical fiction and autobiography, as well as between biography and autobiography, he arrives at the conclusion that it is 'in terms of the kind of reading it engenders, the inherent credibility it reveals, which can be elicited from the critical text' (Lejeune 1982, 220) that autobiography is to be defined. As Lejeune has made clear elsewhere in the chapter, reading as a practice has a historical dimension, while readers themselves are diverse and modes of reading comparative and relative rather than universal and absolute. As well as being bound by convention, autobiography is a product of publishing codes that govern the nature of the contract between reader and writer. Autobiography, then, is 'as much a way of reading as a kind of writing; it is an historically variable *contractual product*' (220). There are a number of threads to be drawn out here: firstly, the search for a particular style of writing or recognizable or agreed generic or structural features, something intrinsic to the text, is shown to be difficult to pin down for all time. Nor is adjudication of a set of truth claims verified in relation to some extra-textual authority a sure-fire method of categorization. Rather acknowledgement is made of the extent to which reading habits change, often as a function of ideas about what constitutes truth in relation to the fictional and the real and their preferred or anticipated modes of narration.

While Lejeune's point relates to changes in reading cultures across time, there is another aspect to reception of Knausgaard's work worth pursuing, namely cross-cultural and cross-linguistic reactions, given the fact that the work was originally produced in Norwegian and has been translated into multiple languages (35 at the last count, according to the Vintage website). In his Introduction to a commentary on the, at that time, yet-to-be published volume 6 in English translation, Barnard Turner points to inclusion in the final volume of reflections on the controversy over publication of *Min Kamp* in Norway. The controversy was generated by a number of things, including reactions to volume 1 by members of Knausgaard's family, including his uncle who took issue with Karl Ove's representation of his father's death. The extent of Knausgaard's disclosure, not just about self, but about other members of his family was seen to be problematic in terms of whose truth prevails or whose story gets told and there was much discussion about the ethics of revelation and ownership of another person's life story, given that *A Death in the Family* revolves around the circumstances surrounding the death of Knausgaard's alcoholic father.

For literary critic and fellow Norwegian Toril Moi, Knausgaard's project has to be seen as a whole and what she calls the ethical turn in Knausgaard comes in volume 6 where, she argues, he opens himself up to 'the presence of the other' (Moi 2013, 210). She sees Knausgaard's whole enterprise as posing a problem for literary critics schooled in a particular way of treating works as objects and artefacts to be kept at a distance. Admitting, as a reader, to 'passionate engagement and identification' (205), with Knausgaard's *My Struggle*, she goes on to position Knausgaard's project in relation to 'a paradigm change' (206) – acknowledgement that authors actually exist – and indicates her view that the role of literary criticism is 'to show how a work, old or new, intervenes in its culture, [...], and make explicit its existential and intellectual challenge to the reader' (206). For Moi, this challenge relates to the relationship between life and form or the quest for a form that does not seek to deny the non-exclusive relationship between literature and life or to negate the dynamics of a work where 'the relationship between shame and openness is fundamental' (206).

Moi's reference to the role of shame and openness in the Knausgaardian project begs the question of the extent to which *My Struggle* relates to a kind of excessive or hysterical self-confession or a relentless search for meaning. Indeed, it might be argued that Knausgaard's treatment of shame and self-exposure has literary potential in *My Struggle*. It was in a newspaper article in *The Observer* from March 2015 that journalist Andrew Anthony drew attention to Knausgaard's 'distinctly unusual' and 'constant grappling with the question of shame'. Certainly, it is clear from reading *My Struggle* that his account of his youth, adolescence and adulthood is dominated by issues of self-esteem and self-image. He seems to suffer from a sense of inadequacy and regularly experiences humiliation, guilt and shame, as he is forced to confront his weaknesses or is made to feel powerless in comparison with others. Most famously, he suffers multiple humiliations as a child at the hands of his father. In addition, Knausgaard refers not infrequently in *My Struggle* to a strong desire to please and to fit in, while recognising that with respect to his writing what is required is isolation, a kind of withdrawal from the world and from engagement in social life. Indeed, Knausgaard's family life is also compromised, if not put at risk, by his overwhelming desire to be left alone to write, a move that could be seen to be shameful in itself.

Yet it seems that at the beginning of his writing career, Knausgaard was less aware of the role of shame in his work than was his editor who wrote the sleeve note to Knausgaard's first novel pointing to it as a kind of monument to male shame. But once Knausgaard recognized the existence of something that was so much a part of him that he took it for granted, he began to see its literary potential, by which I mean the extent to which shame provided substance for his narrative as well as a trigger for his writing. When asked about the role of shame in *My Struggle*, Knausgaard claims that:

> Writing is a way of getting rid of shame. When you write the whole idea is to be free. And what are you free from? *From people looking at you.* I think shame is an essential mechanism in social life. It regulates everything and makes people behave in a decent and appropriate way to each other. But I have kind of too much, an overdose. I'm so restricted I can't do anything. (Anthony 2015; my italics)

The idea that Knausgaard can exorcize shame through his writing is one that requires closer scrutiny, as indeed does the role of writing more generally in the construction of Knausgaard's sense of self.

3.5 Treatment of Shame in *A Man in Love*

The contexts in which episodes involving shame are treated in volume 2, *A Man in Love*, are many and various. Overall, feelings of shame are generated in relation to questions of masculinity, particularly in respect of the observance (or violation) of prototypical masculine attributes and behaviours, such as displays of physical strength; and perceived gender-appropriate behaviour. So, for example, Knausgaard's tendency to demonstrate emotion by shedding tears, not just as a child but also into adulthood, leaves him with a sense of failing to live up to masculine ideals. States of shame in Knausgaard's work tend to be induced by situations in which he feels powerless or weak, such as his failure at a party to break down the door to the bathroom where his heavily pregnant wife Linda has been trapped. Instead, he must ask a boxer to rescue Linda on his behalf and the episode causes him to feel first helpless and humiliated, then ashamed, exposed, as he feels himself to be, to the gaze and negative comparative judgements of others. On returning to their apartment after the party, Knausgaard indicates to Linda how ashamed he feels that he hadn't been able to kick in the door, and her reaction is one of astonishment: 'The thought had not even occurred to her. Why should I have done it? I wasn't the type, was I.' (Knausgaard 2014b, 40). Linda's reported reaction here is indicative of the fact that there is often a gap between

Knausgaard's perceptions and emotions in relation to specific situations and the way in which they are perceived and experienced by others. I wish here not simply to point to the role of different subjectivities in experiencing the world around them but to draw attention also to Knausgaard's narrative focus in this episode on the creation of a sense of self and the dynamics of shame: expressions such as 'my shame seared inside me'; 'I hadn't risen to the task'; and 'I was a miserable wretch' (40) translate a sense of his own psychology. At one level, within the context of an account of his life and his struggle to become a writer, it is only to be expected that Knausgaard is at the centre of his own narrative; at the same time, the mode of narration serves to imitate or replicate the dynamics of shame, giving the reader access to (a version of) Knausgaard's construction of self, whereby he is at times self-absorbed and fixated on his own sentiments at the expense of those around him. Exposure to the contempt or ridicule of others as well as failure to live up to his own ideals of behaviour seem to drive the dynamic that the narrative serves to recreate.

Indeed, many of the contexts in which Knausgaard feels shame have to do with a sense of being emasculated, seemingly provoked by his role as house husband, pushing a buggy around town with his daughter, Vanja, when he would much rather be writing. In essence, he feels deprived of the happiness and invincibility that can come over him when he is writing (79); but other emotions, besides shame, including anger and even rage, are experienced by Knausgaard at different times; these he also attributes to his role as house husband. While acknowledging that cultures change and roles can be reassigned, he indicates in no uncertain terms his unhappiness in assuming a traditionally female role:

> In the class and culture we belonged to, that meant adopting the same role, previously called the woman's role. I was bound to it like Odysseus to the mast: if I wanted to free myself I could do that, but not without losing everything. As a result I walked around Stockholm's streets, modern and feminised, with a furious nineteenth-century man inside me. (Knausgaard 2014b, 101)

Another potent example of this sense of shame and indeed a range of other emotions, including impotence and rage, generated in Knausgaard, is to be found in his narration of the Rhythm Class to which he takes his daughter as a baby. He describes it as a 'hall of shame' (88) and indicates that sitting on a mat on the floor with his daughter in the presence of other mothers and their babies was humiliating and degrading, all the more so, as he found the woman leading the group very attractive.

But sitting there I was rendered completely harmless, without dignity, impotent, there was no difference between me and her, except that she was more attractive, and the levelling, whereby I had forfeited everything that was me, even my size, and that voluntarily, filled me with rage. (86)

He leaves as quickly as he can without drawing attention to himself and once out on the street indicates that he 'felt like shouting till my lungs burst and smashing something' (88). Instead, he hurries away, putting distance between himself and the so-called hall of shame.

These few examples demonstrate some of the situations generative of a sense of shame in Knausgaard but of course they don't necessarily always indicate *why* he felt shame or distinguish with ease or consistency the whole range of emotions that he experiences, including guilt, shame, humiliation, mortification, anger and rage. In his work on shame, Wurmser (2015) indicates that 'shame should not be examined in isolation as affect or just in its social dimensions, but as *embedded in a web of manifold conflicts and traumata*, specifically in profound superego conflicts, and in vicious cycles of narcissism, masochism and self-destruction' (Wurmser 2015, 1616; my italics).

Certainly, in Knausgaard's case, his relationship to his father seems to have caused him repeated feelings of humiliation and shame as a boy, and discovery of the way in which his (by then estranged) father had been living as well as dealing with the conditions of his death seem to have been traumatic. A sense of inadequacy induced by rejection is also experienced in Knausgaard's life on multiple occasions, most notably when, as a young man, his first attempts to attract future wife Linda's attention fail and he repeatedly cuts his face in a display of self-destruction. Of this episode, he writes in *A Man in Love*: 'I had never experienced such shame before' (223), as he is forced to confront first his fellow writers, then the stares of people on the streets of Stockholm. 'The shame burned inside me, he writes, 'it burned and burned and there was no way out, I had to endure it, hold on, hold on, and then one day it would be over' (224).

3.6 Writing as a Mode of Survival

It is important to emphasize that not only is Knausgaard presumed to have experienced these emotions in reality but in writing about them and recreating through words the situations that generated them, he, in effect, lives through them a second time. This, in turn, raises the question of what Knausgaard is doing by seeming to focus on them or at least by incorporating them into his work, ostensibly a lengthy project about his struggle to write. It also begs the question of what he understands his writing to enable and/or to achieve. In other words, why spend so much time recounting episodes that seem to surface his feelings of failure, impotence, rage and shame? And what does such a self-portrait say about Knausgaard, as a man and as a writer?

One answer to this question is undoubtedly that writing is a mode of survival for Knausgaard in the sense that it provides him with a refuge from the gaze and expectations of others and offers him a space of potentiality rather than actuality. In volume 2 he describes a blissful period when, after their first daughter's birth, he was writing daily in his new office in Dalgatan, Stockholm, while Linda stayed at home with Vanja. It was a period of several weeks when, he writes: 'Everything was possible, everything made sense' (79). But the happiness and invincibility that he felt at that time was short-lived and something he claims to have 'searched for ever since, in vain' (79). While writing evidently remains a compulsion, judging from his continued production, how he represents his experience of it varies, even within the pages of *My Struggle*. This may relate to his familial context and shifting sense of self as well as to his understanding of the importance of writing in his life. As someone who avowedly likes to please and who aims to be a good person (cf. 102; 188), Knausgaard struggles with the conflict between living in the world and participating in the routines and obligations of family life, while craving maximum freedom from others and from self. It also relates to the fact that once he has enjoyed some success as a writer, he is torn between public recognition and the knowledge that actual writing requires a room of his own and simply getting on with it.

What writing seems to represent for Knausgaard, as well as an opportunity to rid himself of shame, is a way to 'recapture the world' (618) in all its complexity and multidimensionality. As a human being with a particular trajectory and life experience, Knausgaard wants to be able to express his individuality and represent it in such a way that it rings true. As a writer, he wants to lend his human experience a density, a visceral quality, a truthfulness and an authenticity that he feels to be lacking in a fabricated plot featuring a fabricated character (568). That is not to say that the representation of Knausgaard that the reader encounters in *My Struggle* can necessarily be taken at face value nor that we can simply read off from Knausgaard's self-portrait in the work an understanding of Knausgaard the human being, notwithstanding his espoused aims of getting closer to reality and writing as quickly as possible to avoid the interferences of rationality and a retrospective, more mature view. Indeed, Knausgaard recounts that when he delivered volume 3, *Boyhood Island*, to his publisher, his editor wanted him to add more adult reflection to his representation of events rather than simply conjure up his boyhood as if he were living it again.

In other words, it is important to remember in evaluating Knausgaard's depictions of episodes and events involving shame and associated feelings such as humiliation that the work sits within a culture and history of writing and particularly writing about self, even if its links to that culture and history appear at times oblique and oppositional. We might consider Knausgaard's connections to Proust as a case in point.

3.7 Memory and the Construction of Self

Volume 3 of *My Struggle*, entitled *Boyhood Island* in English translation, focusses on life for the Knausgaard family in the 1970s living on an estate on the island of Tromøya. Through a mix of description, dialogue and narrative recount, it provides a picture of the routines and behaviours, interests and obsessions, fears and anxieties of the young Karl Ove from whose perspective this period is evoked and recreated. There are several aspects of narrative treatment and organization worthy of comment in relation to this volume, which in many ways is somewhat different in tone and focus to the first two volumes. These differences relate partly to the fact that narration of Karl Ove's childhood is rendered in a voice that stays close to that of the child's perspective, creating a sense of immediacy, despite the choice of a past tense and retrospective point of view and the revelation at times, through comments and evaluations, of the presence of the adult narrator. Indeed, the opening pages of the volume appear to reconstruct a journey in seemingly precise detail with stretches of conversation of which the barely eight-month-old Karl Ove would have been entirely ignorant. It is clearly a reconstructed scene complete with short parental biographies and comments that appear to link the Knausgaard family to a particular time and place: Norway in the late 1960s. In addition, there is description of their surroundings as they walk 'on this hot overcast day in August 1969' (Knausgaard 2014c, 4) bearing suitcases and pushing a buggy in the direction of their new home. Reference to the features of the landscape and historical sites such as Tromøya church serve to ground the event temporally and geographically, while giving it all the appearance of reality.

Yet, these first few pages are then undercut by an admission: 'Of course I don't remember any of this time' (6), before the adult Karl Ove indicates that looking at childhood photos of himself from this period causes a sense of disconnect between what he sees – a 'me' he barely recognizes – and the person, a forty-year-old man sitting at his desk writing about his childhood. So already what is brought into play in the writing is a sense of the distance afforded by time between then and now, the different types of evidence that may signal a sense of the real and/or of presence (e.g. the photo; detailed description creating a reality effect), and the author's incredulity or at least uncertainty about the connections between the boy in the photo and the man at his desk: 'Is this creature the same person as the one sitting here in Malmö writing?' (6), he asks and begins to speculate on whether it might not make more sense to have different names attached to the different ages of man from childhood through to old age. Problematization of the assumption of there being in the man something of the child and of a relationship of identity assured by retention of the same, rather than different, names, is already a way of interrogating what it means to have a self or rather versions of self, and how it is possible to gather these different selves together under one name. He finishes by repeating: 'No, I don't remember any of this' (7).

There follows discussion of the role of photographs in constructing images of a past era and of the ways in which they allow subjects to fill in the blanks: 'From all these bits and pieces I have built myself a Karl Ove, an Yngve, a mum and dad, a house in Hove and a house in Tybakken, a grandmother and grandfather on my dad's side, and a grandmother and grandfather on my mum's side, a neighbourhood and a multitude of kids' (9–10). It is this 'ghetto-like state of incompleteness' (10) that he calls his childhood. Such a series of observations, if not actually a manifesto, certainly draw attention to the evidential base or the grounds on which the past is reconstructed and a sense of personhood is manifested.

The section that follows on memory indicates its general unreliability and the fact that there are different kinds of memory: what the narrator calls 'canonised memories' (11), which seem to refer to those whose existence has been established and corroborated through repetition and the words of others; then there are involuntary memories, where things 'rise into [...] consciousness of their own accord' (11) and bring in their wake 'an immediate, intense feeling of happiness' (11). The narrator goes on to pick out memories 'associated with the body' as when gestures or movements recall other occasions when the same gestures or movements were made; then there are 'memories that accompany emotions' (11) and those 'associated with a landscape' (11). The narrator goes on to give examples of landscapes that prompt associative memories: shingle in the driveway in summer, 1970s cars, the paths he took from home to the forest or to the new supermarket. These are literally pathways to the past and as he goes down them, further memories unfold: his fear of a neighbour's Alsatian dog, for example. But more generalized, perhaps representative memories also appear in relation to the estate where Karl Ove grew up which constituted for him 'the world' (15).

In this opening section, the older narrator provides commentary on the past even as he brings it to life. The past is framed, so to speak, by the narrator's current understanding of the place of the new estate in Norwegian society: 'An estate has no roots in the past, nor any branches into the skies of the future, as satellite towns once had' (15). A few essayistic sentences, clearly the product of the older narrator, position reconstruction of Karl Ove's past within a more general societal frame. While globally the narrative is retrospective, locally there are evaluative and explanatory comments from the older narrator's present perspective; equally these more generalizing reflections return to the individualized experiences of Karl Ove whose childhood is recounted in apparently rich detail and specificity. In other words, there is both a contextual societal lens and an individualized account of Karl Ove's boyhood and early adolescence until the age of 13, including his first day at school, his swimming lessons, his love of football and music, initial interest in girls (e.g. Anne Lisbet) and the first stirrings of sexuality, visits to his grandparents and a focus on the day-to-day routine of life: spending time with his mother, keeping out of his father's way as much as possible, yet invariably finding himself at the sharp end of his father's desire for a highly structured, tightly controlled existence. Through dramatization of particular scenes, putting on the TV without permission and apparently managing to break it, losing his socks after swimming, the reader experiences young Karl Ove's fear of his father and witnesses his father's rather overbearing treatment of him.

Of course, given the initial framing of the unreliability of memory and the fact that it is unlikely that Karl Ove will have remembered word for word the dialogues recreated in *Boyhood Island*, the reader may well be asking questions about the extent to which the sense of immersion in Karl Ove's boyhood world is simply an effect of the writing – a kind of reality effect produced by the accumulation of detail and the accretion of examples which begin to point in the same direction. Yet the accumulation and repetition across the volume of episodes that elicit on the part of Karl Ove, an emotional reaction, of fear and anxiety, mostly in relation to his father's treatment of him, or of wonder, excitement, and a sense of immersion in the moment (around music and books, for example, or the stirrings of sexual awareness) serve to render verisimilitude and credibility to a narrative of childhood into which the reader is drawn.

Despite, perhaps even because of, the older narrator's interrogative and evaluative comments, expressions of doubt and uncertainty about the reliability of memory, the environment into which the reader is drawn appears all-encompassing. The world of Karl Ove's childhood is at the same time very specific, in that it relates to a Norwegian childhood in Tromøya in the 1970s and early 1980s, and triggers a degree of empathy, if not identification, with the figure of the young boy as he negotiates relationships, both within the family and beyond, and begins to construct a sense of self and of his place within the world he occupies. The kind of concerns he shares with the reader are realized in such a way through dramatization and discussion or commentary that it is difficult not to experience by proxy the kind of emotions felt by Karl Ove or at least to understand the source of his fears and fantasies. Karl Ove is presented at different times as both victim and victimizer. His treatment by his father seems unkind and over-bearing, even malicious (e.g. 'fifty-two-card pick-up', 312–313), while Karl Ove's arrogance and lack of empathy towards others (e.g. the episode with Edmund, 242–245) is not glossed over but rendered in great detail. The perception of his classmates that he cries far too easily, has rather female interests (e.g. clothes; books), despite his love of swimming, football and music, give the reader a sense of the complexities and idiosyncrasies of his emerging personality. The manner in which the episode with girlfriend Kajsa, and its aftermath, is presented (434–442), is indicative of a gap in young Karl Ove's understanding of how to act with girls. Kissing is rendered as a competition between boys in terms of how long you can snog a girl, rather than seeming to relate to an expression of what are undoubtedly his genuine feelings for Kajsa. The reader learns, for example, that after Kajsa finishes with him, something the reader comes to expect, given his behaviour towards her, the young Karl Ove is devastated. Conscious of Karl Ove's hurt feelings, his brother Yngve takes him in hand and plays music for him, inviting him to listen to the lyrics which express loss but also acknowledge the healing effects of the passage of time (443–445).

The end of *Boyhood Island* coincides with Karl Ove's move with his family to Kristiansand, where his father has got a new teaching post. Brother Yngve refuses to leave, since he has only one year left at school. There is a confrontation between Yngve and his father but Yngve doesn't back down. This is a defining moment in the sense that the balance of power is shifting, at least in respect of relations between Yngve and his father. Karl Ove declares that at the time he was happy to leave this part of his life behind him, given his treatment by peers, but the volume finishes with the older narrator's recognition of the future importance of this period of his life: 'Little did I know then that every detail of this landscape, and every single person living in it, would forever be lodged in my memory with a ring as true as perfect pitch' (Knausgaard 2014c, 490). So contrary to some of the affirmations made at the beginning of volume 3, at least in relation to his early years, the narrator in a rather Proustian manoeuvre, having come to the volume's end, points to the future significance of the landscapes and people he has just evoked in writing, which unbeknown to the young boy at the time have lodged in his memory and are brought to the surface again through acts of voluntary and involuntary memory.

3.8 A Norwegian Proust?

The question of the relationship in terms of similarity and difference between Knausgaard's *My Struggle* and Proust's *A la recherche* is often posed and a range of answers given in relation to the overall Knausgaardian project. In some ways, Knausgaard's seeming insistence on moving away from the conventions of fiction, including away from a focus on structure and fine writing, towards a mode of writing from life that allows him to capture the ordinary and everyday and to let the words fall as they hit the page/appear on screen, is a kind of anti-Proustian aesthetic. Yet, as has been mentioned already in relation to *Boyhood Island*, there are a number of points of contact with Proust, most notably in relation to a discussion of different types of memory. In addition, while at one level mention of Tromøya Church and its history is motivated insofar as Karl Ove's childhood was spent in the area, it is difficult not to read it also in relation to Proust's interest in Combray. Indeed, the seeming attempt to create a kind of boyhood psycho-geography would present further parallels with Proust's endeavour in *A la recherche*. In an article in Spanish that examines the role of the descriptive passages of the church in Combray in volume 1, Violeta I. Garrido Sánchez (2018) uses close textual analysis to demonstrate the ways in which the narrator's recreation of his boyhood experience of accompanying his parents to church points, through the choice of epithets, scenes, and metaphors, to the creation of an aesthetic that 'thickens' time allowing the coexistence of both singular moment and its repetition through time, and presenting the reader with a recollection realized through language as if experienced for the first time.

Whether in Knausgaard, as in Proust, there is an attempt to regain time or simply a desire, even compulsion, to write is a moot point. To produce 3,600 pages of text that evokes the narrator's life from early years to early forties might suggest an attempt to use the material of everyday life to construct a sense of self, if not an essential self, then at least a writing self. The question of the motivation for writing is often complex and we know that Knausgaard's *My Struggle* was at least in part motivated by a desire to leave behind the fake and fictive and try to get closer to his experience of reality. Given that *Boyhood Island* consists of almost 500 pages of recollections and routines, the question of whether the volume represents a kind of nostalgia for the past or is simply an uncovering of the mechanisms and stirrings of boyhood, in terms of the child pre-figuring the man, is also a complex one. At the heart of *My Struggle* is the creation of a life story that depicts a portrait of the artist at a point when family responsibilities mean that time for writing is compromised and constrained by the demands of everyday life. As fellow writer, Rachel Cusk (2013), in her review of volume 2, *A Man in Love*, puts it: Knausgaard 'assumes the central role in what becomes a drama of consciousness in action, as the artist struggles to give a new and complete expression to his interior life in step with his life in the world'. She sees Knausgaard's project as 'perhaps the most significant literary enterprise of our times' insofar as he is trying to return what she calls authenticity to writing through a disavowal or questioning of story. In aligning the Proustian and Knausgaardian projects, she sees a 'readiness to dispense with the illusion of narrative in one's concept of living'.

This could be said to accord with the views of Garrido Sánchez (2018, 229) on Proust who writes: 'Para Proust la verdad del mundo no es referencial, sino simbólica, y se expresa en el arte, cuyo símbolo estético privilegiado es la representación de la cosa a través de la memoria' (For Proust truth about the world is not referential but symbolic and is expressed in art, whose privileged aesthetic symbol is the representation of the thing through its evocation in memory – my translation). The difference between Proust and Knausgaard could be said to reside in Knausgaard's apparent artlessness and in wanting to dislodge concern for structure and fine writing by focusing on the presentation of the everyday.

3.9 Knausgaard as Radical Realist and/or Autofictional Writer?

Knausgaard is aware of the limits of realism as a representational mode and shows himself to be an inheritor of the Romantic tradition insofar as he credits art with singular importance, while subverting, even ironizing, his Romantic tendencies. *My Struggle* is both epic *Künstlerroman* – a lengthy, some might say tortuous, account of one man's attempts to become a writer – and a digressive, self-referential and highly intertextual composition whose resistance to conventional modes of writing is signalled by its unevenness and hybridity in terms of style and substance. Knausgaard's insistence on getting closer to a sense of reality needs to be seen to operate in the context of an awareness of the impossibility of recreating the moment after the moment has passed, except in its cultivation through language. Yet despite, maybe because of, the excesses of Knausgaard's project in terms of its length, intensity and degree of self-absorption, the reader is witness to a profound engagement with what might be termed the existential – one man's search for meaning in life – in the construction of a compelling documentary narrative that does not shy away from self-exposure, a degree of banality, and a preference for telling rather than showing, in its examination of big questions and controversial issues. While Knausgaard's mode of inquiry may not appeal to all, with its confessional overload, and 'excruciatingly exposing' treatment of self (Andrews 2015), for others this 'six-part, wildly revealing autofiction saga', as Glancy (2018) terms it, will seem less a monument to male shame and more a literary and philosophical intervention in an ongoing debate about the function of fiction and fabrication in the construction of autobiographically focussed accounts of experience. In the so-called post-truth era, interrogating constructions of self in relation to a particular treatment of life and its evocation through memory, as well as establishing the kind of connections that pertain between and among perceptual, experiential and interpretive modes, is of the utmost importance. In this sense, Knausgaard's *My Struggle* series is a fascinating attempt to claim art as 'the last remaining place where life could show its true face' (Knausgaard 2014b, 163) and demonstrate the value of literature as an essential field of human inquiry.

The production of Knausgaard's *My Struggle* is also a radical act. It is written against the backdrop of failed attempts by the author to project a picture of his father and to explore his feelings towards him in fictional form, and a realization that the stuff of life is richer, stranger and more multi-layered than the fabrications of fiction. In refusing, at least in volumes 1 and 2 of *My Struggle*, to adhere to novelistic conventions in terms of conscious structuring, and the contrivances of plot, Knausgaard determined to let the writing take him where it would and to refuse, as far as possible, self-censorship. In reality, an argument can be made that despite Knausgaard's aims and intentions, there is, in fact, a discernible structure: the passage at the beginning of *My Struggle* – apparently the only passage consciously written in a literary style – on what happens to the body upon death, can be seen as an abstract precursor to the concrete and detailed account of the circumstances surrounding the death of Knausgaard's father in the latter part of *A Death in the Family*. And, as Knausgaard admits in volume 6, *The End*, he had to exercise more caution in writing subsequent volumes, given reception of the first two published volumes and their effects on his wider family.

It must be remembered, however, that while already a young writer of note, before publication of the *My Struggle* series, Knausgaard did not have to attend to the kind of international reception he solicited at a later date and was, arguably therefore, freer to write what he liked. Thereafter, it became more difficult to ignore public and family reactions. The design of the project, then, while determined in advance with his publisher, was realized, in terms of its completion, within a different frame than had been the case for volumes 1 and 2, despite Knausgaard's attempts to ignore the papers and what people were saying about him and just get on with the business of writing. Only in the final volume, according to Knausgaard, did he return to the roots of the project in terms of lack of self-censorship, detailing episodes of his wife Linda's bipolar disorder and confessing that his determination to write at all costs may have tipped her over the edge. Inevitably, then, volume 6 becomes a kind of reaction to the already published volumes, as well as containing strong meta-critical elements, including the essay on Hitler's *Mein Kampf*. In this sense a work that may have appeared rooted in the familial and life experiences of a single individual becomes much more explicitly a philosophical and existential struggle to understand not only the kinds of social contexts and political circumstances that mould or produce particular types of individuals but also to consider the notion of the will to power. While Knausgaard is not Hitler and *Min Kamp* is not *Mein Kampf*, there is recognition at the end of volume 6 of the destruction that has been wrought in writing and producing *My Struggle*.

The volume famously ends with Knausgaard's determination no longer to be an author, a determination belied by his subsequent publication record which includes a seasonal quartet and a book on the paintings of Edvard Munch, in addition to what has been hailed as Knausgaard's return to fiction, *Morgenstjernen* (2020) or *The Morning Star* (2021) in English translation.

3.10 Concluding Remarks

This chapter has treated both evolving writerly aims and intentions in respect of *Min Kamp* and its variable critical reception as it became available outside of Scandinavia in English translation. It has noted the difficulty in pigeonholing Knausgaard's *My Struggle* with any degree of authority, given its essentially hybrid nature as an autobiographically focussed narrative conscious of the dangers of narrativization and aware of the precarity of memory. It is, at the same time, a work that wants to get as close as possible to the reality of experience, while understanding the impossibility of closing the gap between past and present, experiencing 'I' and writing 'I'. Yet across the six volumes, a combination, to differing extents, of excessive attention to detail in the construction of a temporal and geographic milieu, of a critical self-representation and an evolving sense not just of the problematics of representation but also of the ethics of disclosure, characterize the work. Insofar as Knausgaard is conscious of a necessary degree of fictionalization, both in terms of novelistic techniques, and in relation to the presentation of self, he can be seen as an autofictional writer, yet one who is striving to renew the affordances of the novel in the direction of a radical realism. The line between Knausgaard as author and Knausgaard as narrator and as character (or object of perception) is thin and porous in the work – consciously so. In this sense, he is exploiting the inbuilt equivocation of attachment and detachment that Lanser (2005) draws attention to in relation to the 'I' of the beholder. Serial publication of the work and the time lag between its publication in Scandinavia and in English translation also impacted upon reception of the work insofar as it was framed and gossiped about in advance of its arrival. In addition, Knausgaard's prominence on the literary scene following the phenomenal success, by literary standards, of the *My Struggle* series also had the effect of further diminishing the gap between authorial presence as articulated in the book and the 'real' life of Karl Ove Knausgaard.

In a recent interview in the context of publication of his new work, Knausgaard discusses what he wants to do in writing literature.

> For me, literature is to try to reopen the things that are fixed [...] the things we have to fix for practical reasons, that are risky when they are unfixed. If it's fixed, it's easier – but that doesn't only go for gender; that goes for almost everything, like worldviews and science and religion. But in real life, outside of ideologies, everything is floating and there are no borders. Only in writing and reading can you unlock what you previously locked in, and you can move around, and it is you and the richness of who you are. (Peters 2021)

This suggests that it is in the space produced by writing literature that freedom and flexibility abound in terms of exploring and investigating the big questions and experimenting with the dissolution of borders that appear fixed: borders between life and death, between the image that a person presents to the world and their inner conception of self, between fiction and non-fiction. Knausgaard's new work, while in some ways a departure from what he was trying to do in his *My Struggle* series, insofar as this is an apocalyptic novel, a work bordering on genre fiction, nevertheless retains recognisable aspects of Knausgaard's trademark signature: intense interest in the mundane and the everyday even as his characters wrestle with 'how we think about mortality' (Garner 2021). And as this same critic remarks, Knausgaard, who is 'one of the finest writers alive' has not lost his 'ability to lock you, as if in a tractor beam, into his storytelling' (Garner 2021), even if, ultimately, the work is 'a somewhat programmatic novel of ideas' (Garner 2021). While the *My Struggle* series is certainly no 'programmatic novel of ideas' (Garner 2021), it too is a work that does not shy away from big ideas and from serious consideration of philosophical and existential questions. However, its central focus on the perspective and feelings of a single character-narrator who is both subject and object of inquiry does distinguish it from his most recent work, *The Morning Star*, presented as the first in a series of fictions. What remains constant in Knausgaard's literary production is the desire to interrogate what appear to be fixed generic categories and, to echo his words, to 'unlock' them. Literature remains, for Knausgaard, an open, rather than a closed, field; the novel form requires constant re-invention to escape the strictures of narrative conventions.

Chapter 4

COMPANION PIECES: JEANETTE WINTERSON'S *WHY BE HAPPY WHEN YOU COULD BE NORMAL?* IN RELATION TO *ORANGES ARE NOT THE ONLY FRUIT*

4.1 Introduction

Why Be Happy When You Could Be Normal?, Winterson's 2012 memoir, is described on her website as 'the silent twin' (http://www.jeanettewinterson.com/book/why-be-happy-when-you-could-be-normal/) to the story recounted in fictional form in her now classic *Oranges Are Not the Only Fruit* first published in 1985. *Oranges*, the semi-autobiographical novel that launched Winterson's writing career and brought her to public attention, introduced the reader to WintersonWorld, a world in which a young girl called Jeanette, primed to become a missionary, grew up in a Pentecostalist household with her larger-than-life mother and rather timid father. The story that emerges in Winterson's first novel is that of a young girl, adopted as a baby, coming to terms with the world around her as she veers off the missionary path that her mother has chosen for her, falling in love with another girl and thereby falling foul of the expectations of her family, particularly her mother, and wider religious community. Her rejection of the norms of her community lead to her being forced to leave home and having to fight to continue her education. Books, a love of language and a love of literature, prove to be her saviour.

Yet above and beyond the sentimental education and tough life lessons that the young Jeanette experiences, including what it means to be marginalized and an outsider, it is the manner of the story's telling that is so memorable: a narrative structured around the first eight books of the Old Testament from Genesis to Ruth that combines a story of growing up with humour and flights of fantasy, a mix that was to characterise much of Winterson's subsequent work. For while *Oranges* is categorized as a work of fiction, rather than a memoir, it is one based loosely around aspects of Winterson's own past and is notable for its hybridity, experimentalism and playfulness in terms of style, thematic treatment and mode of narration. What distinguishes, *Why Be Happy?* from *Oranges*, apart from the obvious temporal gap (27 years) and difference in generic classification (*Why Be Happy?* is classified as a memoir, *Oranges* is a work of fiction), is perhaps the fact that *Why Be Happy?*, while not devoid of humour, strikes a more serious note and covers a larger period in Winterson's life than *Oranges* but it is precisely these differences as well as the similarities that this chapter will treat.

As will be seen, many of the themes embedded, and the concerns expressed, in both works are familiar to readers of Winterson's work. We might think, by way of example, of adoption, of lesbian love, and of the transformative power of the word. There is in *Why Be Happy?* much coverage of the period already translated into fictional form in *Oranges* with some key scenes and personalities revisited. In this sense, *Oranges* and *Why Be Happy?* are companion pieces in Winterson's literary corpus and will be treated as such in this chapter. Moreover, their reciprocity is noted by early reviewers and critics of *Why Be Happy?*, such as Mary Eagleton (2013, 248) who draws attention to 'the territory familiar from *Oranges*' in the first 11 chapters, while pointing to the differences in the way the material is 'contextualized or refracted through a different perspective' (248). So the fact that *Oranges* is generally treated as a fiction, albeit one that draws on aspects of biography, and *Why Be Happy?* is considered a memoir, even if 'a highly selective' (248) one, will allow for some discussion of the premises of these different genres as well as their actual realization within the corpus of a particular writer, in this case Jeanette Winterson. Indeed the Winterson corpus as a whole is characterized by a return to themes that, in retrospect, appear to relate to her initial trauma, disclosed in *Why Be Happy?* but covered up for the most part in *Oranges* by humour and the addition of fictional characters such as Elsie, modelled, not on reality but on need, the need to survive, the need to imagine a different existence, the need to tell another story and thereby create another reality.

A later chapter in this book will consider the complexities of the relationship between fiction and non-fiction in the work of another writer, Chinese-born British writer Xiaolu Guo, whose 2017 memoir, *Once Upon a Time in the East*, revisits some territory familiar to readers of Guo's early fiction. In focussing on the ways in which similar material and themes reappear across a writer's *oeuvre*, while taking account of the differences in its shaping, structuring and tonal treatment, I will raise questions about the extent to which generic difference is a relative rather than an absolute category and seek to identify the contextual, as well as textual, factors that impinge upon reading practices and readerly engagement with different text types.

But to return for now to Winterson's work with a view to treating *Oranges* and *Why Be Happy?* as companion pieces, rather than simply as singular texts. It will of course be important to surface a sense of how these individual works have been read and discussed as well as establish the kind of links that have been made between them in the critical literature. I have already alluded to similarities in thematic treatment and in recurrent motifs in both works and will return to these in more detail later.

4.2 Companion Pieces? Critical Reception of *Why Be Happy?* and Links to *Oranges*

To frame the discussion, I shall begin by giving a sense of the reception of Winterson's memoir, particularly, but not exclusively, where there has been explicit recognition of the connections with her much earlier fiction. Described by fellow writer Joyce Carol Oates (2012) as a 'painfully candid and often very funny memoir', *Why Be Happy?* devotes much space to reviewing life with the 'monstrous' Mrs. Winterson and an eventual search for Winterson's biological mother who gave her up for adoption. As readers of *Oranges* will remember, there is a moment when, in the fiction (Winterson 1991, 98–99), Jeanette's birth mother turns up on the doorstep in the northern mill town where the action is set and gets short shrift from Mrs. Winterson. In response to Jeanette's question about whether that was her mother, Mrs. Winterson replies: 'I'm your mother [...] She was a carrying case' (99).

Oates notes that *Why Be Happy?* has 'the unsettling air of the most disturbing fairy tale' (Oates, 2012) in that it appears to lead towards a happy ending yet where the happy ending is itself a kind of delusion. Indeed, she sees the ending as fizzling out somewhat and rather hasty: the real reckoning in the book has been Winterson's recognition of what Mrs. Winterson has given her, despite everything, and her understanding that biology is not everything. Much of Winterson's life post-*Oranges* is glossed over with a focus on her breakdown and subsequent quest for her biological mother. While the story is complete in the sense that Winterson eventually tracks down and meets her mother on several occasions, the book ends on a more tentative note: what happens next is uncertain, unknown. While, on the one hand, this is true in an absolute sense in that we cannot know what will happen in the future, it may also be a way of finding closure in writerly terms to the focus of the memoir. In other words, this part of Winterson's life story has been brought provisionally to an end.

For Oates, the production of the memoir has been 'an act of exorcism on the part of the writer' (Oates 2012), an attempt to free herself once and for all from this very charged love–hate mother–daughter relationship and to accept that alongside the trauma of her childhood came many of the things that have made her who she is today. This reading sees *Why Be Happy?* as an attempt on Winterson's part to rid herself once and for all of the negativity surrounding her sense of self, as a child who has been rejected, at least twice, first by her birth mother, then by her adoptive mother, arguably a third time by her then partner, Deborah Warner, and to come to understand through the process of writing something fundamental about love and loss. In other words, Oates reads the memoir as a quest, a search for answers to the question of who the author is, where she hails from, and what has made her the way she is. In this sense, the memoir has a self-explanatory function, though Oates notes the fairy-tale-like qualities and the delusion of a happy ending. It will be important to bear in mind the elements in both *Oranges* and *Why Be Happy?* that seem to be drawn from the same source and to look more closely at Winterson's treatment of similar events in both works.

Critic Emma McKenna (2016) reads *Why Be Happy?* in terms of doubling, not just in the sense of the creation through writing of an alter ego, a character and a split self (past and present selves, fictional projections and their autobiographical counterparts) that the authorial narrator must try to unify in order to heal, but also in terms of the many doubles that trouble the memoir: birth mother and adoptive mother, love and loss, a desire for self-creation and social mobility, alongside recognition of the value of family and community. Finally meeting her birth mother is for Winterson both end and new beginning: she has realized her quest to find out where she came from and to try to understand why she was given up for adoption, a quest motivated rather late in the day, as she reaches her lowest ebb following the break-up of another long-standing relationship and is forced to confront her constant adequation of love and loss. Yet, it is also a moment in which she discovers or uncovers the fact that she has assumed many of the traits of her adoptive mother and has developed as a person not only in opposition, but also in relation, to Mrs. Winterson. Latterly, she has been forced by circumstances to acknowledge her heretofore unexpressed feelings for her absent birth mother, complex feelings of rejection, anger, uncertainty and to an extent curiosity about her own origins. These feelings mutate over time as she meets her birth mother and responds to what she sees and learns. As McKenna (2016, 305) puts it: 'Her relation to her birth mother becomes ambivalent precisely because she is no longer an ideal: her birth mother threatens the present Winterson with an origin story she has tried to shed'. McKenna's reading is informed by what she sees as Winterson's politics, a politics that align her with the need for social mobility and individual exceptionalism, even as she tries within *Why Be Happy?* to set her own story within the wider history of industrial Manchester.

Where *Oranges* was a coming-of-age novel about a protagonist whose sexuality is deemed sinful by her adoptive mother and the evangelical church where she has been a preacher, causing her to leave home, *Why Be Happy?* is a work that reviews the formative experiences of a by now successful writer who, nevertheless, is forced to confront her childhood demons. *Why Be Happy?* shares with its fictional counterpart a narrative drive based on the notion of quest: however, this is less a romantic quest than a quest for answers to the riddle of Winterson's birth and true origins. It is an attempt to acknowledge the wound and the rupture caused, at least in part, by her unorthodox upbringing and the impact of adoption on the narrator's trajectory and psyche. While in *Oranges* the first-person narrator Jeanette keeps at bay the underlying trauma of rejection through distancing techniques, much humour and intercalated fairy tales and fantasies, *Why Be Happy?*, written at speed following a breakdown and suicide attempt on the part of the author, attends to the silences in the fictional cover version of the story she tells in *Oranges*, revisiting the scene and setting of her childhood and early adolescence to fill in the gaps and try to make sense of her trajectory.

The title itself, *Why Be Happy When You Could Be Normal?*, recalls something Mrs. Winterson is supposed to have said when Jeanette indicated that her relationship with another female brought her happiness and she was therefore prepared to sacrifice appearances in order to be herself. For Mrs. Winterson the idea of putting personal happiness above the observance of family values is not something she can or wants to understand, though as Margot Gayle Backus (2001, 138) points out, the depiction of Mrs. Winterson in *Oranges* can be read as 'the story of a middle-class woman's strategic use of religion, marriage, and adoption to preserve her imperiled class position'. Such an interpretation sees Mrs. Winterson's post-religious conversion, sexless marriage and adoption of a daughter whose life will be dedicated to God, as a means of atoning for previous mistakes, such as her declared youthful attraction to Pierre, her French beau, but she does this at the expense of both her husband and of Jeanette. In the case of her husband, she does so by denying him sexual relations and in Jeanette's case, it is by limiting her 'access to basic information concerning her own origins and identity' (138) and cutting her off from a sense of her place in the wider world.

In many ways Winterson makes a virtue of the narrowness of her world insofar as she develops a set of skills as a child and young adolescent that will enable her eventual progress as a writer: she learns to value language (e.g. the language of the Bible) and an ability to tell a good story (modelled on her ever-expanding repertoire as she hides a range of books under her bed) alongside prodigious skills as an orator (she was after all a child preacher). In interview with Anne Robinson discussing her favourite books, for example, Winterson picks out *Jane Eyre*, mentioned in *Oranges* as one of the few books to be found in the Winterson household, a surprising choice perhaps, but one adapted by Mrs. Winterson to the circumstances of growing up in a religious household. The latter is said to have altered the ending such that Jane marries not Rochester but St. John Rivers and goes off to be a missionary's wife. Only later does Winterson realize on reading *Jane Eyre* for herself that Mrs. Winterson had changed the plot to model a new reality. So, as Winterson puts it, in interview, it was a very postmodern moment but one that left her with a sense of just how 'you can do anything with language if you make it your own' (Robinson 2011).

In an early *Late Show* interview (1994) with Jeremy Isaacs, Winterson is asked to what extent *Oranges* is autobiographical. Her answer reveals her slight irritation with the premise of the question, but she nevertheless replies to the effect that as a literary writer she is playing with form and with genre. While acknowledging the similarities between the set-up, the characters and aspects of her own experience as a person brought up by Pentecostal parents in a working-class Lancashire town, she asserts that writing entails transformation and that it is not always possible to remember what happened. 'And if you cannot remember', she says, 'you must invent'. She goes on to stress that she is a writer of fiction and to say that 'she has very little time for realism. If you want that, you can get it on the street', she says, somewhat dismissively. The challenge, for Winterson as a writer, is to speak not just about what she knows but to transform into words what she can imagine. She sees herself not as a novelist but as a fiction writer who tries to incorporate into her work the discipline and denseness of poetry. In apparently dismissing the novel form, she is thinking of more traditional nineteenth-century novels which by implication are more interested in recreating a particular social reality and in following a linear structure. By comparison, Winterson sees her own work as following in the footsteps of more daring and experimental writers such as Virginia Woolf, whom she famously sees as a precursor.

Interestingly, writer and critic Lauren Rusk (2002, 108) considers *Oranges* as 'innovative life writing', even as she acknowledges 'its roots in the tradition of developmental fiction', by which she means in the tradition of the *Bildungsroman*. In fact, she sees *Oranges* as a work that is seeking to defy categorization (110). In the context of *The Life Writing of Otherness*, Rusk looks closely at the work of other writers, including Woolf, Kingston and Baldwin alongside that of Winterson with a view to showing not only how these writers represent a sense of their own otherness but how they position themselves in relation to others in and through their writing. According to Rusk, '[t]he creation of hybrid forms to enact transgressive female experience is an approach that Winterson, Kingston, and Woolf all share' (110). In the chapter on *Oranges* she looks closely at how this works in terms of the text's allusiveness, its intercalation of fantasy elements alongside depiction of the main protagonist's development and the blurring of boundaries between narrator, protagonist and author.

In a work that articulates correspondences between life and art and subverts more broadly the logic of binary thinking, Rusk points to the presence in *Oranges* of 'a compelling narrative voice, an especially important aspect of life writing' (131). She characterizes the narrative voice as insistent and intense, exactly the kind of voice one might expect from someone trained as a child preacher. While this link between the distinctiveness of voice and elements of the writer's biography inscribed in her narrative of development is interesting, it rather begs the question of whose voice it is the reader hears, that of the narrator-protagonist and/or that of an authorial narrator and if the latter whether there is a difference in voice from novel to novel in Winterson or even a difference in voice between *Oranges* and *Why Be Happy?*

Of course, at the time of publication of Rusk's work, Winterson had not yet published her memoir. In some ways, this makes it all the more important to look again at these companion pieces, as I am describing them, and to review them in relation to one another in terms of their narrative construction and narrative voice as well as thematic treatment, readerly reception and writerly motivation. In this sense, Rusk's designation of *Oranges* as a piece of life writing preceding publication of Winterson's memoir provides a kind of interpretive bridge or connective alleyway between semi-autobiographical fiction and memoir, the designations that to date I have been using to characterize *Oranges* and *Why Be Happy?* It is as well, however, to also keep in mind Winterson's own characterization of the relationship between the two works where the latter is the former's 'silent twin'.

I take this to mean that *Why Be Happy?* fills in some of the gaps in *Oranges* and that the two texts are siblings bearing a strong family resemblance, even if their generic classification appears to differ. What may seem on the surface a contradiction in terms is, in fact, the continuation of a life story already seeded in *Oranges*, an autobiographically focussed narrative fiction, which is then reviewed and extended in *Why Be Happy?*, a memoir that revisits and reframes the semi-fictional representation, evaluating it anew and commenting on it. Both contain elements of the quest, both can be read as searching for answers to questions about how best to live one's life, and both recognize in their textual construction, albeit with a difference, the importance of story in understanding one's existence and the role of the imagination in helping to change the plot.

Yet fancy and fantasy can occupy an ambivalent position in life, as in art, depending on the contexts in which they appear and the functions they fulfil. In this sense, in looking more closely at both texts there will be elements that will require particular focus, such as the role of fairy tales in *Oranges* and the ways in which fantasy is intercalated into what might be considered a narrative of everyday life, even if that everyday life is itself somewhat unusual by virtue of being unfamiliar to most readers. Growing up as an adopted child in a Pentecostal family where the expectation is that you become a child preacher is perhaps already far from the experience of many and to that extent the material itself may already have a somewhat fabular feel to it. And while the lesbian coming out novel may not seem unusual today, it must be remembered that the climate was rather different when *Oranges* was first published in the mid-1980s. Given Winterson's avowed preference for literary, rather than genre, fiction and a spiral, rather than a linear, narrative (Winterson 1991, xiii), it is perhaps not surprising that *Oranges* resists a straightforward reading and is essentially a multidimensional text with much narrative interweaving. Neither is *Why Be Happy?* unproblematic in its designation as memoir, as we will see, but displays many of the hybrid narrative features characteristic of the Winterson corpus as a whole.

4.3 Oranges Are Not the Only Fruit

> All in all, the text offers strenuous interpretive activity. It urges us to supply the missing links between the main story and the interpolated fantasies. It challenges us to consider the meaning of unconventionally used conventional sources, such as the Bible and Arthurian legend. And as a densely self-referential work, *Oranges* invites us to piece together, retrospectively, correspondences among its images and motifs.
> (Rusk 2002, 108)

What this quotation from Rusk makes clear are the interpretive complexities of what might otherwise appear to be simply a linear story of growing up and coming out. Reference to 'the main story' and 'the interpolated fantasies' suggests a narrative that, depending on your perspective, is either complemented by, or interrupted with, fantastic tales whose meaning relative to the ongoing narrative requires some deciphering. And the reference to *Oranges* as 'a densely self-referential work' indicates that readers may need to keep in mind, or refer back to, imagery and narrative threads that may initially pass unnoticed or seem arbitrary but turn out, on closer inspection, to be motivated in some way by the unfolding textual dynamics.

In her 1991 introduction to publication of the Vintage paperback edition of *Oranges*, Winterson discusses her motivation for writing the book and alludes to her writerly aims and ambitions. She indicates that throughout 'the making of the book' (Winterson 1991, xii), she asked herself the question: 'Why art instead of nature?'. Such a question needs further unpacking within the context of her introduction and rationale for writing the book. It comes just after she has talked about the circumstances that gave rise to her, a young 23- to 24-year-old, living unhappily in relative poverty in London and deciding to put her energies into writing *Oranges*. At that time, she was most concerned to 'do something large and to do it well' (xi), avoiding if possible 'that dinginess of soul that says that everything is small and grubby and nothing is really worth the effort' (xii). While in some ways, Winterson's mode of expression might be considered to display a youthful arrogance, there is nevertheless in what she says a desire to break free of the constraints around her and to invest in something that she sees as worthwhile, that is art, in general, and her own art in particular.

The second point to make here is the fact that in characterizing her book in the introduction, she ensures that the reader is aware of the extent to which, in structure and thematic treatment, *Oranges* stands out from the pack: it is, she says, 'an experimental novel', 'a threatening novel', and 'a comforting novel' (xiii–xiv). According to Winterson, its experimental nature resides largely in the fact that *Oranges* incorporates an anti-linear narrative which can be 'read in spirals' (xiii) and that it represents the beginning of what would become characteristic of Winterson's 'experiment with style, structure and language' (xv). She sees it as 'threatening' insofar as it exposes the hypocrisies as well as the comforts of the evangelical church and draws attention to its patriarchal nature. And it is 'comforting' 'not because it offers any easy answers but because it tackles difficult questions' (xiv) in that its 'heroine is someone on the outside of life' (xiv) who nevertheless 'has to deal with the big questions that cut across class, culture and colour' (xiv). In this sense it represents a drama that at some point in the lives of everyone must be played out, even if the material facts are different or the manner of resolution varies. Of course, not everyone will, like Winterson, seek to write about such a drama.

It is also, Winterson indicates, a quest novel: 'this quest is one of sexuality as well as individuality' (xiv). The links here are again complex in the sense that within the context of a novel with a main protagonist whose story is narrated in the first person, the reader's focus is invariably on that individual. Jeanette's situation in *Oranges* leaves her with few allies, though she does have some, particularly Elsie and those who make it possible for her to continue to live and study within her Lancashire industrial town, when she is forced to leave home because of her unrepentant sexuality. Winterson's representation of Jeanette in *Oranges* reflects the protagonist's awareness of the extent to which survival and self-preservation entail rejection of compromise and moving away not just from family but also from a place where horizons and ambitions are limited. In this sense the protagonist's insistence on being accepted at university and moving to the kind of university town (Oxford) usually reserved for those from a different background is both evidence of a class struggle and the refusal of an individual to accept the diktats of convention.

Finally, in answer to the question of whether the work is autobiographical, Winterson playfully and perhaps frustratingly writes: 'No not at all and yes of course' (xiv). This is, however, an issue that she takes up again in more detail in the new introduction written for the reissue of *Oranges* by Vintage in 2014. Here she admits to having based the story in *Oranges* on her own life but insists that there is nothing unusual about that (Winterson 2014, xi). Indeed, she goes on to mention male authors such as Paul Auster, Milan Kundera, Philip Roth and Henry Miller, all of whom have introduced into their work characters with the same name as that of the author (xiv). Winterson contends that while critical reaction to the use by these authors of a fictional version of themselves has generally been positive and seen to be playful, ironic and metafictional, in the case of women writers, such a ploy is 'assumed to be confessional' (xiv). She rejects what she sees as a gender bias and evidence of the application of different notions of 'creative authority' (xiv), indicating instead that throughout her work she has gone on writing in the first person and that these first-person narratives both are and are not (aspects of) herself: 'I am I and I am Not-I' (xiv).

Lest this provocation be misunderstood, Winterson goes on to say that life is part fact part fiction, suggesting that we all tell stories about ourselves (xiv). The author as creator of a work projects or builds through language a fictional universe containing characters and their interactions, events, imagery and motifs. The extent to which such a world resembles the world of actuality may depend on the kind of universe configured (e.g. fantastic, realistic, utopian, dystopian), the type of characters drawn (e.g. familiar or alien, prototypical or highly individualized, rounded or sketchy) and the extent to which the book conforms to or appears to challenge a recognizable genre (e.g. literary fiction, memoir, science fiction). Of course, to a certain extent all writing involves a degree of artfulness, if not artifice, in terms of organization, structuring of ideas and mode of expression, which is why seemingly categorial distinctions (e.g. fiction v. non-fiction) can become blurred or present difficulties upon further investigation.

Autobiographical writing, in particular, with its assumed identity between and among author, protagonist and narrator, is, as Micaela Maftei (2013) has shown in *The Fiction of Autobiography*, an area where such an assumed unity needs to be problematized. In discussing a number of examples along what might be called an autobiographical spectrum from storied fictional lives to works that relate to or are modelled on the life of a real individual, Maftei re-examines some of the premises of autobiography and interrogates them in relation to a range of carefully chosen examples, from Woolf and Nabokov to Barthes, Didion and Ginzburg. Through analysis of individual works such as Stein's *The Autobiography of Alice B. Toklas*, *Roland Barthes by Roland Barthes*, Didion's *The Year of Magical Thinking* and Ginzburg's *The Things We Used to Say*, she dismantles this assumption of unity, showing the extent to which 'identity in autobiography is fluid, as it is in life' (Maftei 2013, 59). Given the multiplicity of selves evident over a lifetime, as we move from childhood to adulthood, the distancing effect of time and the unreliability of memory, alongside the fact that a writer must re-create and therefore potentially transform the past, there is for Maftei an inevitable separation between the here and now and the then and there. This is true whether the writer's goal be a predominantly truth-telling one in the sense of 'this is what I remember to have actually happened' or in terms of developing greater understanding about a life through the singularity, and the truth-telling potential, of fiction. Of course, even as an autobiographical fiction may focus on an individualized or singular character, for it to speak to an audience, it must also to a degree be representative of aspects of the human condition.

As Maftei (2013, 59) puts it: 'Autobiography necessitates the removal of its author to a place outside the experience, in order to write about it'. What is also required is 'a splitting of selves [...] in order to feature within the text while constructing it' (59). In this sense, the 'I' that a writer is today is not the same 'I' as she was yesterday or the day before, never mind in childhood or adolescence. In summary, as well as temporal distance (past v. present, then v. now), there is a splitting of selves into writer as experiencing subject and as object of the narration; and as observer of and participant in a drama or life story that is constructed, framed and evaluated. The very act of writing, regardless of genre, involves selection, ordering and transformation of primary material. While the degree of mediation and the manner of shaping that primary material may to a degree be conventionally determined depending on whether it stems from lived experience or relates to a projected, fictional universe, there is in the process of storying and narrating a life a necessary distance between idea or image and their realization and embodiment in language. In addition, there will be in the case of work aimed at publication an impetus to engage readers and sustain their attention.

Indeed, Maftei sees the creation of story as 'the instrument of selfhood' (62), a phrase that suggests the importance of narrative construction in the process of understanding our lives and who we are. It is by storying existence and using language purposefully that the co-ordinates of selfhood surface and the fiction of autobiography is held together. It is perhaps important to state that purposeful use of language does not necessarily mean that the author is aware of all the resonances of her writing; it simply suggests that in putting together a work of autobiography, whether fictional or based on a real life, a writer tries to use language as effectively as possible in the light of her aims. Clearly, language and the manner of its structuring may also be read in relation to unconscious motives by readers in a post-Freudian, post-Jungian world. All texts have gaps, silences and points of indeterminacy (Iser 1981), and stories can be narrated and re-articulated in different terms at different times depending on the goal of the telling. In this sense, it will be particularly pertinent to examine Winterson's re-telling of some of the episodes originally recounted within the fictional context of *Oranges* in relation to their later reconfiguration in her memoir. But before focussing on Winterson's revisiting and reworking of primary scenes within a different context, let us turn in more detail to her first foray into WintersonWorld in *Oranges*.

4.3.1 Structure and narrative organization of Oranges

The first chapter of *Oranges*, named for the initial book of the Bible, begins with Jeanette's origins. In some ways, the narrator-protagonist positions herself as both just like everybody else ('Like most people I lived for a long time with my mother and father' (Winterson 1991, 3)) and, at the same time, as different or special ('I cannot recall a time when I did not know that I was special' (4)). What distinguishes her is the fact that she was adopted, that her upbringing was somewhat unusual in a household where religious ritual reigns, and the fact that Jeanette's mother kept her at home until receipt of a letter forced her to send the child to school. The initial chapter's narrative organization is motivated in that it introduces the main characters and themes as well as pointing to future events. On re-reading, seemingly passing mention of some episodes and incidents (e.g. Pastor Finch and the exorcism of demons; the fact that Jeanette, according to a gypsy woman, will never marry) turns out to relate to the story-in-progress. The first chapter also introduces a kind of textual chunking, with narrative breaks, intercalations, and the requirement to read the text not at the literal level or solely in a linear way but to seek coherence at the level of theme or by virtue of recurrent imagery and motifs.

Reading Winterson's work, then, becomes a multimodal affair where typography, spacing, wordplay, rhythm and imagery are as important as accounts of what happened next. The first few paragraphs already set this up where words are milked for ambivalence or for their dual meanings: 'My father liked to watch the wrestling, my mother liked to wrestle' (3), where 'wrestle' turns out to be both literal and figurative combat or struggle and where the symmetry of the phrasing nevertheless reveals difference: Jeanette's father is passive – he likes to watch – while Jeanette's mother is active – she engages in combat. Depiction of Mrs. Winterson as being in 'the white corner' (3) both continues engagement with the wrestling metaphor – we think of wrestlers in their corner between bouts of fighting – and adds new information, given that the colour white is usually associated with virtue and spotlessness. The first sentence of the very next paragraph – 'She hung out the largest sheets on the windiest days' (3) – again picks up on Mrs. Winterson's combative qualities, while inferring a link between 'the sheets' and 'the white corner'. The comedy and visual quality of pinning out the largest sheets on the windiest days is followed by reference to Mrs. Winterson's provocations both in a religious and a political sense: she's happy to engage the Mormons in discussion on the doorstep, and she doesn't hesitate to put a picture of the Conservative candidate in the window in a predominantly Labour town.

In this way the narrative proceeds associatively, visually and playfully. The typographical effect is evident in the listing of enemies and friends (in that order) on the first page and in the positioning of Jeanette as having been 'brought in to join her [Mrs. Winterson] in a tag match against the Rest of the World' (Winterson 1991, 3). Where reference to a 'tag match' relates back to 'wrestling' and the idea of opposing teams, capitalization of the 'Rest of the World' draws attention to the enormity of the task, as well as continuing the comic note: two against a multitude! As the chapter continues, so the reader gets a sense of the main characters (principally Jeanette and her mother) and their routine, in addition to passing reference to others with a part to play in the drama (members of the church); the location (a small house in a 'stretchy' street (6) in a northern mill town); the themes (nature and art; the power of imagination to transform reality; growing up, education and self-invention); the structure (blocks of text linked associatively; the intercalation of fairy tales and quest narratives into the linear sequence of events) and tone (comic, interrogative, didactic).

It is important to recognize that the narrative is related in the past tense as the protagonist looks back on her early life and development. At the same time, however, use of dialogue alongside the narrator's ability to reconstruct selected visual scenes from her early life gives the impression of immediacy despite the marked temporal distance. In addition, the narrator shifts on occasion from past tense to present tense, as she moves from relation of completed events to evaluation and comment on them in the present. But the very concept of present is complicated by the fact that there is the present of the story (in terms of the presumed temporal ordering of events or storytime) and the narrative present where the comments made can be attributed to an older narrator. So, for example, having relayed Mrs. Winterson's conversion story, originally told to her by her mother, narrator Jeanette moves from narration of a completed past event ('Pastor Spratt **came to stay** with them' (8)) to description of the scene 'now', i.e. the present in terms of the story ('We **have** a picture of him [Pastor Spratt] surrounded by black men with spears'). This is followed by evaluation of Mrs. Winterson which is from the narrator's adult perspective ('My mother **is** very like William Blake'). This is not the kind of comment likely to have been made by a young girl growing up in a household with a limited selection of books.

Immediately thereafter in a subsequent paragraph, we return to relay or report of the past ('She [Mrs. Winterson] **walked** out one night and thought of her life and thought of what was possible' (9)) but this too is from the perspective of the older Jeanette since it attributes motivation to her mother which she may not have been aware of as a child. The paragraph continues: 'She thought of the things she couldn't be. Her uncle had been an actor. "A very fine Hamlet," said the *Chronicle*' (9). The change of tense to the past perfect ('Her uncle **had been** an actor') is indicative of temporality: Mrs. Winterson's uncle is now dead but it is potentially also an indirect report of what Mrs. Winterson said to the young Jeanette at the time (She said that her uncle had been an actor). The quotation attributed to the *Chronicle* could be a continuation of Mrs. Winterson's indirectly reported speech or ostensibly be something that the older Jeanette has come to discover and be part of her narration. The verb tense is interesting in this regard: 'said' rather than 'had said'.

The final paragraph before the break in the story is worth looking at in full, since it demonstrates the narrative complexities:

> But the rags and the ribbons turn to years and then the years are gone. Uncle Will had died a pauper, she was not so young these days and people were not kind. She liked to speak French and play the piano, *but what do these things mean?* (Winterson 1991, 9; my italics)

The first sentence with its present tense verb suggests that this is an evaluation by the older narrator. Uncle Will is Mrs. Winterson's uncle, not Jeanette's and the return to a past perfect ('had died') suggests a report of what happened or was said in the past. However, the italicized part seems to me to be a return to commentary on the part of the narrator (the older Jeanette), though ostensibly it could also be a continuation of Mrs. Winterson's thoughts on the subject in the manner of free indirect style. There is an ambivalence here which may be calculated but which certainly complicates not just temporal relations within *Oranges* but also illustrates the range of voices 'speaking' within the text at a local level. So even though we have in *Oranges* a first-person retrospective narrative in a global sense with implied identity between narrator and protagonist, it is not just focus that shifts (from one character to another or from one episode to another) but also at a local level, the voices that as readers we hear are disparate and varied. Through a range of narrative techniques (dialogue, reported speech, free indirect speech, omniscient narration) employed across the work, it is not just the narrator that we hear but some of the characters, both directly and indirectly. And there are temporal, as well as narrative, dislocations and polyphonies.

Alongside the narrator's reconstruction of episodes, events and routines from the past, and her commentary on them from the perspective of her mature as well as her younger self, the reader has access to other stories and acts of storytelling: religious stories, fairy tales, stories of transformation. The question of who narrates these embedded tales is also more complex than might appear to be the case. Take, for example, the story of the very sensitive princess who agrees to take over responsibility for 'a small village of homely people' (9) from an old woman. This story has the outline structure of a short fairy tale in that it starts with 'Once upon a time' and it involves an encounter in a forest between a princess, both beautiful and brilliant, and an old hunchbacked woman, who understands 'the secrets of magic' (9). Gifts and tokens are given to the princess in exchange for her agreement to take over from the hunchback and fulfil her duties, of which there are three. These three duties are numbered and outlined on the page such that they stand out. As well as reflecting the fact that some numbers are credited in Western culture with significance in certain contexts (e.g. the Trinity, the Three Bears), they also point forward to the subsequent section of text where a parallel story is narrated. The story outlined here, which ends with a transfer of power and a release through death for the old woman, conforms thematically and structurally to the genre of the fairy tale and as such seems to emanate from general culture rather than from a named narrator.

As indicated above, the story that follows in many ways parallels the one just told but is attributable to the narrator and relates her mother's dream of getting a child and dedicating it to the Lord. The story continues in a pseudo-biblical manner ('And so it was that on that particular day [...] she followed a star [...]'), thereby aligning Mrs. Winterson's journey to the orphanage, and her selection of a child over whom she watched, with the journey of the Wise Men to follow the star and attend the birth of Christ delivered to the Virgin Mary. This story draws a parallel between the Immaculate Conception and Mrs. Winterson's sexless delivery of Jeanette. Just as there are three duties in the tale of the princess, so there are three things in Mrs. Winterson's dream or vision: 'She would get a child, train it, build it, dedicate it to the Lord (10)'. What follows indented on three separate lines is a list of three attributes of the child in question:

a missionary child,
a servant of God,
a blessing (10)

The layout draws attention to the kind of child Mrs. Winterson is to seek and even though this is not a numbered list, unlike the duties in the previously related fairy tale, the coincidences of structure and typography suggest a link between the stories. Mrs. Winterson's dream of finding a child to devote to the Lord, a child whom she takes away 'for seven days and seven nights' is a biblically fashioned story which brings to the fore a relationship between mother and child built on renunciation of the flesh and allegiance to an Old Testament God, where sacrifice is uppermost. Reading the two stories analogically, the implication is that the old woman in the fairy tale finds a way out of her dilemma via the princess's assumption of her duties, while Mrs. Winterson is freed from the duties of the flesh through 'water and the word' (10). Thus, analysis of the tropes and narrative structure of only one chapter, 'Genesis', in *Oranges*, named after a book in the Bible, is indicative of the degree of complexity, allusiveness and foreshadowing, not to mention tonal range and interpenetration of voices and temporalities at play in the work. In some ways, its very density and multivocality both conceal and reveal. Its relationship to *Why Be Happy?* is anticipatory and indexical, the links symbiotic and associative.

4.4 Why Be Happy When You Could Be Normal?

As indicated, *Why Be Happy?* (Winterson 2012, 8) is the 'silent twin' of the story told in *Oranges*. As such, Winterson's first novel, characterized as 'semi-autobiographical' (1), is referenced throughout the work and provides a point of departure for the memoir. The memoir is divided into 15 chapters with an 'Intermission' between chapters 11 and 12, and a 'Coda' at the end. The Intermission is an extremely short section at just over a page. It does not even have a chapter number. In terms of content it indicates that linearity and clock time have never been of interest to the authorial narrator and that she intends to skip over twenty-five years. The sentence that precedes this declaration – 'I would rather go on reading myself as a fiction than as a fact' (154) – is suggestive: it provides a bridge between *Oranges* and *Why Be Happy?* insofar as neither is a purely linear account of a life and both are the result of a degree of consciously creative work.

In addition, the Intermission sits between an account of Winterson's final visit to Accrington, with a friend, to see her adoptive mother and an abbreviated account of her breakdown, descent into madness and erratic road to recovery. Unlike the final chapter of *Oranges* which provides what I'm calling a synthetic resolution to the book, by which I mean to refer to its artful, rather than necessarily 'truthful', way of bringing things to a close, Winterson's revisiting of her final home visit in *Why Be Happy?* is a rather more sombre affair, which alludes to Mrs. Winterson's challenging behaviour and madness. In the chapter following the Intermission Winterson writes of her own madness and eventual return to mental health, following a breakdown. The manner in which she does this is, in some ways, reminiscent of her grappling with the demon in *Oranges* (Winterson 1991, 111). In other words, there are aspects of her account which follow a familiar Wintersonian pattern right down to the splitting and externalization of a part of herself. In *Why Be Happy?* this is a creature who tries to take her down and make her submit to suicide. Her cure is affected through creative work, gardening, and conversing with the creature. She ends up writing a children's story involving a creature sawn in two, one half male, the other female. In taking herself off to the shed every morning to write and submitting to a daily routine of writing, conversing with her 'creature' and gardening, she begins to exert more control over her mental health. 'Creativity', she writes, 'is on the side of health [...]; it is the capacity in us that tries to save us from madness' (Winterson 2012, 171).

The coda is a short set of reflections following the end of the narrative, a narrative which ends with the word home. The coda speaks of adoption stories in general and of Winterson's own adoption story in particular and conveys her mixed feelings about having discovered her birth mother. On the one hand, she is 'pleased' that her mother is 'safe' (Winterson 2012, 229); at the same time, she is conscious of the gap between her own life and that of her biological mother. She discovers that the life that she has led as a result of being raised by her adoptive mother is one that she prefers to 'the me I might have become without books, without education, and without all the things that have happened to me along the way, including Mrs. W' (228). Winterson considers herself lucky. So finding out about her origins has been a mixed blessing. It was something she finally felt compelled to do. Yet, for all that it is a true story, 'it is', she writes, 'still a version' (229). This notion of *Oranges* having been a cover story, with *Why Be Happy?* its silent twin, alongside the conclusion that there is no single truth, just versions of truth and that life is part fact, part fiction, can be seen as a kind of throughline across the two works. Not only are they interdependent, they can also be seen to represent different points along a life-story continuum. For just as *Oranges* employs 'a strand of autobiographical writing as an experimental device' (Preda 2019, 26) in a work, containing inset narratives, that juxtaposes the worlds of reality and imagination, so *Why Be Happy?* can be seen as a reflective response to and commentary on Winterson's fictional creations in the light of a critical episode in her own life that led her back to some of the questions at the heart of her fiction. The wall between art and life for Winterson the writer has always been porous and two-way. The 'doubleness at the heart of things' (Winterson 2012, 168) that she speaks of in *Why Be Happy?* is consistent with the duality of things in *Oranges*, including the double narrative voice where 'little Jeanette's perspective mingles with the adult-narrator's focalisation of past events' (Preda 2019, 30).

Indeed, most of the chapter titles in *Why Be Happy?* pick up on aspects of Winterson's early life and return to territory familiar to readers of *Oranges*. The fact that there is contextualization of the earlier work in terms of motivation for writing it, for example, and that references to it are threaded throughout *Why Be Happy?*, providing a kind of episodic counterpoint, means that the two works have a symbiotic relationship. Like much of Winterson's fiction, including *Oranges*, the memoir is written in a way that requires the reader to connect the blocks of text into which individual chapters are divided. Analysis of the first chapter of *Oranges* demonstrated how this worked in terms of the kind of connections posited or inferred at a thematic, structural and/or metaphoric level. The first chapter of *Why Be Happy?*, entitled 'The Wrong Crib', begins with a kind of character sketch of Mrs. Winterson ('a flamboyant depressive' (1)) who, when angry with Jeanette, would often indicate that the devil had led them to the wrong crib, before the narrative turns to the year 1985 and publication of *Oranges*.

Winterson makes much of the fact that her mother demanded a phone call after she had read *Oranges* and goes on to dramatize the scene. She paints a picture of a larger-than-life Mrs. Winterson filling up the phone box (3) and reports an exchange between them that is at once poignant and recuperative, insofar as it was clearly a key moment for both Winterson and her adoptive mother and in representing it, she is also trying to understand it from her current perspective. The manner in which Winterson records the exchange is explanatory for the most part ('I tried to explain [...]' (3)), and there are passages of reported speech ('She said, "It's the first time I've had to order a book in a false name"' (3)) and free indirect speech ('Why should a woman not be ambitious for literature?' (4)), as well as temporal shifts reflective of the way in which the present is coloured by the past as memories that have been repressed come flooding back, having been triggered situationally by similarity or difference. The temporal shifts are indicated here typographically as well as in terms of tense usage: '*The pips – more money in the slot –* and I'm locked out and sitting on the doorstep again' (4)). And so the narrative transitions to the past and Winterson's memory of being put out on the doorstep as a child. The historic present is used to convey the vividness of the memory: 'Inside our house the light is on. Dad's on the night shift [...]' (4). The gaps, and what is not said, help to convey the pain of revisiting episodes from the past.

So within the frame of a section dramatizing an episode from the past in which Winterson talks to her mother and feels again like the child she was, the coexistence of different temporalities and perspectives serves to layer the narrative. Explanatory discourse from Winterson's present narrative perspective – that of an author who has had a breakdown, gone in search of her biological mother and in the process been compelled to revisit childhood traumas rendered to date in semi-fictional and comic mode – creates a kind of mise-en-abyme of layered and embedded text secured by relations of similarity and difference. In recounting a phone call made to her mother after publication of *Oranges*, she moves further back in time to childhood experiences, such as sitting on the doorstep overnight, and then returns to the narrative present, one imbued with a perspective that dates from the more recent past. As she recalls the dramatized scene in the phone box, she frames it in more general terms: 'I can't remember a time when I wasn't setting my story against hers' (Winterson 2012, 5). She goes on to talk about the fact that adopted children are 'self-invented because we have to be; there is an absence, a void, a question mark at the very beginning of our lives. A crucial part of our story is gone, and violently, like a bomb in the womb' (5).

This turn to 'we', which includes Winterson as an adopted child whose 'story' bears similarities with that of other adoptees, reflects her more mature consciousness of what it means to be separated from a birth mother and be handed over to an adoptive mother. The reflections that follow, this feeling 'that something is missing never, ever leaves you' (5), are indicative of a reckoning with the past and a consciousness of the negative consequences that have flowed from adoption. But there is also recognition of the positives that have emerged, one such being that Winterson the writer can retell stories from her own perspective: 'To avoid the narrow mesh of Mrs. Winterson's story I had to be able to tell my own. Part fact, part fiction is what life is. And it is always a cover story. I wrote my way out' (6). Writing, therefore, is, and has always been for Winterson, a mode of survival. She goes on to reflect on the kind of books she has written and their over-arching themes of love and loss, about which she has written 'obsessively' (7). This retrospective and overarching view is a way of making sense of her history and the stories she and others (e.g. journalists, reviewers, critics) have told about it.

That Winterson is aware of the extent to which stories are always framed and positioned relative to an audience, and an idea of truth and fiction, is made clear in what follows (8–9). Her characterization of stories as 'compensatory' (8) reflects the extent to which she sees narration as a kind of reversioning of reality and that this reversioning may have various functions, including perhaps to make up for what is missing in reality (compensatory) as well as to change that reality (transformative). If *Oranges* was a version of the story that Winterson 'could live with' (6) at the time, *Why Be Happy?* is an attempt to bring to the surface the silences latent in the previous text. This is, at least in part, the motivation for revisiting many of the episodes recounted in fictional form in *Oranges* in the context of her memoir. However, the assumption that *Why Be Happy?* represents the truth and that *Oranges* is a mere fiction can be unsettled by comparative analysis and by the ties that bind the two works together, as much as by what separates them. What remains consistent across these two apparently different generic works, one marked fiction on the back cover, the other memoir, is much of what is characteristic of Winterson's style: a preference, within a chapter heading, for juxtaposed blocks of text, whose resonances with preceding and subsequent blocks must be found at the level of theme or motif and/or through the ties of metaphor.

Conversely, Winterson's tendency to employ, in her fictions, generalizations and synthesizing statements is also typical of what can be found in her memoir. If there is a difference (and I think there is), it is to be found at the level of narrative discourse: there is, for example, lots of explanatory discourse in *Why Be Happy?*, though this is not entirely missing in *Oranges*. In addition, *Oranges* operates more firmly in terms of a sequenced, developmental story and a retelling of 'romances', including fairy tales and quest narratives, or to put it slightly differently, it alternates between the world of the everyday and that of the imagination. These are, however, relative terms, insofar as the everyday in *Oranges* is for many readers already an unusual set of family circumstances, related with humour and a degree of bravura. *Why Be Happy?*, on the other hand, is a text that has been driven by crisis and that bears a symbiotic relationship to its progenitor, *Oranges*.

4.5 A Comparative Analysis

Table 4.1 is an attempt to capture some of the differences and similarities between *Oranges* and *Why Be Happy?* with a view to showing at a glance their inter-relationship. One of the questions that this chapter has been interested in posing and in answering, at least provisionally, is the extent to which there are textually defined differences in genre and the extent to which these differences are anchored in and supported by context. By context, I mean to refer primarily to paratextual cues and readerly expectations elicited by these, but I am also gesturing to a more general understanding of context

Table 4.1 A comparative analysis of *Oranges* and *Why Be Happy?*

Name of book	*Oranges*	*Why Be Happy?*
Type (paratextual indicators)	Semi-fictional autobiography/fiction	memoir
Type of narrator	Past tense first-person homodiegetic narrator (narrator = character) Narrator-protagonist shares name with author	First-person narrator: autobiographical contract in place? (author = narrator = protagonist)
Narrative characteristics	A **developmental story** (female *Bildungsroman*) with moments of crisis (illness, sexuality). **Quest narrative** Part fact, part fiction	**Autobiographical narrative prompted by crisis** (breakdown/attempted suicide) that causes narrator to review parts of her life story in order to understand the moment of crisis and get beyond it. **Explanatory narrative: quest to find biological mother and understand life's trajectory** Healing/transformation through power of narrative
Story arc/narrative progression	Linear first-person narrative interrupted by external narration of fairy tales. Juxtaposition and embedding	Degree of linearity with embedding and juxtaposition
Type of ending	*Synthetic* resolution (my term) to indicate approach to novelistic closure	Open-ended resolution/degree of uncertainty: 'I have no idea what happens next' (230).
Temporal coverage and focus	Early life through adolescence to young adulthood (approx. 20–25 years). Division into 8 chapters. Events recounted by older narrator but filtered through consciousness of younger protagonist. Some use of dialogue.	Period covered: cradle to aftermath of late-life crisis (approx. 50 years); **approx. half of narrative devoted to early life and early career**. Intermission of 25 years (154). Relation of crisis (168); road to recovery, search for biological mother and aftermath (coda).
Overall tone of work	Largely comic but with undercurrent of tragedy. Strong sense of need to escape/turn towards other realities. Compensatory, transformational.	Explanatory, tragic, reflective, compensatory, transformational.

in terms both of cultures of reading and of writing, given that reading and writing practices can be shaped, if not conditioned, by culture, as will become apparent in the chapter on Xiaolu Guo's memoir, *Once Upon a Time in the East*. Genres across cultures and indeed specific periods within those cultures do not always map neatly onto one another and writers such as Guo who work across linguistic and cultural borders have access to a broad range of writerly conventions and assumptions about genre from both Eastern and Western perspectives. For as narrative specialist Mieke Bal (1997) points out: 'Endorsing the view that interpretation is both subjective, and susceptible to cultural constraints – framings – that make the process of interpretation of more general interest, turns narrative analysis into an activity of "cultural analysis"' (11). How material is framed, as well as shaped, in addition to questions of voice, modes of narration, reader expectations, and writerly intentions are all determinants of a culturally complex and finely nuanced tradition of meaning-making. Meanings are not given nor always textually transparent but are made in situated acts of reading by culturally informed readers in relation to contextually and temporally relevant cues.

One of the conventional differences between a fictional account of a life and an account of a real life is said to rely on the autobiographical contract which depends on the reader being able to equate narrator, protagonist and author in terms of their identity (Lejeune 1982). Yet such an apparently straightforward process of identification is in practice trickier to determine without reference to additional contextual factors. In the case of *Oranges*, for example, there is evidence to suggest that the teller of the story and the subject who is the focus of the story are one and the same. Yet, even this seeming adequation of narrator and protagonist is more complex than might at first be apparent, given the retrospective nature of the narration and the fact that the older narrator is looking back at her younger self and, as it were, also to an extent evaluating that younger self, as well as representing it. As has already noted, the character shares a first name with the work's author and the implications of this relative to the work's overt generic designation have also been discussed. It should also be noted that reference to their character's 'dual outward-inward exploration and the pre-eminence of the quest for self' (Preda 2019, 34) is seen as characteristic of all of Winterson's novels. While narrative distance between older and younger homodiegetic narrators is nothing new, it does serve to complicate the relationship between narrator-commentator and representation of an earlier period in the character's life, pointing to the important role of commentary and evaluative discourse in permitting a narrator to interrogate (versions of) the past.

When it comes to the question of the role of the author, as has already been discussed, assumptions based simply on the fact that all three (character, narrator, author) are named Jeanette can be misleading, without reference to other factors, such as the paratextual. In addition, narratological practice would want to distinguish the person ultimately responsible for writing the book in the world of reality – its author – and the implied author of a constructed but ultimately fabricated world set in motion through words attributable to the narrator of a story in which she happens to feature as actor or protagonist, as well as the presumed purveyor of a storyworld. Even where there appears to be congruity or alignment between the author's name, the name of the character and that of the narrator, the question of shared identities is, in reality, a somewhat more vexed affair, as we have seen. The fact that an author shares a name with a character-narrator does not, of necessity, mean that the author intends the reader to connect the writer's real history with that of the character-narrator.

There may be other reasons for the choice of naming practice, such as the projection of an authorial persona such as that in Brett Easton Ellis's *Lunar Park*. This authorial persona may be an object of critique, an object of fun/self-parody and/or an attempt on the part of the writer to blur the boundaries between so-called fact and fiction by surfacing and playing with the metafictional possibilities implicit in all acts of mediated and narrativized verbal communication. Life and art may be said to be separate domains, to mirror one another, or to be irreparably entangled. These different, even oppositional, positions are all tenable and can be justified or argued in a relative, if not an absolute, sense. The postmodernist mantra of 'I write, therefore I am' (Hampel 2001) lends credence to the creative power of the word, suggesting as it does a becoming through writing, and playfully posits not an a priori but an a posteriori human subject that comes into existence through writing and the written word. The question of the difference, then, between 'real-life author' and her avatar or narrative instantiation becomes all the more fraught, particularly in respect of an autodiegetic work, where the narrative focus is on its narrative creator.

In the case of *Why Be Happy?* it seems that despite the explicit paratextual generic marking – 'memoir' on the back cover – the question of identity between and among author, narrator and protagonist is no less fraught, insofar as the narrator of Winterson's *Why Be Happy?* both is and is not the author herself. She is in terms of names and naming practices, she is not insofar as the narrator of *Why Be Happy?* is, to an extent, no less a construct and a persona than was the narrator of *Oranges*. And the retrospective view that she invariably adopts on the meaning of past episodes and events, realized in different versions of the 'same' story, still has the effect of splitting off the experiencing subject from the observer and analyst of that subject just as is the case in an autobiography deemed fictional or semi-fictional. While

Why Be Happy? appears to have been written quickly and as a way out of madness, the work nevertheless shows sufficient evidence of structuring and of narrative distance both temporal and psychic that it cannot be said to be lacking in the kind of design features characteristic of Winterson's work as a whole. Of course, a text marked by structure and design cannot simply be deemed artificial, a construct, or even false or fictional (as opposed to authentic, truthful and non-fictional) without taking account of other, largely extratextual, factors.

4.6 Voice and Narrative Persona

We might posit the question: if the difference between *Oranges* and *Why Be Happy?* cannot be said to lie unproblematically at the level of names and identities, wherein might it lie? Might it be that the kind of narrative discourse employed in *Why Be Happy?* involves more frequent affirmations or that explanatory discourse is more of a feature than in *Oranges*? Perhaps the questions of voice – of who speaks? – alongside the question of narrative persona might be a way of further untangling some of these issues.

As Jahn (2017) points out, in classical narratology, the question of voice relates to modes of narration and the question of who speaks. He also indicates that, strictly speaking, insofar as it is the reader who 'hears' a particular way of speaking or narrating and identifies it with a specific narrator or character, voice is, in fact, a readerly concept:

> [V]oice can only enter into a text through a reader's imaginary perception; hence, unless the text is an oral narrative in the first place, or is performed in the context of a public reading, *voice is strictly a readerly construct*. (Jahn 2017; the italics are mine)

Jahn distinguishes intratextual and extratextual voices, where the former relates to the voices of characters and narrator/s within the textual world; the latter refers to that of the author which is of interest 'in two scenarios only', these being where there appears to be identity between the author and narrator, 'also in nonfictional, real-life, or historiographic narrative'. The other scenario that Jahn points to is the converse: 'when the author's and the narrator's voices are likely to be significantly different – in other words, when one assumes that the author intentionally uses a narrative voice distinct from his or her own' (Jahn 2017).

For a writer such as Winterson whose work has been variously characterized as predominantly modernist, quintessentially postmodernist, or simply (post)-modernist, the question of how to approach her work and how to read and interpret it in respect of its overt paratextual generic designations and/ or generic markers is again a complicated one. As a self-confessed follower of a modernist tradition – Preda (2019, 24) speaks of 'the author's pledge of allegiance to modernism' – Winterson is a self-consciously literary and hugely ambitious writer. At the same time, as a product of a different age and ethos, for whom the modernist mantra of new forms for new times means constantly pushing the novelistic envelope and developing a mode of narrative communication appropriate to the period in which she lives, Winterson is also aware of the affordances of historiographic metafiction, the inherent playfulness of language, the citational force and parodic value of intertextual allusions and their role in the construction of generic hybridity and a dialogic text.

Temporally, therefore, her positioning as a (post-) modernist writer also affords her an understanding of the ways in which the taken-for-granted assumptions of one era provide fodder for critique, parody or outright rejection by the next. Winterson's seemingly unquestioning belief in art, articulated in *Art Objects*, alongside its creative and transformative potential may to an extent place her in a high modernist camp but equally she is aware of the politics of representation and a history of reading that would differentially categorize writers as metafictional or confessional; experimental or conservative; bold and outward-looking or preoccupied with interiority and the personal, according to gender and genre-based assumptions. In this sense, her preference for a post-modernist playfulness, generic hybridity and a failure to comply with the assumptions of gender reflect her refusal to be compartmentalized according to essentialized modes of being. The kind of narrative strategies used in *Oranges* and *Why Be Happy?* are designed to sidestep a reductive set of dualisms and keep in play a potential continuum of possibilities relating life in its plenitude to its artful and manifold representations.

A brief look at Chapter 2 entitled 'My Advice to Anybody is: Get Born' will help illustrate Winterson's choice of narrative strategies in *Why Be Happy?* and gives an indicative sense of the mix of fact and contextualizing detail that seem to go hand in hand with her stylistic signature: a tendency to locate her characters – in this case herself – within a story and to employ metaphor and a kind of associative logic to move from one block of text to the next. Chapter 2 starts with the year and place of her birth – 1959 in Manchester – and moves into a kind of characterization of the city alongside a potted history of Manchester from the nineteenth century onwards. There is a strong sense that place and time are important components in underwriting the possibilities open to people of a certain class. There is also a suggestion or implication that Winterson's early experience of life played into her sense of self and helped make her what she is. From this perspective it might be said that the chapter relates a kind of psychogeography of Manchester with some of its attributes equally applicable to the formation of the young Jeanette. Manchester, 'a double city rooted in restless energy and contradictions' (Winterson 2012, 14), alongside the specifics of growing up in Accrington, a working-class town, with her adoptive parents, were the things underpinning her development. Early on, Winterson 'dreamed of escape' (17) from the kind of life she saw around her: hard graft, a week's holiday by the sea.

This chapter, then, is about her inheritance: both genetic and sociocultural. It treats the so-called facts of her adoption, 'picked up from Manchester and taken to Accrington' at some point 'between six weeks and six months old' (18–19), though in reality there is little that is solid and substantive about her life before adoption. Only the reality of her screaming until the age of two, most likely as a result of 'the trauma of early separation from the love object' (20) but seen as evidence at the time of being 'possessed by the Devil' (20). What Winterson knows of her adoptive parents' existence prior to her arrival is scant: essentially that they had a life before and after religious conversion. Winterson dwells on the opposition between her adoptive mother and herself in terms of their ability to enjoy life and focusses on her own 'dream of escape' (21) from the narrow confines of what Accrington had to offer. The function of stories in this scenario was to provide not just solace but a road map, a way through the difficulties of everyday life.

What comes through Winterson's selective narration of her birth and early years is the importance of the quest and a sense that she was destined to be different. Her rejection of binary oppositions is also in evidence (25) and she uses affirmations and explanatory discourse in equal measure. For example, the paragraph beginning: 'We were matched in our lost and losing' as far as 'We both wanted to go Home' (23) pits Mrs. Winterson against the author as a child, while explaining their differences and where they stemmed from. Winterson's ability to generalize from her own experience: 'Adopted children are dislodged' (23) and to link one sentence to another via materially similar language and the power of metaphor – 'My mother felt that the whole of life was a grand dislodgement' (23) – are equally in evidence here. This is a trait characteristic of some of Winterson's fiction as well, much of which incorporates grand statements and associative links. *Art and Lies* (1994) is full of such examples but even *Oranges* is not devoid of them. After Mrs. Winterson searches Jeanette's room and removes and burns the love letters, notes and jottings that she finds, the narrator in *Oranges* comments: 'There are different sorts of treachery, but betrayal is betrayal wherever you find it' (110) and goes on to indicate that this was the moment when her mother lost her regard and she began to see her faults. Statements, and their sequencing, such as 'Walls protect and walls limit. It is in the nature of walls that they should fall. That walls should fall is the consequence of blowing your own trumpet' (110) are very much a part of the Wintersonian landscape, regardless of genre.

But it is the final paragraph that most resembles what could be the beginning of a piece of fiction by Winterson: 'When I was born I became the visible corner of a folded map' (25). She goes on in that paragraph to elaborate life as a journey on which you set out from a fixed location; thankfully, however, the destination is not fixed and there are multiple options: 'The map has more than one route. More than one destination. The map that is the unfolding self is not exactly leading anywhere [...] But you can pack for the journey [...]' (25). The notion that the self is an unfolding map is richly suggestive of change/s over time, of possibilities that reveal themselves as you travel, and of alterative routes to be explored. This is Winterson, the novelist at work. We might think here of *Sexing the Cherry* (1989) with its focus on travel both geographic and temporal. So a chapter that purports to start with placing the limited facts of individual biography within a larger social and historical context (time and place) ends with a set of co-ordinates and a quest, the suggestion being that what is to follow is also a quest narrative, a story of love and loss, of happenstance, of meeting one's destiny, of trying to live 'a meaningful life' (24).

Given the often philosophic and playful nature of some of Winterson's fiction, it is perhaps not surprising that her non-fiction (e.g. essays), including her memoir, have much in common stylistically with her novels. It is not that they are the same but that there is a stylistic and perhaps a thematic continuity across Winterson's *oeuvre* that makes it recognizably hers. What differentiates parts of *Why Be Happy?* from *Oranges*, apart from the fact that the former incorporates explicit references to the latter, is that it provides context and explanation where in *Oranges* the text was sometimes more oblique and less charged in terms of mining past trauma so as to understand its impact and to heal. *Oranges* covers up some of the early trauma through humour but equally the symbiotic relationship that develops between the texts is a factor of time and experience, as well as rupture and breakdown.

4.7 Concluding Remarks

To say that fiction and non-fiction are cut from the same cloth, given that they both avail themselves of language and potentially of narrative resources is of course to overstate the case and is, in fact, the kind of statement to which Arnaud Schmitt, a long-standing critic of autofiction, takes exception. For Schmitt, while the frame that the reader applies to a text may vary in the case of ambivalent or apparently generically hybrid works, it is simply not possible to read with uncertainty in mind. One must either read a text as (predominantly) fact or as fiction, even where the strategies used to present the non-fictional draw on those that are commonplace in a fictional universe. In a recent article in which Schmitt (2020, 1) rethinks autofiction, he concedes that one argument in favour of autofiction is the view that its use is 'an opportunity for the author to enter a fictional world while retaining her/his name, or her/his psychological/physical features; in other words, describing or even using oneself as an avatar'. The notion of the avatar is of interest here for a number of reasons. Firstly, because it has been explored already in Emilie Walezak's 2018 article where she picks up on the notion of the avatar in relation to Winterson's representations of her mother in her *oeuvre* including *Oranges, Sexing the Cherry* and *Why Be Happy?* Secondly, the avatar suggests a distancing of self with an image or representation standing in for the 'real' person, yet nevertheless embodying their spirit. Indeed, looking across Winterson's works, Walezak (2018, 129) writes of Winterson's 'capacity to experiment with multiple selves'. While Walezak's article centres on the mother–daughter relationship and its re-inscription and transformation over time, she reads the different conjunctions and interpretations as consistent with Winterson's growing radical consciousness and feminist politics.

Mention of autofiction earlier begs the question of whether and why such a term should be applied to Winterson's memoir or even some of her first-person fiction, such as *Oranges* where there appears to be identity between and among protagonist, narrator and author. If we understand autofiction in terms of treatment of the author as a persona within the work, then *Oranges* may be a candidate for such a designation. For Schmitt (2020, 6), autofiction is 'simply a form of autobiographical novel', though he concedes that in the past his objection to the term autofiction may have had something to do with maintaining the integrity of life writing. What has become clear in the course of this chapter is that for Winterson, her first semi-autobiographical novel was foundational in more than one sense. Not only did it start her successful career as a writer of (mainly) fiction but the story that she had to tell within its pages is one that bears a strong similarity to the outline, if not all the details, of her own life up to that point. The unfinished business relating to her adoption, early life and adolescence is then re-explored in *Why Be Happy?* and certain key scenes are revisited alongside commentary and evaluation from a much older, more mature Wintersonian narrator whose experience of life has taught her to look more deeply at her preferences as well as her commitment to literature to understand where they came from and what they mean.

In some ways, Winterson's life and her art go hand in hand in the sense that she stories her experience and mines it for meaning, yet the degree of identification between narrator, protagonist and author is variable throughout her work. Only in *Oranges* does the protagonist bear the same name as the narrator and author. At the same time there is a degree of playfulness and humour alongside the literary allusions and recounting of tales, a self-conscious knowingness about how best to structure the narrative for effect that suggests a writer intent on establishing her authorial credentials. I am not suggesting that *Why Be Happy?* is not a memoir insofar as it claims to recount a part of Winterson's life as truthfully as possible. What I am suggesting is that in concentrating so firmly on the territory charted in *Oranges*, it binds itself to that book and makes it foundational in yet another sense: *Oranges* contains the founding myth of Winterson's writerly existence and introduces her mother as a larger-than-life character. Winterson's insistence on referring to her adoptive mother in interview as either Mrs. Winterson or Mrs. W. compounds a sense of both distance and proximity: distance because it is unusual to refer to one's mother by her married name; proximity in the sense that Winterson's adoptive mother seems to have exerted such an influence, evident in other fictions such as *Sexing the Cherry* in the character of the Dog Woman, for example.

Winterson's genesis as a writer is founded on the facts of her early life and on the influence exerted by her adoptive mother in raising her as she did. It is the crisis that she undergoes in later life and the subsequent quest for her biological mother that allows her to see afresh the role of Mrs. Winterson in helping to form her and shape her life, both positively and negatively. *Why Be Happy?* is indeed a companion piece to *Oranges*, not simply its silent twin and painful fulfilment but a kind of revisioning and resetting of residual Wintersonian myths with a view, perhaps, of making peace with the past and affording a permissive view of a future where 'the possibility of love' (230) includes self-love as well as love of and for others. To change the future, Winterson knows that she needs to change the narrative.

Chapter 5

A CROSS-CULTURAL MEMOIR: XIAOLU GUO'S *ONCE UPON A TIME IN THE EAST*

5.1 Introduction and Aims

Reception of Xiaolu Guo's *Once Upon a Time in the East*, published in the UK in 2017, has been variable, as might be expected, perhaps, of a work that seems to combine trauma and personal revelation, with a style of narration in keeping with much of Guo's fictional output, that is to say, a blending of fiction and autobiography. Just as Winterson's memoir, *Why Be Happy When You Could Be Normal?* was sparked by a desire to overcome the trauma of her past, and come to terms with her biography, in its cultural, as well as personal dimensions, Guo's work, referred to, among other things, as a 'tale of survival' (George 2017, 32) presents Guo's life-story in terms of a mix of deprivation and poverty and a stubborn determination to overcome the sufferings and limitations of her upbringing and environment, including a period of sexual abuse. Yet such is the manner in which her story is told that for many reviewers, Guo's tale of survival reads more like a grim fairy tale, a kind of 'Cinderella in China', as the title of a review in *The Spectator* has it (George 2017, 32). In another review in *The New Statesman*, it is the book's title that is picked out for its fairy-tale-like qualities (Walsh 2017, 51), given reading conventions which equate 'once upon a time' with the beginning of a fairy tale.

One of the things that this chapter will set out to achieve is to understand why reception of Guo's memoir has included a strain that reads it not so much as an account of an eventful life but as a fabular tale (Feigel 2017), and to consider why this might be, in conjunction with a sense of what Guo sees herself as trying to achieve, in order to understand the kind of relationship that is in place between Guo's earlier fictions and her memoir. Moreover, the chapter will be concerned with interrogating further received ideas, assumptions and expectations about genres, as they relate to notions of fiction and non-fiction, life and art, narrative personae and the so-called autobiographical contract. The complicating factor here will be both linguistic and cultural insofar as Guo has been writing in an acquired language since publication of her first English language novel, *A Concise Chinese-English Dictionary For Lovers* (2007); she continues to rework and add to her cross-cultural tales, as evidenced by publication of *A Lover's Discourse* (2020), a kind of sequel to her dictionary novel and one which makes explicit its connection to Barthes' work of the same name in English translation. Indeed, as I have indicated elsewhere (Doloughan 2019), translation, including self-translation, is a useful way of understanding the complex, performative dynamics at play in Guo's work.

5.2 Framing Guo's Work

Interestingly, in discussing the publication of *A Lover's Discourse* (2020) on Radio 4's *Front Row*, an arts and culture programme in the UK, Guo admits that her novels are really quite close to her own life story and are, in fact, versions of it. She also mentions that *A Concise Chinese-English Dictionary for Lovers* was not the work she had originally intended to publish, which is, in part at least, why she has returned to the themes explored there. Indeed, in many ways, *A Lover's Discourse* displays some of the same qualities as Guo's 2007 dictionary novel insofar as it treats a relationship between a couple from different backgrounds and linguistic and cultural communities; and both works allude to, and take their inspiration from, the work of Roland Barthes. In interview with presenter Tom Sutcliffe Guo talks about Barthes as an early influence and about the fact that we are all multiple (rather than singular) beings with different selves. She indicates that her new book is pared down, minimal in terms of plot – not that any of her novels can be described as plot-driven – and that she wants to focus on language and the ways in which it constrains as well as permits creativity. For Guo, there is a kind of psychic and emotional experience of reality whose articulation in a particular language relates to, and may be constrained by, deployment of the specific lexical and grammatical resources available. For those who have access to more than one language, translation of a feeling and/or insight into language is therefore potentially even more fraught, as the speaker seeks to express herself using the multiple resources at her disposal. In an article on her writing day for *The Guardian* newspaper in the UK, for example, Guo expresses her frustration with writing across languages, when she thinks in one but writes in another: 'I still feel there's so much in me screaming to be heard [...]. I try to write a transcript which is in both Chinese and English, a text that is alive and true for both cultures I am living in' (Guo 2016).

A Lover's Discourse is also a novel about the search for home and roots: one of the homes that the couple in the novel inhabits is a narrow boat, a choice whose properties play both on the literal and the metaphoric in that the narrow space of the boat keeps movement in check, while at the same time, its location on the water means that it can be unmoored and anchored elsewhere, just as the female character's life in the UK is subject to constraint, instability and dislocation. Guo indicates in the *Front Row* interview (2020) that she is also using the image of the narrow boat to refer to a vision of Britain cut adrift and unmoored in a post-Brexit world. In the same interview, when asked if she now feels at home in Britain, Guo deflects the question somewhat to indicate that while the familial ties that she has created help to make her feel more grounded, she also refuses to see nationality, nation, and family as guarantors of belonging. Instead, it is her artistic practice that is her home and without which she does not flourish. In *The Guardian* newspaper article quoted earlier, she says something similar insofar as it is her books that are her travelling companions and whose presence makes her feel at home: 'Without them, I feel I've lost my glasses. Everything blurs. In this perpetual living abroad, I need to locate myself through these authors [Mishima, Laozi, Bolaño, Joyce] through their particular ways of using language, ways of dreaming' (Guo 2016).

In addition to being a translingual writer who has adopted English as the principal language in which she constructs her work, Guo can be seen as a transcultural writer, a term used to categorize 'imaginative writers who, by choice or because of life circumstances, experience cultural dislocation, follow transnational life patterns, cultivate bilingual or plurilingual proficiency, physically immerse themselves in multiple cultures, geographies, or territories, expose themselves to diversity, and nurture plural, flexible identities' (Dagnino 2015, 1). When considering Guo's memoir, its structuring, its content, and generic features, alongside some of Guo's fiction, insofar as that also speaks to her trajectory as a writer, it is important to keep in mind Guo's self-declared cosmopolitanism and her persistent linguistic and cultural border-crossing. It is equally important from the perspective of reception of Guo's work to bear in mind that her points of reference extend beyond those favoured by many readers from the West; as a young woman growing up in China in the 80s and 90s and a product of the Beijing Film Academy, her access to literature incorporated a wide range of Western and Eastern books, including film theory and literature in translation. In interview she often refers to the 1980s in China as a time when, post-Mao, there was a boom in literature in translation in China and a relative openness to new ideas following the Cultural Revolution.

'What's on Weibo?', a website devoted to information about social trends in China for those interested in learning about Chinese society, includes a list (from December 2018) of the top 25 fiction books to read in English in order to learn more about modern China. Joint number 10 on the list is Guo's memoir,

Once Upon a Time in the East, referred to on the cover of the hardback edition as autobiography, alongside *Falling Leaves* by Adeline Yen Mah. They are positioned together, despite the age difference in the writers who come from different generations, on the basis of perceived similarities in terms of their themes, identified as 'Chinese family dynamics and culture' (Koetse 2018). Given that there is also a page on the same website for the 30 best non-fiction books on China, it is interesting to note the positioning of Guo's memoir in the fiction section. This may be telling, the more so since, for Guo, *Once Upon a Time in the East* might more accurately be described as 'a documentary novel' (Guo 2019).

5.3 Authorial Aims and Intentions: A Portrait of the Artist

The question of what Guo intends in *Once Upon a Time in the East* is a complex one. What is clear, however, is that she is not entirely comfortable with the publisher's label. She sees memoir as a 'big, heavy word' and understands what she is trying to achieve in slightly different terms. In discussion in 2017 with Isaac Stone Fish, a New York-based journalist and international affairs analyst, Guo reveals that she came to a point where having written so much fiction, she began to see the novel as a commodity and wanted to write something more like an essay. However, since essays are difficult to sell and she had already started publishing some separate pieces (in *The Guardian* and *The Financial Times*, for example) about her childhood, she decided to collect these few fragments and continue them so as to form a more or less coherent whole. As a diary writer, she was able to draw on her observations and create a more continuous picture of growing up in China and eventually leaving for the West. Above all, she wanted to produce for her new daughter an account of her life in China before moving to the UK. Clearly, *Once Upon a Time in the East* is not a comprehensive account of Guo's life up to that point. There are many lacunae and whole periods of existence (in France and Germany, for example) are left out. It is, in many ways, best read as a series of vignettes that nevertheless coalesce into a kind of cross-cultural narrative that tells the story of a young Chinese woman's struggle to become an artist. In this sense, it bears affinities with the *Künstlerroman*, a kind of portrait of the (emerging) artist. Moreover, there is a pivotal scene, discussed in what follows, that begs reading within a Joycean frame.

The title also requires comment, insofar as the US title is different from the UK one. The US edition takes its title – *Nine Continents* – from the scene in the book with the Taoist monk where the young Xiaolu's grandmother asks the monk to read her grand-daughter's palm. The monk looks diagonally at her hand and eventually replies that she will be a peasant warrior and will cross the Nine Continents. The Nine Continents refers to China in its vastness but also, by extension, the whole world. For a young child living with her illiterate grandparents in a small fishing village in Southern China, this is indeed a startling revelation and something for the young girl and her grandmother to cling on to. The UK title signals a point of origin in the East but, as inclusion of italicized extracts in English translation from *Journey to the West* by Wu Cheng'en signal, this is also the story of a journey to the West. Guo indicates that unlike her fiction, the book was written quickly in 11 months. She had reached a point in her writing career where she felt that fiction embodied a certain lack of immediacy given the requirement for narrative filtering and structuring. Such a viewpoint suggests that she sees the fast pace of writing *Once Upon a Time in the East* as a guarantor of immediacy or a degree of authenticity; however, a closer look at the memoir, if this is indeed an appropriate term to use of *Once Upon a Time in the East*, displays a measure of structuring, and its use of imagery would seem to be consistent with a degree of (more or less) conscious design.

5.3.1 Structure and design

On re-reading Part 1 on 'Shitang: Tales of the East China Sea', what comes to the fore is inclusion of imagery pertaining to the sea and despite the unremitting poverty and desolation, a sense conveyed through the writing of the development of an imaginative capacity on the part of the young protagonist. For example, in describing Guo's grandfather's suicide, the authorial narrator writes:

> My grandfather's eyes were wide open, but not moving. They looked like the eyes of a dead fish. (Guo 2017, 46)

She goes on to describe his corpse in the following terms:

> His mouth was grey and dry like the lips of a dead shark. (Guo 2017, 47)

To cite a different example: in talking about the kind of things washed up on the shore which the inhabitants of Shitang, the fishing village, scavenge, the narrator recounts the episode of a metal box being washed up and found to contain 'small pills packed in different glass bottles, each bottle labelled with foreign letters' (50). In continuing the description, the narrator writes:

> The pills had various colours and shapes; some were big white tablets, others round like fish eyes, brown and transparent. (Guo 2017, 50)

The point I am making is that scrutiny of the linguistic choices made and of the use of imagery would suggest a degree of care and thoughtfulness in their selection and articulation. In some ways, use of colour in this first part is also telling: in evoking the village of her early years, Guo uses a palette that consists mainly of browns and greys. This is partly why the episode, 'Tourists on the Beach' (57–59), stands out. Of course, it is significant in a more fundamental way too, insofar as it highlights for the narrator the possible difference between art and reality. In this episode a group of student artists appear in Shitang and paint the sea, the sky and the sunset. The colours they use seem to be at odds with what the narrator sees in actuality and she points this out to the artists, who are unperturbed by such observations, since for them what one sees is in the eye of the beholder. The scene represents a kind of epiphany for the young narrator who calls it 'one of the happiest days of my life' (58). In understanding, if only viscerally, the power of art to change reality, the narrator writes: 'From that afternoon onwards, I knew I wanted to become an artist. I would devote my entire life to that end' (59).

It might be said, more generally then, using the words of Vancouver-based Chinese-Canadian poet, Natalie Lim (2018), that Guo has turned 'foreign soil/into survival'. By devoting her life to becoming the artist she always dreamed of being, she has produced, in her filmmaking and in her writing, versions of herself, based on experience/s reconstructed in memory, and expressed narratively, poetically and visually. Guo is clear that 'memory is always a narrative reconstruction' (*CBC* interview 2018). In speaking about *Nine Continents*, she indicates that she did not really know about her 'real' grandfather or what he thought about, she could only observe his behaviour and its effects on her grandmother and reconstruct in her imagination and through her writing a scene that evokes in the reader a sense of this figure who cast a shadow on their lives. Her grandfather's suicide, she indicates, helped shape her life at the time because it was not very common for someone from the peasant class, as opposed to intellectuals during the Cultural Revolution, to commit suicide; later she thought about the fact that her long-suffering grandmother just kept going, uncomplainingly, unlike her grandfather.

5.4 Links in a Translational Chain

So far, I have hinted at a couple of aspects of *Once Upon a Time in the East* that may account for its reception as fabular: firstly, it sends signals to the reader through the language used that it is a story with fairy-tale elements ('Once Upon A Time [...]'), and it incorporates references to *Journey to the West*, a classic novel of Ming dynasty Chinese literature that blended folk religion, philosophy and mythology. In addition, the author's comments on the book's generic classification would suggest that for her as a writer it is both a break from the requirements of the novel form and another version of the kind of protagonist represented in previous works: a young Chinese woman who leaves China for the West and recounts her experiences of living in a different culture. As I have argued elsewhere, a narrative thread links some of Guo's early fictions to her self-portrait in *Once Upon a Time in the East*. *Village of Stone*, a novel originally written in Chinese (我心中的石头镇/Wo Xinzhong de Shitouzhen) and published in 2003 by Shanghai Literature & Art Publishing House, was translated into English in 2004 by Beijing-based American translator Cindy M. Carter and published by Chatto & Windus. It tells the story of Coral, living in Beijing with frisbee-throwing boyfriend Red, who having received a mysterious package of eel, is reminded of her early life in Shitang, a fishing village in the South China Sea where she grew up. Returning there with her boyfriend, she evokes the place in descriptions not unlike those applied to Shitang as it is depicted in part 1 of *Once Upon a Time in the East*. Moreover, a line can be traced from *Village of Stone* via *A Concise Chinese-English Dictionary for Lovers* to *Once Upon a Time in the East* in terms of their depiction of the central character, a young Chinese woman from the provinces with aspirations who moves to the city (usually Beijing) and eventually leaves China for the West (usually London).

In other words, it is as if Guo's earlier fictions present a version of parts of her own story, at least in their essentials. What is different in the memoir is the fact that Guo uses her own name and discusses her origins. It is also revelatory insofar as she names for the first time a sexual abuser, though depictions of rape and sexual abuse do feature in the earlier fictions mentioned previously. In conversation with myself in the context of a series on 'Life Stories' (2019) at the Institute of English Studies, University of London, Guo talked about her memoir in relation to her early fictions. She described herself as essentially a diary writer and made clear that her preferred mode of writing is the production of short prose pieces with some kind of connecting thread holding them together. In conversation she acknowledged connections between *Village of Stone* and the later memoir, preferring to call the latter a documentary novel, rather than a memoir. In her capacity as a writer, rather than a human being – she sees a tension here – she claims to live without much moral concern, and notes that memoir is also a creation, something reconstructed in memory and rendered in language; she is, she says, first and foremost, a storyteller and that is her priority (Doloughan and Guo 2019). She points out that the US version, *Nine Continents*, has a different ending to the UK version and that quite often her works change in translation as she revisits them with her translators and decides to take things out or revise them. So while *Once Upon a Time in the East* sees the protagonist moving from one flat to another within London and receiving news of the death of her mother, *Nine Continents* ends in Berlin. Guo's tendency to change even already published texts is something I can confirm from personal correspondence with her German translator Anne Rademacher (2015). With respect to the translation of *I Am China*, Rademacher indicates having discussed edits with Guo in the translation process from English into German.

It is important, therefore, to be alert to the continuities, as well as the differences, across some of Guo's fictions and to understand the extent to which some of them are versions of what becomes her autobiography, the term used on the back cover of *Once Upon a Time in the East* in the UK, while the US title highlights the term memoir, *Nine Continents: A Memoir in and Out of China*, as if they were synonyms. Arguably, memoir as a term is more likely to be applied to a portion of a life or episodes from a life, as in the case of Winterson's *Why Be Happy When You Could Be Normal?* Indeed, to an extent, there are similarities here with Winterson's revisiting of elements of her childhood, many of which had already been explored in fictional form in *Oranges*. The trigger for production of *Why Be Happy?* seems to have been Winterson's suicide attempt, breakdown and quest for her biological mother, as we have seen. While Guo's motivation is less clear, we do know from interviews that she wanted a break from the commodification of fiction and that the cycle of death (her parents) and birth (her daughter) provided a frame for publication of *Once Upon a Time in the East*.

In many ways, it is the Prologue, 'The Past is a Foreign Country', that does the work of providing a lens through which to view Guo's story. And, according to Guo, inclusion of the Prologue was a necessary addition to her book-in-progress, and a strong motivation for, if not a condition of, publication. As a new mother in a country far from her birthplace, she decides after 15 nomadic years to finally 'pay a debt of filial duty' (Guo 2017, 2) by returning to China to see her surviving parent (her mother), pay her respects to her dead father and help move her grandmother's ashes. In this case it is a joyful event – the birth of her daughter – that motivates her long-distance telephone call to her mother, with whom she otherwise has had little contact, and which informs her decision to accede to her mother's request to return for the Qingming Festival. Qingming Festival takes place in April and is a time when Chinese people pay their respects to the dead. It is also the case that the narrator would like her daughter to be more grounded than herself; she knows that she will have to explain to her half-Chinese, half-Western daughter something of her life before becoming a mother. She also wishes her daughter to know where she comes from. In Guo's case, then, there is seemingly a positive motivation for revisiting the past. Yet, it must be remembered that in the course of the book, she also reveals the name of her abuser during a period of her life in Wenling when she was sexually abused. This confrontation with a traumatic past is also part of the motivation for revisiting this period of her life and perhaps laying its ghosts to rest. So the picture is more complicated than it might at first appear. The life story is wrapped in a warm blanket, like the newborn, who travels with her mother to China, but this is also the story of a young Chinese girl who has overcome poverty, deprivation and emotional and sexual abuse to realize her dream of becoming an artist. In this sense, it *is* a fabular story and may seem larger-than-life in that Guo manages to realize her ambitions despite significant obstacles, not least her success in learning a new language in her twenties and getting her work published to critical acclaim.

Comparisons with Winterson's artistic trajectory may initially seem far-fetched, given the cultural and linguistic differences that separate them in addition to the fact that they are the products of different generations and cultures. Yet their initial social location in terms of class and gender, and the somewhat unusual, even exceptional circumstances of their early life, show a surprising degree of commonality. As we have seen, Winterson's family circumstances were unusual, in that she was adopted and grew up in an evangelical household; the fact that she spent much of her writing career re-presenting her adoptive mother in different guises in her fiction (as the Dog Woman in her 1989 novel *Sexing the Cherry*, for example) and playing out aspects of her early life is witness to its impact on her formation as a writer. Winterson, like Guo, presents dramatized aspects of her life in her work and while these are transformed and incorporated into whatever story she is telling, it becomes clear, in retrospect, that she is mining similar seams and returning, almost obsessively, to the same set of themes (of loss and love, of art and life, for example). Both writers present versions of themselves in their writing and their main protagonists share a sense of their difference and uniqueness. Just as in *Sexing the Cherry* Winterson presents in Jordan (the traveller and dreamer) and the Dog Woman (the larger-than-life mother figure and fierce fighter) conflicted aspects of family life and potentially a self at war, so Guo uses her novel *I Am China* to present in her two characters Mu and Jian, conflicts about art and life that have characterized her own existence.

Moreover, despite their very different histories, both writers reveal in their memoirs and in their commitment to art more generally an inner strength and ambition that leads them to hold on to their dreams despite serious obstacles. For example, Winterson overcame obstacles to get into Oxford, while Guo returned to Beijing to compete a second time for a place at the highly prestigious Beijing Film Academy. Winterson was her adopted mother's only child, though as she discovers when she meets her biological mother, she has, unbeknown to her, a larger extended family circle. However, the pattern of her early life has established itself and, just like the characters she presents in her fiction, Winterson comes across as very self-sufficient and determined to fight for her beliefs and to protect her writing life. Interestingly, while in reality Guo has a brother, she nevertheless sees herself as an only – indeed a lonely and somewhat alienated – child. Like Winterson, she identifies herself as an orphan, despite having parents; she turned to literature and art more generally as a means of salvation. In addition, for both Winterson and Guo, art has the capacity to transcend reality and literature, and the arts more generally are the means whereby reality can be transformed. Both, too, focus on language and its possibilities for transformation. And art for both is the primary means by which they define themselves and through which their identities are established.

It is worth quoting in full a passage from the end of *Once Upon a Time in the East* which articulates Guo's philosophical and literary leanings and pinpoints the moment in her young life that she sees as significant:

> The protagonists of my favourite books were all orphans. They were parentless, self-made heroes. They had had to create themselves, since they had come from nothing and no inheritance. In my own way I too was self-made. I was born and then flung aside, to survive in a rocky village by the ocean. If I had to pinpoint a moment when this thought crystallised in my mind, it was that day on the beach in Shitang when I met the art students drawing in their sketch pads facing a sunless, wavy-grey sea. I was six years old and consumed by an ineffable loneliness. I watched the young girl in particular as she contemplated the monotonous scene before us, and then started to apply paint to her paper. Her brush made a shimmering blue and a burning sunset appear across the page. I was suddenly captivated by the girl's imaginative act: that one could reshape a drab and colourless reality into a luminous world. (Guo 2017, 314)

Much could be said about this passage within the context of *Once Upon a Time in the East*, and in relation to Guo's work more generally, as well as in relation to wider intertextual resonances. In terms of the memoir itself, there is both a linear and a cyclic quality to the narrative, both in evidence here. While the Prologue has set up the motivation for Guo's return to her birthplace and an encounter with the sites of her childhood and adolescence, the final section, 'The Circle of Life', of Part V, 'In the Face of Birth and Death', returns the reader to the writer's present life in her new flat in London with her child, having understood that she has now created her own family unit and is 'free of the burden' (314) of her Chinese familial past. She is, she writes, 'my own home now' and she could at last take 'fresh new air into my own lungs' (314).

So the moment of her mother's death, while it generates sadness, is also a moment of liberation from the negativity of the ties to an oppressive past. Guo has laid her ghosts to rest in writing her book and in finally confronting the demons that have haunted her. She indicates in a sentence just before the passage quoted that she has been orphaned for a second time (314), the first having been when she is given away by her parents to the childless couple in the mountains. To lose one's parents might normally be considered a sad, if not tragic, event but for Guo it represents a new beginning, alongside the birth of her daughter whose future she wishes to assure. Unlike the nomad she feels herself to have become, she wants her daughter to be 'a grounded person, unlike me, a peripatetic peasant, a cultural orphan' (1).

The working title for the memoir was *A Global Peasant*, a title intended to point to Guo's wandering and sense of dislocation, while flagging up her peasant roots. Not perhaps as marketable a title as *Once Upon a Time in the East*, it nevertheless encapsulates important aspects of Guo's trajectory and points to the conflicts and tensions played out in her work, in both literature and film: what happens when the juggernaut of globalization hits people in rural areas and small town locations in China (cf. *UFO in Her Eyes*), what happens when people are separated, either by choice or as a consequence of political and/or economic forces, from their home environment or cultural point of origin (*A Concise Chinese-English Dictionary for Lovers*; *She, A Chinese*; *We Went to Wonderland*; *I Am China*; *A Lover's Discourse*). These big questions are played out in her work from the perspective of individual characters embedded in particular societies, often characters who are rebellious or marginal(ized) in some way, and who don't always fit the societal mould. Much of Guo's fiction involves a female character who leaves a rural backwater, first for the big city (usually Beijing) in China, and who then leaves for the West (usually London). In this sense, finding a place for oneself and trying to construct an identity seems to demand crossing borders, both literally (leaving one place or country for another and experiencing different linguistic and cultural realities) and metaphorically (extending the self by appropriating new linguistic and cultural identities).

Yet it is precisely Guo's cultural nomadism that has allowed her to translate herself and her art to different locations and to draw on it as a wellspring of creativity. Her work is the product of a range of influences and voices that she inhabits and animates: her long-standing fascination with the work of Roland Barthes which directly underpins at least two works, *A Concise Chinese-English Dictionary for Lovers* and *A Lover's Discourse*; and her experience as a documentary filmmaker which allows her to bring to her prose narratives a visual quality and concern with space and place, even as her films incorporate a lyricism and poeticality that disrupt the narrative flow (Doloughan 2015). In addition, her sources and influences in *Once Upon a Time in the East* are marked in paratextual ways in her dedication to Marguerite Duras, for example, and in her choice of quotation from Eva Hoffman's *Lost in Translation*. While the former is a long-standing point of reference for Guo, alongside other French writers such as Jean Genet and Boris Vian, the latter is a more recent point of contact and reflects Guo's recognition of the fact that other translingual writers have experienced similar emotions when crossing cultural and linguistic boundaries. The fact that the Hoffman quotation speaks to issues of alienation, internal exile and selfhood is important in indexing Guo's own struggle to overcome a deep sense of alienation both in China and the West by creating a new identity as a translingual, transcultural writer.

5.4.1 Intertextuality

That Guo is familiar with the work of James Joyce is apparent not only in what she says in interview but is also visible in her work. In the long passage just quoted, it is difficult not to hear Joycean echoes as evidenced in selection of the word 'luminous'. Insofar as *A Portrait of the Artist as a Young Man* tells the story of the making of an artist, one concerned with aesthetics, and 'the clear radiance of the esthetic image' as it is 'apprehended luminously by the mind which has been arrested by its wholeness and fascinated by its harmony' (Joyce 1979, 321), the reader is likely to hear in Guo's story of her own artistic development a particularly Joycean resonance. Like Guo, Joyce had to leave his homeland to pursue his creative life; he, too, led something of a nomadic existence and made sacrifices for his art.

It is also worth returning to Guo's inclusion of translated passages from *Journey to the West* in her narrative both as a structuring device and as an intertextual reference point. *Once Upon a Time in the East* is a work divided into five parts, preceded by a prologue; each part is introduced with an italicized extract from *Journey to the West*. In many ways, these extracts parallel, at an abstract level, the content of the text to come. So, for example, the extract that introduces Part 1 'Shitang: Tales of the East China Sea' (5–67) is a creation myth which features the birth of a monkey destined to go on a journey with a Buddhist monk to find 'the purest Buddhist scripture on earth' to enable mankind to 'achieve real knowledge of life and death' (7). This parallels Guo's arrival in the world and suggests that she too will go on a journey, as indeed the Taoist monk predicts. The little monkey in the extract is also described as being 'no ordinary monkey' (6); it is a monkey that feels sad and lonely and has a 'great urge [...] to do something deserving with his life' (6). In the Shitang section, the reader becomes conscious of the young Xiaolu's sadness and loneliness and of her desire to do something meaningful with her own life, although at the age of just six, she may not have articulated it this way! It is clear from the narrative, however, that Guo's destiny will be to leave her small backwater and go on to achieve great things: the recounting of her epiphany on watching the art students on the beach suggests that it is art that will occupy her future.

The extract that begins 'Part II, Wenling: Life in a Communist Compound' relates the moment in the Tang dynasty when having secured the basis for a rich material existence, the emperor decides that the country needs 'to be animated by a strong spiritual life' (70). Together with his pilgrim companions, the monk Xuanzang, chosen for this mission, goes off to India in search of the original Buddhist sutras; they meet the monkey, whom the monk names Wukong, meaning 'Emptiness Knower', on the way. Wukong's job is to serve the monk and help him on his journey. If there are parallels with this phase of Guo's life, they are perhaps at the level of an improved material existence: the compound in Wenling is a step up from the house in the fishing village of Shitang and, initially at least, conditions are better in that the young Xiaolu has better food and accommodation. However, her emotional life is still difficult: she doesn't get on with her mother and she and her brother have little in common. Yet she does have the support of her father and they have shared interests in art. It is her father who takes her to Beijing to sit the highly competitive entrance exam for the Beijing Film Academy and who buys her lots of books after she fails to gain a place on the first attempt. In some ways, what is related in this part is a series of trials and tribulations, obstacles to be overcome, as the young protagonist begins to find her own path in life. The journey towards realization of her goal to become an artist will be a long and fraught one but writing, described as 'one of my closest spiritual companions' (165), will be key on this journey to leaving the 'sweaty, drowsy south' (169) and heading for the freedoms Guo sees Beijing as offering at that time.

The next section entitled 'Part III, Beijing: The Whirlpool of Life' (173–238) is introduced by an extract from *Journey to the West* that relates the monkey's trickster nature and ill-discipline and shows the monk having to tame Wukong through use of a magical headband that tightens, and causes pain, to ensure the monkey's obedience. The counterpart in Guo's narrative is the fact that once in Beijing, while initially studying hard and being content to follow the curriculum, she soon begins to follow her own path by immersing herself in the revolutionary art scene. While she laps up everything she can, she turns away from state-sanctioned art and seeks out avant-garde artists in the East Village in Beijing to film. In fact, she is called in by the director to explain her presence at an event at the Great Wall with avant-garde body artists. She indicates that she 'wanted to have a real artistic experience rather than only watch French new wave films with sexy actresses in them' (184).

During this period she also begins to write what will become *Twenty Fragments of a Ravenous Youth* (in English translation), telling the story of Fenfang, 'the country girl who ran away from home for Beijing and tried to become an artist' (Guo 2017, 201). This is a plotline and thematic concern that will permeate quite a few of Guo's books and films, the protagonist in many ways a version of herself. The books Guo had at her side during the writing of this first novel, she describes as 'Salingeresque books, slim but with vivid first-person narratives' (201). Thus began her search for a voice, one capable of rendering aspects of her own experience into a narrative.

Part IV relates Guo's arrival in Europe on a Chevening Scholarship to study at the National Film and Television School in Beaconsfield. The extract from *Journey to the West* that introduces it relates the pilgrims' journey to India and charts the monk's long years of study before finally arriving at his destination. It also narrates the difference between the pilgrims' expectations and the reality of what they find and, in this sense, parallels Guo's arrival in London, where she claims to have 'ended up in the ugliest parts of the city' (249). The London she experiences seems rather brutal and desolate unlike the city of her dreams and her travels with a boyfriend to south-west Wales are no better in that she fails to find in the countryside the kind of beauty that the poets extol. She is forced to confront the kind of cultural differences, explored in more depth and with great humour in *A Concise Chinese-English Dictionary for Lovers* that prevent her simply ditching her own cultural assumptions for those that predominate in another country. She notes a sense of dislocation and abandonment resurfacing in Wales as she recalls her life in Shitang; she understands that she must return to the hustle and bustle of the city. Her negative experience in west Wales is a moment of learning in more than one sense: 'I needed China as the driver of my imagination, a source of creativity, thought and understanding' (257).

Soon after this, she settles down to write what will become her first novel in English, *A Concise Chinese-English Dictionary for Lovers*, a work that enjoys great success and cements Guo on her path as a writer, as well as a filmmaker. 'Being an artist', she writes, 'defines who I am. Not my passport, my gender, my language, or my skin colour' (268). Part IV ends with the arrival of her parents in London and Guo's decision to film their encounter with the English capital and then to document their trip to Paris and Rome. The section entitled 'An old couple in a land of wonders' is an allusion to the making of Guo's 2008 film, *We Went to Wonderland*. While Guo's interactions with her parents are at times strained during their surprise visit, she reflects after they have gone on the 'sense of nakedness' that returned to her after their departure and describes their absence as 'another unwanted presence' (294). Yet when she returns to China a few months after their European tour to watch her father die, she tries to reconnect with him by reminding him of episodes from their trip and sheds tears when she realizes he is in no fit state to react and that 'his body was shutting down' (296).

'Part V, In the Face of Life and Death' (300–315) is introduced by the final extract from *Journey to the West*. In this extract, the monk's journey has come to an end and he is ready to dedicate himself to translation of the sutras; the monkey returns to the wild. Guo's return is to China for a final time to pay her respects to the dead; her life with her new child and a family of her own has begun, thus completing the circle.

In sum, inclusion of extracts from *Journey to the West* acts as a cultural counterpoint to the narrative fulcrum and represents access, in English translation, to a classic and popular Chinese story for Western readers, as well as providing a reference point rooted in the East. It is a kind of cultural fulcrum around which Guo's own story stands in a relationship of part playful parody, part earnest search for the truth of her own existence. Given the many references to Western authors and filmmakers within the text who have been crucial to Guo's intellectual and artistic development, inclusion of these extracts is also a way of locating herself within an Eastern tradition. It is also potentially a means of educating Western readers who may not be as familiar with Chinese culture as might be expected. Much of Guo's work sits in the space between cultures insofar as she uses her position as someone with access to both Eastern and Western cultural codes or more precisely as a multilingual writer who has crossed cultures to point to cultural similarities and differences, misunderstandings and failures in communication. While she does this often with humour and in a light-hearted way, thematizing the kind of differences that can make it difficult for people from different cultures to communicate, there is also an underlying critique in her work of the kind of intellectual laziness that results from much Western ignorance of Chinese cultural and literary history, except in translation. A writer and filmmaker such as Guo who has access to cinematographic and literary traditions from both East and West is in a position to use her linguistic and cultural knowledge as a resource which affords opportunities for enhanced creativity, as I have argued elsewhere (Doloughan 2016).

As for questions of genre and reader expectations, it is my contention that without understanding the cultural basis, if not cultural bias, of certain generic conventions, there is a danger that dominant modes of writing and reading at particular historical moments are privileged, particularly those which assume a monolingual and monocultural standpoint. Indeed, we have seen already that the question of genre in Guo's case is a complicated one insofar as she hails from a country with a rich cultural tradition with its own literary norms and conventions. Guo's trajectory, as a multilingual reader and writer, has equipped her to understand the constraints and possibilities of generic conventions in Europe, as well as to have familiarity with key texts from the East, and specifically from China.

In general, Guo's favourite writers appear to be those who play with genre and/or extend the boundaries of literature in some way. Mention of Marguerite Duras as a role model alerts the reader to Guo's interest in and dedication to writing that has a sensuous and visual quality, as well as writing that transforms, while staying close to, (versions of) experience. In other words, Guo's literary models are, broadly speaking, European and American, rather than British; her periods of living abroad and residencies in Germany, where she now has a second home, France and Switzerland have helped to cement a sense of both playfulness and philosophical reflection in her work. Yet there are, arguably, traces in her writing of exposure to certain strands of writing in China too and this has already been discussed in relation to inclusion of extracts from *Journey to the West* in *Once Upon a Time in the East*. In addition, when asked in interview in response to questions about Chinese writers she would recommend, Guo often mentions writers such as Eileen Chang, Ha Jin and Su Tong.

As Guo indicates in *Once Upon a Time in the East*, the novel in the Western tradition was a relatively new form for China, the dominant literary forms being poetry, essays and short stories (201) at that time. She claims to have taken her cue from French and American literature in translation in beginning to write her first books and we have seen already how writers like Roland Barthes play an important part in her repertoire, even down to providing a title for *A Lover's Discourse*, described, incidentally, as a book which engages in 'subtle upending of Western perspectives' (Cummins 2020). However, while her Western influences and reference points are often discussed, there are fewer mentions in reviews and interviews of possible Chinese sources and mediating contexts.

Yet it seems that there is also a Chinese form of *Bildungsroman* or *chengzhang xiaoshuo* (Li 2011) in the twentieth century, whose features are consonant with aspects of her work, much of which involves a journey, in both a literal and a metaphoric sense, on the part of a female protagonist who rejects her often painful past and parochial upbringing to realize her future in an urban environment in China or beyond. As previously indicated, much of Guo's fiction relays versions of her own biography, though there are notable exceptions, such as *UFO in Her Eyes*, where the concern is more focussed on processes of globalization and their effects on a small community in rural China, than it is on the trajectory of an individual as she navigates the social world around her in her desire to make something of her life. If, as Li surmises, the *Bildungsroman* is characterized by 'the attributes of mobility and interiority' (Li 2011, 16), this is certainly in evidence in Guo's semi-autobiographical fiction which focusses on the protagonist's reflections on her experience of the world around her and her social, intellectual and sexual encounters, as she navigates both the possibilities and constraints of her situation. Indeed, as Li (2011, 25) suggests: 'It is sometimes difficult to draw a sharp line between autobiography and the autobiographical novel'.

5.5 Companion Pieces

While the focus in this chapter has been primarily on Guo's memoir and its cross-cultural reception, an argument has also been made that throughout her writerly trajectory to date, Guo has been disclosing aspects of her own biography or, at the very least, using and transforming the 'facts' of her biography within fictional contexts. In this regard it is useful to return to *A Lover's Discourse*, given that it is in many ways a companion piece to *A Concise-Chinese English Dictionary for Lovers*, Guo's first English-language publication, and because it is yet another example of the ways in which different versions of self, albeit in relation to other, are constructed within the Guo corpus. Guo claims that *A Lover's Discourse* is in many ways the book she wanted to write at the time she was working on her first novel. Both books bear a connection to the work of Barthes and in previous interviews Guo has discussed her interest in Barthes' *Fragments d'un discours amoureux* (*A Lover's Discourse: Fragments*) in respect of providing her with a structure for her dictionary novel, *A Concise Chinese-English Dictionary for Lovers*. *A Lover's Discourse*, published 13 years after her initial engagement with Barthes' work in an English-language context, declares its influence much more clearly, from the quotation preceding the opening pages, to the Prologue, which is a discussion of a translated aphorism from Barthes, to explicit references within the text to Barthes' life and work, discussed in conversations between the two lovers. The narrator's long-standing interest in Barthes comes under pressure, as she learns more about his biography (Barthesian Love Discourse I, 80–82) and begins to wonder if she has been misreading his work, given that she had assumed he was talking in his work about love between a man and a woman. As she reflects on the reality of Barthes' knowledge and experience of love, she begins to reconsider his work: rather than a dialogue, or 'a personal document' (80) speaking to her, it was more 'like a solipsistic monologue' (Guo 2020, 80). Ruminating further on this, the narrator wonders if she has completely misunderstood Barthes or herself. In the days following this revelation, she reads up more on Barthes' life and begins to understand that his deepest love was for his mother. From her partner's perspective this deep maternal love left no space for romantic love. The narrator then considers whether the love she has for her partner and he for her might not be 'strong and complete' (85), given that neither was tied to their family in a Barthesian way. In the third Barthesian Love Discourse (86–87), the exchange relates to a love that goes beyond the sexual. In this way, reflections on Barthes' work act as a spur and a counterpoint to the lovers' discussions in *A Lover's Discourse*.

While there are similarities with *A Concise Chinese-English Dictionary for Lovers*, there are also differences. The similarities reside in the organization of the two works and in their structuring insofar as they both rely on headed entries, important terms around which discussion between the two lovers from different cultures takes place; and both have a skeleton narrative, since the books are not so much plot-driven as dialogic and enact a working out of positions via a lightly sketched storyline. Another similarity relates to the focus on cross-cultural differences and how to navigate them within a relationship. The differences relate to the further paring down of conversations – the design of *A Lover's Discourse* is more aphoristic – and the sections within chapters are for the most part very short. Each chapter, if chapter be the right word, has a heading that relates to orientation: West, South, East, North, Down, Up, Left, Right. In some respects, the points of orientation are clearly marked, since the section marked East includes the narrator's trip to Shenzhen, and to the village (Dafen) in China where art reproductions are made, and Down relates a trip the lovers make to Queensland, Australia, but not all sections reflect such a clear orientation. Moreover, for one critic, these points of orientation are 'vague and disorienting in a way that points out their arbitrariness' (Shea 2020). Shea reads this as 'structuring devices [which] intentionally flatten and fragment the story that occurs between them. They mimic the expanding structure of a mind carefully built to house experiences that might otherwise prove indecipherable, collapse, or disappear entirely'.

In this sense, the overarching chapter headings are a catch-all for observations and meditations, many of which recur across the work (e.g. thoughts on 'originality' and 'reproduction'). As in *A Chinese-English Dictionary for Lovers*, the narrator of *A Lover's Discourse* is concerned with cross-cultural difference and its impact on relationships between those with different histories and originating from different locations, and there remains a focus on language as an entry point to culture and a means by which to flag up and express identity. Yet, unlike in Guo's first novel, where the narrator's increasing access to and ability to manipulate the English language marks the shifting power relations between the lovers, one British, the other Chinese, in *A Lover's Discourse* identity markers are more complex and hybrid. Neither partner is native to British culture; both are, in effect, observers of the world around them, looking to find a mooring, both literal and metaphoric, or at least a place they can call home. The range of languages and cultural references that permeate the text – mainly English (British and Australian), German, and Chinese, with some French – and the focus on identity as hybrid and intersectional, complicates the narrative. As *Guardian* reviewer Aida Edemariam (2020) puts it, *A Lover's Discourse* is 'a fragmentary meditation on the nature of love, on desire and on connection between two humans. It is a kind of autofiction in the mould of Rachel Cusk or Meena Kandasamy: an unapologetically intellectual project where thoughts on female desire, or memory, or work, are strained through a sieve of Walter Benjamin, Yuan dynasty poetry, Le Corbusier, Marguerite Duras'.

5.6 Guo's Autofictional Narratives

The reference to autofiction in Edemariam's (2020) review is interesting for a number of reasons. Firstly, as has been shown in the course of this chapter, Guo's memoir has been read as Cinderella-like, fabular and a mix of personal mythology and biography, rather than a realistic, slice of life, narrative. Secondly, I have demonstrated that an autobiographically informed thread links many of Guo's fictional works in which aspects of self are developed and exploited, alongside a return to a prevalent set of thematic concerns that revolve around human communication in the face of cultural and linguistic difference, concepts of home, and the meaning and value of art. In addition, Edemariam's remark draws attention to a thread connecting the projects of a number of contemporary female writers keen to rework given forms to reflect more clearly the truth of their experience and express their intellectual and critical concerns. As Alex Clark (2018) puts it, 'to capture 21st-century experience writers must breach borders – blend fiction, memoir, history, poetry, the visual and performing arts'.

This breaching of borders is particularly apt for a writer like Guo, originally from China but steeped in European cinematographic and critical theory at the Beijing Film Academy, now an English-language writer, with a prior publication record in China. In addition, as someone who has had to navigate different writing traditions and readerly expectations concerning the role and construction of narrative, Guo has drawn on her experience and cross-cultural and cross-disciplinary knowledge to create an episodic and fragmentary storytelling practice which combines the aphoristic, the epistolary, the poetic, and the narrative in a way that challenges categorial distinctions and blurs generic boundaries.

Of course, publishers draw on conventional generic labels as well as library and bookstore classifications in deciding how to position and market a writer's work and this can be further complicated by the extent to which a writer's work is well-known, or unfamiliar, to the public, as well as the extent to which it feeds reader expectations, reflects a particular *Zeitgeist* and/or interrogates given narrative forms. Yet critical references to autofiction as offering 'an alternative, experimental narrative of self' (Clark 2018), alongside Guo's remarks in relation to her memoir as a documentary novel, would suggest that for many writers today connections between fact and fiction, autobiographical trajectory and fictional re-presentation of aspects of self, is more like a work-in-process or an episodic or serial re-versioning than a definitive self-portrait in either fictional or factual form.

Indeed, Deborah Levy's self-designated living autobiography trilogy is further testimony to the fact that there are many ways of producing accounts of a life and that increasingly they tend not to conform to traditional models in terms of chronology, focus and design. For many female writers in particular the interest lies in juxtaposition, recurring themes and images, and the creation of a multidimensional text where subjectivity is layered and approached from different angles and perspectives. Such texts foreground the provisional, rather than the definitive, nature of self, self in relation to or projected via another; they also focus on the role of language and imagery in the creation of self, evidence criticality and self-reflexivity, and use genre as a resource, rather than a conventional mould, in the sense that they often combine the aphoristic and the essayistic with the narrative and the poetic. In this sense use of 'I', the first-person pronoun, even within the context of an autobiography poses questions about the status of the narrative persona. For example, is the Deborah Levy, author of *Real Estate*, the same person as the narrator and chief protagonist in that volume, the third in her living autobiography, particularly when writer Levy tends to talk about herself as a character in discussion of her work? (See, for example, 'In conversation: Deborah Levy with Julia Bell (Arts Week 2020: Online)'. Levy's insistence that the word 'living' be added to the trilogy's designation would suggest interest not just in potential changes in relation to understanding and appreciation of the self over time but that the various roles she is required to play in her work – narrator, and designer of the narrative, sometimes major, sometimes minor, character, and person who authorizes the book in the sense of determining, alongside the publishers, when it is ready to be released – is suggestive of her awareness of the dynamic, complementary and sometimes overlapping selves that are foregrounded in relation to the roles a person plays. These roles may be shaped by different briefs, contexts and intentions. Selves, then, like stories, 'exist in their doubleness' (Ward 2011), if not multiplicity, an expression taken from work on Aleksandar Hemon and applied here to the work of Deborah Levy, a writer very much interested in the double, the shadow text, as well as the *Doppelgänger*, and for whom all thinking is porous, as are the genres on which she, like Guo, draws. As Levy (2021) writes in *Real Estate*, 'All writing is about seeing new things and investigating them. Sometimes it's about seeing new things in old things' (257).

5.7 Concluding Remarks

What is at issue here is the status of the autobiographical 'I' in fictional and non-fictional contexts. At one level, it appears self-evident that fictional and non-fictional narratives imply a different relationship to truth, set different expectations on the part of the reader, and propose a different triadic relationship between and among writer, narrator and character. It seems reasonable to suggest that the autobiographical contract in force in real, as opposed to fictional, autobiographies, acts like a warrant underscoring the identity of the various subjects and their relationship to one another: author = narrator = character, helping to differentiate the non-fictional from the fictional. Yet, as has been seen in relation to Winterson's *Oranges* and *Why Be Happy?*, ostensibly a semi-fictional novel and memoir respectively, questions remain about the extent to which choice of narrative person/a, degrees of identity between and among author, narrator and character, and generic markers cohere to clarify or interrogate relations between what are essentially subjects in process. By subjects in process, I mean to refer to the necessary difference that both the act of writing and the passage of time effect on the construction of personhood. This is not tantamount to panfictionalism; rather, it is an acknowledgement of the kind made by many writers that the process of selection – what to recount – and the mode of narration – how and in what manner to write – are as much a function of narrative epistemologies as shifting conceptions of self. The author has, over time, a different relationship to her own history and to its linguistic and generic articulation.

In considering the nature of life-writing (autobiography and memoir) and the ways in which it may draw on, yet differ from novelistic forms, writer and critic Shirley Geok-lin Lim (2009) draws a distinction between what she sees as the difference between life ongoing writing and ongoing life writing. For Lim (2009), there is a paradox at the heart of writing from life/life-writing insofar as writing takes the writer out of the flow and experience of life, at least for the duration of the writing, to create textual memories and/or dramatizations of scenes from life. 'Life, as writing, is no longer life'

(306), she states, pointing to the difference between experiencing/living a life and writing from or about a life. Yet there is potentially another paradox in that memories are not just felt, but also created in imagination, and shared through writing. What is remembered is as much the product of imagination and/or personal vision, as of anything evidence-based or supported by historical and/or biographical facts. In visiting academic colleagues in Taiwan, Lim began to appreciate how even the 'same' genre (memoir) can be differently shaded across cultures, 'not shadowed by memory but led by life, shape-shifting to the borderlands of travel writing, social commentary, and other forms of creative non-fiction' (307).

Yet despite being conscious of the different shadings and understandings of what goes by the same name or passes under the same generic label, Lim feels it important not to collapse generic distinctions entirely but to recognise both that categories may be stretched and interrogated, and that modes of reading as well as modes of writing impact upon a work's reception. 'The autobiography', she writes, 'as it has been produced in the twentieth and twenty-first centuries, despite Lejeune's attempt to legitimize it, has proven very much an illegitimate form, often openly defiant of the strictures he had set down, slyly disobeying as much as seeming to be observant of the laws of the genre' (2009, 303). She goes on to offer, by way of example, two pieces of her own writing, each of which treats memories of her father who died of cancer and aspects of the father–daughter relationship. Comparing a poem written closer to the time of her father's death to an autobiographical record that dramatizes the moment of learning of his death, while apparently offering more evidentiary clues, Lim (2009) questions which of these responses – prose narrative or poem – is more real. Yet despite the complications and troubles of genre, Lim does not see all acts of imaginative writing as having the same status (311–312).

For a writer such as Guo, there is a certain fluidity between and among the various generic forms at her disposal. As a translingual, transcultural writer and filmmaker, she draws on the multiple and hybrid generic, cultural and linguistic resources to which she has access, reworking them for her own artistic, critical and creative purposes. In setting *Once Upon a Time in the East* in the context of Guo's writerly trajectory, what comes to the fore is her reversioning and updating of autofictional narratives that draw on and explore her life experience to date, presenting it in different, context-dependent, guises. Like the other writers on whom I have focussed in this monograph, Guo's concerns are philosophic and existential, and are rooted in considerations of the extent to which self-knowledge and identity is a function of narrative formations and/or cultural, linguistic and generic preferences. For writers such as Knausgaard, it required an extensive as well as intensive investigation of the making of a writerly subject across time, balancing the biographic, the documentary, the narrative, and the expository. Pushing back against invention and fabrication, he sought to elucidate and frame subjective experience against a highly textured and extensively documented personal narrative that nevertheless created an immersive, intersubjective experience for many readers. In a much more minimalistic and tightly controlled fashion, Cusk has reframed what it means to write a life by turning the spotlight away from the directly experiencing female subject to the ways in which that subject is vacated and reconstructed through the discourse of others. For Winterson and Guo, an apparent investment in the memoir form is less about turning their backs on the novelistic, which was always for them a generic blend, and more about reframing their autofictional projects from a documentary perspective.

Chapter 6

RACHEL CUSK'S SEARCH FOR NEW FORMS: SELF-PROJECTION AND REFRACTION IN FICTION AND NON-FICTION

6.1 Introduction

As a writer of novels, memoirs and essays, Rachel Cusk has engaged with a variety of literary forms over the course of a career that has had its share of controversy as well as kudos. From *Saving Agnes* (1993), winner of the Whitbread Prize for first novel, to *Second Place* (2021), longlisted for the Booker Prize, via the somewhat mixed reactions to, and controversy surrounding, her memoirs of motherhood, and of separation and divorce, in *A Life's Work* (2001) and *Aftermath* (2012), followed by the almost universal acclaim afforded the 'Outline' trilogy (2014–2018), Cusk has never rested on her laurels but has always challenged herself as a writer by pushing the boundaries and conventions of genre in relation to reader expectations and critiquing gender norms in terms of what it is possible and/or deemed desirable for a female writer to say, and in what form. While, in many ways, her interests have been consonant with Knausgaard's concerns insofar as she became wary of 'the artificiality of the novelistic "occasion"' (Booker Prize 2021 website) and has infused her fiction with episodes from real life, there are also differences between both writers, which will be explored in this chapter, in terms of their trajectory and the locus of their interest.

Moreover, in the broader context of the themes and focus of *Radical Realism*, the chapter will connect Cusk's trajectory with current trends among writers 'trying to expand the possibilities of the novel', whether this be by 'incorporating the techniques of memoir and essay, of hewing closer to the author's subjective experience' or by 'effacing the difference between fiction and their own personal nonfictions' (Blair 2015). It will frame what is often seen as the 'sharp break from the conventional style of Cusk's previous work' (Blair 2015) in relation to broader literary and cultural developments, including contemporary interrogation of the fact-fiction borderlands, and to the work of other writers, including that of Knausgaard, whose work Cusk has reviewed positively in the past and with some of whose concerns her work dovetails in terms of a rejection of plot and fabrication at the expense of an interrogation of the real and of what constitutes reality.

Suffice to say by way of introduction that Cusk is very focussed on form and on issues of voice – particularly the female voice – and perspective. The world created in books, for Cusk, regardless of genre or mode, should be true to experience, rather than based on fantasy and invention. That is not to say, however, that as a writer she is unaware of the impact on readers of elements of style, as well as choice of substance, and of the force of metaphorical language in steering readers' responses to the kinds of worlds projected or conveyed in her writing. Indeed, such tendencies are very much in evidence in her memoirs with whole passages in *Aftermath* dependent upon extended, embedded metaphors which draw together different domains through a conjunction of images, thereby creating particular stylistic, cognitive and emotional effects (e.g. images of pain and decay ostensibly in relation to a visit to the dentist which apply in actuality to the state of her marriage. See 'Extraction', in Cusk 2012, 29–42).

In general terms, across her work, Cusk is particularly interested in the way in which institutions and societal structures tend to constrain or afford certain types of behaviour and reproduce, rather than challenge, gendered outcomes. A life lived within such structures without reflection is, for Cusk, a life unexamined. This reflection and examination become possible through writing and art more broadly. In this sense there is constancy across Cusk's *oeuvre*: her focus has always been, broadly speaking, on the situations, dilemmas and experiences of middle-class, well-educated protagonists, whose lives reflect and refract aspects of the lived experience of the books' author. Cusk sees knowledge as deriving from reflection on experience; her books examine what we think we know and what society, or segments thereof, tells us, in the light of the realities of experience, examining the difference between story and truth, or that between societal script or narrative and subjective experience of reality.

In moving from the memoir form and returning to the affordances of the novel form, Cusk has been continuing her struggle to find her own truth and to represent that struggle in a form that rings true more generally. Form, for Cusk, is a 'vessel that comes from something real' (Louisiana Channel 2019), which I take to refer to the search for a means of shaping material that may derive from or be close to experiences from life such that they hold together in a meaningful way, which heightens rather than distorts the reality and truth of the situation represented. In a sense, then, literature, for Cusk, is a form of philosophical enquiry insofar as it is seeking, if not answers to questions, then certainly to set out and examine those questions as they relate to, and emerge from, the embodied experience of the characters that Cusk draws and gives substance to. These characters are not invented in the sense that they have been plucked from the world of the imagination and bear little relation to Cusk's own lived experience. On the contrary, they are close to her experience of life at different stages of the life course and reflect or refract her concerns at each stage.

At the same time, the 'Outline' trilogy represents a break with Cusk's memoirs insofar as she was trying to find a form that would represent not just personal loss but loss of institutional forms of being. Insofar as the 'Outline' trilogy concerns the life and experiences of narrator Faye, who has removed herself from the institution of marriage, and is trying to establish a place for herself within (or outside of) structures that seem to favour men, Cusk is looking for a form conducive to treating the situation of a woman in midlife coming to terms with a change in her status. In opposition to the subjectivity on display in the memoirs, the challenge for Cusk in the 'Outline' trilogy was to find a form consonant with the situation of a woman who has taken a back seat and seemingly erased herself, becoming a kind of filter or listening device for the stories of others. For readers of Cusk, the labels on the books identifying them as either 'fiction' (the novel) or 'non-fiction' (the memoir series, the essays) provide a point of entry which guide their expectations but given that Cusk is also known to be a genre-defying writer, it is important to look more closely at her *modus operandi* in terms of the shape of her works and to consider whether there is anything intrinsic to the way in which she delivers her ideas and investigations according to genre. While *A Life's Work* and *Aftermath* were published as memoirs and may therefore be perceived as true accounts of particular slices of life, there is an artfulness to the writing that is not dissimilar to that employed by Cusk the novelist.

For example, *Aftermath* contains a final chapter entitled 'Trains' which acts as a kind of coda to the work, while presenting another perspective on events, that of Sonia, the au pair staying in the Cusk household during the dissolution of their marriage. This section, narrated in the third person, tells the story of Sonia's arrival by train and eventual departure by taxi from the author's household to join the author's sister's household in London. Sonia's narrative re-presents some familial episodes from the outside, so to speak, and, as well as teasing out Sonia's backstory, offers an alternative version to the subjective authorial first-person account of the aftermath of the dissolution of her marriage. Given that Sonia's story is told in the third person and that her perspective is ultimately filtered through language selected for the purpose by the authorial narrator, it can be said that it functions not just as a kind of antidote to the intensity and subjectivity of the autobiographical lens but also as a consciously wrought parallel account of female experience. Sonia's backstory in terms of her abusive treatment at the hands of an older man on a train and her mother's reaction to this sexual assault – that she must, in some way, have provoked it – is also illustrative of the harms that can be done to women and girls in a male-dominated society and of their aftermath. Given the overarching themes of *Aftermath* in terms of what happens when institutionalized rituals and forms of discourse break down, this is significant and links Cusk's concerns in the 'Outline' trilogy with those expressed in her memoirs.

In an article in *The New Statesman* entitled 'The Mirror and the Self', Cusk (2013) writes about narcissism, giving expression to societal concern that we in the West inhabit a culture where many individuals are deemed to be obsessed by an image or articulated vision of self. She evaluates the case for a measure of healthy narcissism or self-love, drawing a distinction between having a sense of autobiographical occasion 'whereby the self is not merely declarative but representative' (35) and simply being self-obsessed. She goes on to distinguish self-disclosure from self-examination, the latter requiring a degree of analysis rather than mere confession. Taking by way of example criticisms levelled by some at British artist Tracey Emin and in the US at the Obamas, she points to the difference between an attempt to seek personal truth and narcissism, presenting them as opposite ends of the spectrum. She goes on to suggest that for a working-class artist in the UK and the first black President and First Lady of the United States of America, personal history and narratives of selfhood acquire different meanings not so much because of the narrators' outsider status compared to those in the mainstream but as a consequence of their embodiment of 'change through their own being' (37). For a writer who has herself been criticized for exposing her own private dramas to public scrutiny in her non-fictional works on motherhood and on marriage and separation, who has been perceived as self-absorbed, if not self-obsessed, in her 'making use of real personal experience' (O'Reilly 2007, 3), and whose fictional representations often document the domestic and the so-called trivial, as opposed to 'the culturally sanctioned "important" (male) subjects for the novel' (Cusk 2013, 37), questions of self-love, self-regard and self-understanding in relation to the production and contestation of societal myths and 'the struggle of creativity' (37) and transformation for the (female) artist are pertinent indeed. Her latest work, *Second Place*, continues this exploration of the positioning of female artists in relation to their male peers and of the othering of women in male-dominated societies.

6.2 The 'Outline' Trilogy: Context and Motivation

Critical reception of *Aftermath* (2012), Cusk's exposé of family life in the wake of separation from her husband and her decision to fight to keep the children, was such that she felt silenced by the press and suffered from writer's block for some time before embarking on her recently published trilogy, consisting of *Outline* (2014), *Transit* (2016) and *Kudos* (2018), reception of which has been largely positive. It is important to see the design and composition of these three volumes against the backdrop of the particularly harsh criticism Cusk had previously engendered in respect of her non-fictional work and her subsequent decision to move away from memoir. The first novel in the series, *Outline* (2014), presents a narrator whose name (Faye) the reader belatedly learns (Cusk 2014, 211), while the title relates to an episode recounted to Faye by her successor on the Creative Writing residential, Anne, who recounts her experience of listening to a fellow passenger talk on the journey over to Athens and of feeling like 'a shape, an outline, with all the detail filled in around it while the shape itself remained blank' (239–240). As will be seen in the course of discussion of the trilogy, the apparent obliteration of self or more precisely the construction of a self who is refracted through narrative recount of the lives of others stands in opposition to the mode of self-presentation embedded in Cusk's non-fictional works. What has been termed 'the concept of negative identity' in Cusk's trilogy (Peterson 2015) contrasts with her previous representations of first-person narrative protagonists and may be said to be a strategic reaction to the 'violently negative response' (Peterson 2015) to *Aftermath*. As Peterson (2015) puts it: 'Both traditional, realist fiction and memoir had failed her, and so she went looking for a new kind of storytelling mode altogether'.

Characterized 'as a masterpiece intervention in the form of the novel' (Oyler 2020, 54), the 'Outline' trilogy presents a first-person character-narrator who keeps herself at a distance from much of the action relayed and the stories recounted, thus undermining expectations of a visible connection with and focus on the thoughts, aspirations and inclinations of this central narrating and perceiving figure. The distance created is a feature of grammatical structure – the stories of others are reported and tagged – as well as a feature of perspective: what has been called the obliterated or annihilated perspective, whereby the narrator deflects attention away from herself onto the reported conversations of others. Her minimal reactions to, and comments on, the behaviours and stories of others serve as a proxy for, and index of, her own views and situation, sometimes by contrast. As the series progresses, the reader learns more about the narrator whose very name is withheld for much of volume one, and whose biography, while scanty, parallels in broad outline that of the author herself.

> With the *Outline* books, she [Cusk] hit upon a form that illuminated the complicated 'relationship between the story and the truth', and between fiction and autobiography. These novels put forth a provocatively inverted form of autofiction […]. (Olyer 2020, 54)

This 'inverted form of autofiction' relates to the fact that Faye 'relays stories that other people have told her without revealing much about herself' (Olyer 2020, 54). Yet the question remains: precisely how does Cusk choose a form (or mode or genre) in which to present her work? What are the affordances, conventionalized or otherwise, of novelistic form, essayistic form or memoir form and how are they deployed? And why has Cusk felt it necessary to abandon memoir in favour of an arguably reinvented novel form?

6.2.1 Outline (2014)

What strikes a reader on opening *Outline* is the way in which the narrator deflects information about herself and moves within the space of a paragraph to relate what she is told by those whom she meets. Beginning with the billionaire who has invited her for lunch before her flight to Athens, the reader encounters a series of stories from the lives of others reported and paraphrased by the first-person narrator. The novel's structure is reminiscent of that of W. G. Sebald's *Austerlitz* in so far as the novel insists on reminding the reader through the use of reporting verbs alongside some passages of direct speech complete with verbal tags, that the narrator is summarizing and conveying to the reader the gist of what she has been told, as well as recording some actual speech. Within the world of the narrative report a second level of reporting is on occasions brought to the reader's attention such that there is a kind of embedded conversational structure, of a story-within-the story type. So, for example, the narrator recounts to the reader what her neighbour on the aeroplane from London to Athens tells her, ensuring that in reporting what he says, she makes clear where there is a change of speaker in the embedded narrative when he talks about his marriages, introducing the actions and reactions of his wives as well as of himself. One of the features of *Outline* is, therefore, that it almost entirely consists of verbal processes rather than a representation of actions.

To give a flavour of how *Outline* is structured, I shall focus on the opening chapter by way of example. Chapter 1 is 27 pages in length and can be summarized as follows: the first-person narrator has lunch with a billionaire and takes a taxi to the airport where she catches a flight to Athens. In the course of the flight she engages intermittently in conversation with her neighbour who tells her about his life, including accounts of two of his failed marriages; he asks her a couple of questions seemingly for politeness' sake and she reports her verbal responses to him and conveys her thoughts to the reader. Close attention to the use of pronouns (i.e. 'I', 'he', 'she', 'we') as well as to verbal processes (i.e. 'say', 'tell', 'add', 'continue') throughout this chapter is helpful in drawing out its characteristics. The narrator's presence is felt indirectly for the most part in her summarizing and reporting of what she hears; there are some points in the conversation with her neighbour on the plane when she takes the floor and conveys her responses, comments and occasional evaluation but for the most part, she just listens and transcribes albeit, one imagines, selectively and with a degree of artifice, the narratives relayed to her. So, for example, at the beginning of the conversation with her neighbour, we read: 'I asked him what his nationality was' (7). Later, the narrator interrupts her neighbour's direct speech to correct a mistake he has made: he uses the word prolixity instead of proximity (8), a correction that reflects perhaps on the narrator's need for linguistic precision as much as it does on the fact that her neighbour is a Greek businessman who was educated in England and lived for a time in London. The novel ends with a further correction when the narrator turns down an invitation by 'phone from her neighbour whom she has seen on a couple of occasions while in Athens: he uses 'solicitude' in place of 'solitude' (249). Not only have we come full circle in terms of Faye's conversation with the Greek businessman but the fact that the final word of the novel is solitude is also significant.

The reader is constantly reminded not only in this first chapter but across the novel as a whole that they are dealing with reported speech, both direct and indirect, through the steady use of speech tags and reporting verbs embedded in the recount: 'This, *my neighbour said*, created familial tensions [...] on his arrival in England' (8–9; the italics are mine); 'This unusual situation, *my neighbour said*, had ancient causes' (9; the italics are mine). The reader is reminded from time to time in this chapter of the location of the conversation through references to the cabin and to the progress of the air hostess along the aisle. Indeed the safety demonstration at the beginning provides an opportunity for the narrator to draw parallels between the rituals of a priest leading his congregation through the liturgy and the air hostess demonstrating the use of safety equipment, as passengers 'listened or half-listened' (5). The narrator returns at the end of the chapter to the oxygen masks, 'dangling from a length of clear tubing' (5), when she comments on the fact that their provision is premised on their non-use rather than on their use. This comment elicits a response from her neighbour who indicates that 'he had found that to be true of many aspects of life' (31).

Analysis of the structure and composition of the chapter demonstrates that despite the seeming informality and relative transparency of the narrative, it is in fact carefully crafted and artfully arranged. This is true of the novel as a whole, each chapter of which is built around an encounter, whether this be with her fellow writing teacher, Ryan; her neighbour with whom she goes on a boat trip; or her students who respond to her prompts by telling tales. The conversations generated by each encounter are relayed via Faye's part transcription, part narrative summary of them. It almost seems that as time goes on, the narrator is less and less visible as a subject in her own right, even if the reader is aware of her shaping hand in the construction of the narrative. There is an assumption on the part of the reader that the selection of topics recorded and the choice of interventions on her part are reflective of her own concerns or at the very least constitute an evaluation of the conversations she recounts. It is fairly clear from the section in which she meets with her fellow writing teacher Ryan that the narrator is critical of his behaviour and self-absorption. He only remembers to ask if she has been working on something just as she is about to leave the café where they have been having a drink. The conversation has been rather one-sided, as Ryan recounts his trajectory as a writer in between flirting with the waitress and talking about his family. Ryan's egotistical behaviour, with the merest nod to the norms of social interaction, when he asks Faye about herself, is a clear example of the kind of distinction that might be drawn between narcissism or self-absorption and the kind of critical self-analysis that for Cusk it is important to pursue in writing.

That Faye has adopted a kind of passivity as her *modus operandi* is made clear in a conversation with her neighbour from the aeroplane when he takes her out in his boat. She indicates that she has 'come to believe more and more in the virtues of passivity, and of living a life as unmarked by self-will as possible' (170). She is conscious of not wishing to have to fight for what she wants; rather she appears resigned to the discrepancy between what she wants and what she has. In response to a question from her neighbour about whether there had really been no one in her life since her divorce, she mentions having had a relationship with someone who remains a friend but that she wanted to live differently. Her neighbour comments that she is still in pain and is reminded about episodes in his own life that he proceeds to recount. On admitting to infidelity, he seems to blame his wife for the manner in which she extracted his confession. The narrator is disappointed in her neighbour and characterizes his confession as 'self-serving' (174).

While Cusk's trilogy postdates the Preface she wrote for a special issue of *Literature Compass* on 'Life-Writing', it is nevertheless interesting to note that in her abstract she writes:

If the writer writes books in part to be liberated from herself – to create an external version of herself from which she can disappear – then as a teacher she may find that self concretised and made visible instead. (Cusk 2011, 873)

The notion of being liberated from self through the creation of an external version is doubly interesting in the context of discussion of the construction and characterization of Cusk's trilogy in the wake of reaction to her memoirs and in the light of her narrator's profession as a writer and teacher of creative writing. It would seem that far from being able to escape through her writing of a memoir, Cusk found herself in the eye of a storm of critical reaction which began to undermine her ability to write and to escape from self. The return to fiction with a strong autobiographical trace in terms of similarities between Faye's familial and professional situation (a divorced mother of two sons who eventually remarries; a writing teacher) and that of Cusk (divorced – remarried – mother of two daughters; a writer and former teacher of writing) is also interesting insofar as it invites comparison. What is equally intriguing is the extent to which, if we are right to see in narrator Faye a kind of Cuskian alter ego, she has adopted in the trilogy a different pose: rather than the strong-willed, articulate and self-determining female protagonist, we have a woman who promotes 'the virtues of passivity' (170) and who seems to substitute argumentative reason and self-directed activity for a structure that promotes listening, a kind of echo chamber in which the first-person narrator becomes a vehicle for conveying the stories of others. Yet these others can be seen to be projections of aspects of consciousness that are vital in terms of the focus of Cusk's larger novelistic and writerly interests in relation to the power dynamics of human, particularly male-to-female, interaction; the construction of identity; the loss and maintenance of face in human communication; and modes of representation and understanding the truth of experience. For a writer for whom form is so important, her decision to try and find a new form in the trilogy is significant. As indicated in an interview for *Diacritik* (2016), Cusk was trying to find a form that could express silence and nothingness. She wanted to dispense with plot and narrative as a 'fantasized story of life'. Rather than populate her work with description and a novelistic hinterland, she wanted to maintain a slight distance from reality and create sentences that would be surrounded by silence such that readers could bring their own experience to bear on what they read and empathize with the narrator.

Reviewers of Cusk's trilogy point to her project as 'nothing less than the reinvention of the form itself' (Ali 2017) with narrator Faye who 'seemingly exists only to draw others into conversation' (McArdle 2015, 163). However, as Lockwood (2018, 12) points out, Cusk is 'very explicitly exploiting the public conversations of men, which they consider genial and beneficent, but which women very often consider a burden or an intrusion'. In other words, her feminist agenda is still very much in evidence. Despite the fact that Faye's self seems to be obliterated, she is in fact the person who is orchestrating and directing the transcription and paraphrasing of the stories of others. There are moments when she intervenes to ask questions to keep the story moving, just as in her role as teacher of writing, she sets the parameters for the students to tell their stories (e.g. they must have an animal in them). This, then, is a novel about writing as much as it is a novel about the construction of self or a composite image of self, one derived from the serial reflections of others with whom one interacts.

The two chapters in which the teaching of writing is represented bear further scrutiny, the more so since in interview Cusk (2016b) refers to her interest in trying to understand what she sees as a generalized desire to write and relates her own attempts to get to the bottom of what creative writing might be. In chapter six of *Outline* (132–158), she meets the class of ten she is to teach. She begins by asking them to tell her about 'something they had noticed on their way here' (134) and records a series of stories elicited by the prompt. The stories range from a simple account of something seen (a beautiful dog on the shoulders of a tall man) to more elaborate tales with accompanying commentary and reflection such as that narrated by Marielle on hearing her husband sing a particular song in the shower and realizing he was being unfaithful to her. Some of the stories, filtered through the reporting voice of narrator Faye, focus on the performative aspects of storytelling, others mine experience for meaning and significance, while one student, fifteen-year-old Georgeou, declares himself to be concerned about 'the tendency to fictionalise our own experience' which he sees as 'positively dangerous' (137). Woven into the relation of stories, reflections and observations are comments on the process of storytelling itself: the question of whether life has or is a story, whether so-called facts speak for themselves or whether meaning must be derived from an account of experience. There is one student, however, Cassandra, who has been getting more and more irate during this game of talking, rather than writing. She finally explodes and makes clear her dissatisfaction with the manner in which the class has been conducted:

> She had obviously been mistaken: she had been told this was a class about learning to write, something that as far as she was aware involved using your imagination. She didn't know what I thought I had achieved here, and she wasn't all that interested in finding out. (158)

She continues with a negative comparison between Ryan and Faye as teachers: at least Ryan, she felt, had tried to teach them something! While there is no explicit evaluation of the fairness or otherwise of Cassandra's comments, the dynamics of the scene and what the reader knows of Ryan already would suggest that Faye's teaching does not warrant such an outburst. Rather, Cassandra's expectations of what is involved in writing may need rethinking.

For in some ways talking here is a proxy for the process of writing. The act of storytelling and finding a form suitable for conveying the narrative is performed by the students who recount what they have seen or use the prompt to create a narrative. Each story feeds off and speaks to aspects of the preceding one and/or invites comment. Cassandra's inability to make connections between the exercise and learning to write demonstrates her lack of imagination, while at the same time bringing into play the notion that creative writing depends on a process of fictionalizing or inventing rather than, for example, an ability to present a storyline in an appropriate form or to use what is at hand – the material of reality – in interesting or explorative ways. Cusk seems to be suggesting that creative writing has more to do with constraint and discipline than with imagination *per se*.

One of the strands evident in this chapter is the debate between fact and fiction or more accurately between a process of observing and recording versus a process of fictionalizing or inventing. Part of what Cusk is attempting to do in her trilogy is to change the plot, literally and metaphorically. As someone who believes that there is a point at which experience of suffering and trauma can undermine fiction as a feasible or tenable mode, the search for a new form becomes synonymous with change and evolution. Cassandra's intervention points to the ironies of the creative process at a number of different levels. Talking is not writing but the art of making a story and finding a form that will hold the audience's attention through its mode of delivery and ability to create an expressive or meaningful narrative thread or to embody a sense of occasion is already illustrative of some of the things that are pertinent to the creation of a written narrative. Comparisons with W.G. Sebald's *Austerlitz* are again fitting here inasmuch as the form of the work departs from that of a more conventional novel. It is a work composed of visual and verbal narratives and it also has an embedded conversational structure with long, complex sentences and use of a register more akin to academic writing in places. Yet, as the reader learns if they persist in reading *Austerlitz*, the form can be seen to mirror the subject matter: Jacques Austerlitz is a character whose personal history is discovered to be traumatic. He has repressed the fact of being a child brought over to England on the *Kindertransport*. Only when the structures that he has so carefully erected break down – he has a nervous breakdown – is he able to begin to focus on his own history and to research his past. While Cusk and Sebald are different writers with different concerns, they have this in common: they are both pushing the bounds of novelistic form in a search for something more authentic and more pertinent to the complexities of our relationship with fact and fiction, with self and other and with the inscription of individual lives and personal histories against the backdrop of social and political histories.

The second chapter devoted to the teaching of creative writing involves the students talking about the assignment they have been given in which they are to tell a story involving an animal. Christos begins by talking about the difficulty he had in doing the assignment, finding it almost impossible to introduce an animal into a story about politics and a recent public debate. However, he eventually manages through serendipity to find a solution to the problem and is quite pleased by the outcome. There is representation of the usual disruption in class by young Georgeou who nevertheless manages to insert an animal into his otherwise accurate account of a conversation between himself and his aunt. Clio indicates that the assignment caused her to look at things differently on her way home yesterday: she heard birdsong all around her and remembered a piece by a French composer incorporating patterns of birdsong heard whilst in detention. Georgeou sees this as evidence that 'the role of the artist might merely be that of recording sequences' (206). In an attempt to find inspiration for a story, Sylvia goes to a collection of short stories by D. H. Lawrence and starts to read 'The Wintry Peacock' only to find that she can't continue such is the dissonance between her own situation in sunny Athens and that of the characters in 'a remote part of the English countryside in winter' (210). After an interruption, during which narrator Faye learns that her application to increase her loan on her mortgage has been declined, Penelope tells a meandering story involving a dog that she had bought a couple of years ago for her children. Finally Marielle talks about the cats her ex-husband has left with her after they separate and their impact on her current relationship. Aris sums up what he takes to be the point of the exercise insofar as it is through our interaction with animals that 'we access the story of ourselves' (225).

What Cusk through narrator Faye seems to be discussing in these chapters set in the creative writing classroom is the process by which stories come into existence and the way in which they are shaped and given direction. She also explores the varying relationships between literature, or more accurately narrative structures, and life. For some students, the assignment brief was a constraint that turned into an opportunity for creativity, for others inclusion of an animal compelled them to think more deeply about the human dimension. What it takes to be a writer not only in terms of finding a subject, a voice and a form but also in terms of finding a place from which and in which to write are some of the themes that surface through the voices of the students as they tell their stories, commenting upon their genesis and elaboration. The amount of space devoted in the novel to the creative writing classroom (51 pages in a work of 249 pages) suggests that it is not incidental but rather integral to some of the themes being explored: sense-making through symbolic systems; articulating perceptions and making meanings; the construction of a narrative thread in literature and in life. In many ways, the student stories can be seen as ways of treating theories and practices of narrative and reflect different methods and sources of creativity. Students are guided in the art of observation and are encouraged to use experience and/or what they see and hear, as well as their thoughts and evaluations, to string a narrative together. For some, inspiration will come from other works of literature, for others their lives will offer material for mining, for others still conversations will prompt a response.

What seems to be the case for the most successful stories is that the narrator has realized something or made a discovery or that something – or someone – has changed as a consequence of the story being told. There is also a critical level in the sections on storytelling, that is to say that production of stories leads to discussion of their reception and evaluation. The listeners on occasion comment on aspects of storying or story-making, such as when Georgeou says that he 'sensed that any system of representation could be undone simply by the violation of its own rules' (206), a sentiment that acknowledges the conventionality of storytelling, while pointing to the ways in which rules can be broken. Sylvia's story contains within it a critique of storytelling both in terms of what her mother says: 'You should be living […] not spending more time thinking about books', a sentiment that opposes literature and life, while Sylvia's abandonment of the D. H. Lawrence story she is reading represents a moment of dissonance between the here-and-now and a reconstructed and storied past which seems to have no purchase on her present. So while literature at its best can connect one subjectivity to another across time and space, Sylvia's experience shows that this is not always the case. Sometimes there is too big a gap between the two: 'I couldn't bear it any longer, the feeling that I was the helpless passenger of his vision, so I closed the book', says Sylvia, 'and I went to bed' (210). This male vision from a different time and place no longer speaks to Sylvia, the teacher of literature. From interviews the reader may know that D. H. Lawrence is a writer much admired by Cusk. However, literary tastes change and modes of writing – and of reading – prevalent at one time may be unsuited to another period. In other words, the literary corpus is dynamic rather than static; what constitutes good, effective or imaginative writing will change according to time and place. Sylvia wants to inhabit and craft her own space and not be 'the helpless passenger' (210) of Lawrence's vision. She wants to take control and create her own (female) vision.

6.2.2 *Transit* (2016)

The second book in Cusk's trilogy, *Transit*, takes its title in the first instance from an astrological term and by extension it can be applied to protagonist Faye's situation, as she appears to be moving from her state of utter passivity to a more active state by the novel's end. The novel opens with receipt of an email from an astrologer, likely to have been computer generated, indicating that 'a major transit was due to occur shortly in my [Faye's] sky' (Cusk 2016a, 1). While initially sceptical about astrological influences, Faye does later pay to have an astrologer's report done, the day 'of particular significance' (176) being the day when her Polish builders are taking down a wall in her house, causing her neighbours from downstairs to become irate because of the noise; on the same day, she teaches a fiction class and later goes to dinner with a man who has been introduced to her via a mutual friend. By the end of the novel, Faye has let herself out in the early morning from a house in the country where she has attended a dinner party and stayed the night. The novel ends with a sense of change in the offing:

> I felt change far beneath me, moving deep beneath the surface of things, like the plates of the earth blindly moving in their black traces. I found my bag and my car keys and let myself silently out of the house. (260)

The final paragraph reflects some of the novel's themes: a concern with fate and the extent to which individuals are in charge of their own destiny; conceptions of self and notions of self-definition and self-regulation; and the family unit and male-to-female relationships.

As in *Outline*, the novel is structured mainly around chapters in which the central protagonist, Faye, whose name is again only mentioned late in the book on page 206, meets with and listens to a series of others (a former lover, her builders, her hairdresser, fellow writers at a literature festival, a student writer, a friend, students in a fiction class, a dinner date) and attends a dinner party at her cousin's house in the country. Just as in *Outline* there is little direct recording in *Transit* of Faye's conversations but rather for the most part summary statements or an indication of her thoughts are given. As the book progresses, the reader hears a little more from Faye in addition to a simple record of the questions she poses to others, the former evidence of her presence and her attempts to steer the conversation in particular directions.

One of the points in the novel where the difference between the speech of others and that of Faye is most pronounced is at the literary festival, where both before the event in the green room and during the public session with the writers onstage, the two male writers – Julian and Louis – are given extensive coverage; Faye's talk/reading is simply summarized: 'I read aloud what I had written. When I had finished I folded the papers and put them back in my bag, while the audience applauded' (113). Both Julian and Louis appear to have been on the writer's circuit promoting their books for some time and have become a kind of double act, able to entertain the audience and talk about themselves and their writing in a rehearsed and self-absorbed manner; Faye's summary sentence is in stark contrast to the space given to their self-narration and points to a gender difference which is explored further in the novel in the stylized, self-conscious and increasingly uncomfortable dinner party in the final chapter of the novel. Faye's cousin, Lawrence, who has just remarried, comments on how Faye has been left by her husband to take care of things after their break-up; his new partner Eloise's ex-husband was the same. Lawrence characterizes these men as children, unable to accept their responsibilities (240). There follows a section in which Lawrence explicitly addresses gender differences, taking Faye to task for not respecting the codes: '"Someone like you", he said to me, "would never accept that femininity entailed certain male codes of honour"' (240). Faye refuses to accept that her fate as a woman is powerlessness and indicates that there are many different ways of living. In listening rather than talking, in studying the 'forms and patterns in the things that happened' (243) and seeking their truth, Faye is in essence refusing the role assigned to her and learning to create a new identity. There is a certain irony in Lawrence's position. For, while appearing to be a man supportive of women asserting themselves, it could be said that he is the one to apply rigid principles with regard to the children, what food they eat and how they behave as well as having quite a fixed view in reality of Eloise's and his role in their new family unit. His stance and interventions in the conversation more generally ensure that the evening reaches its climax with wailing children and a tearful Eloise.

Described by writer Helen Dunmore as 'a very fine novel indeed' (2016), *Transit* is applauded for its technical brilliance and 'the compelling nature of her subject matter' where the rebuilding of a house stands in for the rebuilding of a life, as the reader follows Faye from her post-divorce world and feeling of self-obliteration and utter passivity to a gradually renewed sense of self and of possibility. Faye's decision to invest in a flat that requires such effort that even the builders' view is that she is opening a can of worms (40) reflects a certain resolve and persistence on her part to rip out the old and begin again. Like the builders whose roles are divided into those of Destruction (Tony) and Construction (Pavel), Faye needs to work through the fall-out from her divorce and rebuild her life as a single woman with two sons. There are signs throughout the novel that things are beginning to change for her, that she is indeed in transit. The novel's ending leaves the reader with a sense of possibility and a feeling that the man with whom she has had a dinner date following her fiction class may be about to enter her life.

One of the features of *Transit* that deserves further comment is the tension and unexpected violence at its heart. This is evident in a number of episodes such as that in the hairdresser's salon where a young boy, who has been monosyllabic while having his hair cut, pulls the door handle to leave with such force that glass bottles on a shelf shatter and the door itself revolves 'all the way round on its hinges after he had let it go' (Cusk 2016, 81) before it too shatters. The build-up of drama and an eventual over-spilling of emotion into tears at the dinner party is another example of the ratcheting up of tension. Behind the well-groomed façade of the dinner guests and the focus on fine food and the rituals of dining, the conversational script begins to veer off course or rather the interpersonal and power dynamics become increasingly charged. Faye's description of the scene the next morning as she moves among the 'ruins of dinner' (259) captures the aftermath of the dinner party where much has been laid to waste.

In a review of *Transit* in *The Wall Street Journal*, the book is characterized as featuring episodes that 'represent the unsettled challenges of constructing a new identity after a collapse' (Sacks 2017), while reading it is described as 'a frustrating, fractious experience' (Sacks 2017). It is true that the measure of destruction and violence evident in the novel, alongside the wry humour, may seem unnerving or even gratuitous, but this second novel in the trilogy has to function as a 'bridge to another destination as yet unknown' (Franklin 2017). In other words, *Transit* functions to move Faye and the reader from one state to another, while respecting the mood and movement of the trilogy as a whole. If Cusk is negotiating the terrain between fiction and autobiography (Franklin 2017) and attempting to find a new form conducive to twenty-first century concerns about the truth of experience and notions of the real, then part of that project is surely to show what lurks just below the surface of civility in society and to point to discrepancies between illusory appearances and deeper realities. In this sense, Cusk is continuing a tradition of social critique and psychological realism already apparent in the nineteenth- and early twentieth-century novel. Indeed her use of summary statements and stretches of dialogue is reminiscent of the techniques of writers such as Balzac or Henry James. Yet the leanness and spareness of her writing departs from that of her predecessors. There is a minimalist quality more in tune with the new novel (*le nouveau roman*) in France with a focus on the outside as a kind of reflector of interior states of mind. In terms of the gendered nature of relationships and the power dynamics of male to female interactions, Cusk continues her investigation of the consequences of failing to fit the normative familial patterns and assuming what appear to be pre-assigned roles. That she does this in a work where the familial situation and professional trajectory of fictional narrator Faye parallels in many ways that of Cusk herself lends to the trilogy a measure of self-consciousness and reflexivity.

In an article on 'Fiction in the "Post-Truth" Era: The Ironic Effects of Autofiction', Marjorie Worthington (2017) discusses the recent boom in memoirs alongside increasing interest in autofictions in the US. She sees these trends as relating both to a desire on the part of the reader for a truthful account of experience even where fictional techniques are used to enhance the narrative and simultaneously a desire on the part of novelists to assert their authorial authority. Autofiction, a form that she defines as occupying 'a liminal space between fiction and nonfiction' (Worthington 2017, 472) is a way of capitalizing on readers' ability to navigate the fact-fiction borderlands through its combination of the referential and the metafictional. While Cusk's trilogy would not qualify as autofictional in the sense in which Worthington uses it, inasmuch as first-person narrator Faye is clearly not the same as the narrator of Cusk's non-fictional account of marriage and separation, whom we meet in *Aftermath*, for example, and whom we assume to be Cusk's narrative alter ego, there is nevertheless sufficient complementarity in the outline of the lives of Faye and Cusk to encourage speculation about the work's autofictional potential.

As a former Professor of Creative Writing, Cusk has taught writing courses including contributing to a course in Athens (e.g. June 2013) organized by the British Council in collaboration with the University of Kingston, a situation that might be expected to feed her portrayal of writing classes in her novels. Likewise, as a contemporary novelist promoting her work, Cusk has on numerous occasions taken part in literary festivals both in the UK and abroad. In the trilogy there are a number of representations of writers in conversation with other writers, with publishers and with the public at large. In other words, many of the situations represented in the trilogy will have been experienced personally by Cusk, even if the details and their novelistic presentation vary and/or are used for dramatic effect within the context of a particular work. While contemporary readers are generally experienced in differentiating the writer from her narratorial and fictionalized selves, as Worthington (2017) points out, the autofictional form plays with the boundaries of fact and fiction, sometimes to ironic effect. Insofar as context is important in the reading process, knowledge of the extratextual life of the author can impact upon how readers interpret a work's content, even as they understand the important shaping effect of style and genre and appreciate the intratextual resonances in a work in addition to engaging with its design and structure as a whole. In Cusk's case, critical reaction to her non-fictional trilogy and her experience of writer's block in the wake of criticisms of *Aftermath* were such that she wished to distance herself from her former approach to writing and find an alternative form to investigate what in many ways are similar or recognizable themes: the positioning of and response to professional middle-class women; family life and societal expectations of who does what; the obligations and rewards of motherhood; and male-female interactions and conceptions of self.

As well as nods to the referential, there are discussions in *Transit*, as in *Outline*, of the writing, and indeed reading, process. In the context of the literature festival, Faye engages in discussion with the Chair, following the literary event, of the nature of the reader-writer exchange. She suggests that it doesn't matter whether the writer is known to the reader or not. What is important is that the writer manage to hook the reader and keep him or her interested in reading on. She talks about 'the fundamental anonymity of the writing process' (114), characterising reading and writing as 'non-physical transactions' (115) that 'might almost be said to represent an escape from the actual body' (115). It would seem, then, that writing and reading are predominantly cognitive and affective activities that displace or take the place of embodied reality. In the chapter in which Faye engages with a writing student, an exploration of the motivation for writing takes place, though somewhat indirectly. Faye's student Jane is looking for advice on how to make use of the 300,000 words of notes she has already taken over the past 4 or 5 years on the work of a painter. Faye tries to get to the bottom of her fascination with the work and Jane talks about the context in which she first came upon the paintings. She leaves not really having gained the opening she expected but rather a suggestion from Faye that she may simply let it go, a suggestion that Jane roundly rejects.

Jane's narrative, partly in response to questions from Faye, suggests that her engagement with the project is as much bound up in a desire to prove herself as in a wish to explicate the work of painter Marsden Hartley. Her personal context alongside serendipity – she chances on or is drawn to an exhibition of Marsden's work in Paris – seems to motivate her writing. While she is not terribly encouraging, the questions posed by Faye bring out these contextual details: in effect Jane's narrative is autobiographical. Her interest in Hartley's paintings has as much to do with herself as with his biography and trajectory, something she freely admits: ' "He's me", she said' (134). Narrator Faye tries to draw out what she means by this. Jane rejects her suggestion that this is simply a form of identification, such as that made by readers with a character in a book. Rather, she suggests, it is a kind of transmigration of souls. Whether by the end of the hour, Jane has found an entrée into her work remains unclear. If Faye's final reflection on the encounter is indicative, it is unlikely she believes Jane to be a writer:

> I imagined her [Jane] in the dusk of a Paris garden, untouched in her white dress, an object thirsting if not for interpretation then for the fulfilment at least of an admiring human gaze, like a painting hanging on a wall, waiting. (151)

In effect, it is Faye who demonstrates the kind of writerly transformation required to turn life into literature. She has taken some of the elements of Jane's narrative and rearranged them, while maintaining something essential about them. In essence, she has summed up Jane's desires and motivation in an image – that of the painting hanging on the wall – appropriate to the story that Faye has told. Jane's story has been captured in some well-chosen words within a single sentence, and Faye has demonstrated her own process in this imagistic realization of Jane's story drawn out through her questions and interventions.

Just as in *Outline* the telling of stories in the creative writing classroom is a way of discussing writing and what it takes to engage a reader and create a narrative, so this chapter in *Transit* featuring a student–teacher interaction is a way of dramatizing the process of writing and the kind of transformations required to turn elements of life experience into an artful storied image that speaks to the reader. In this sense, the truth of experience is shown to be consistent not with sequenced relation of a series of events on the part of a protagonist or group of protagonists but rather with an artfully composed image that gathers together and fixes the different strands of the story. Perhaps the volumes of Cusk's trilogy might be read both singly and together as a kind of Cubist portrait of the artist reflected through the eyes and stories of others. The composite picture created obliquely by the reader on the basis of Faye's interventions and evaluations tells them something about the character and experience of the narrator as she navigates the fact-fiction borderlands and learns anew how to draw on life to create a narrative fiction or conversely and simultaneously to create in a narrative structure sufficient distance whereby the stories of others come to mirror aspects of self.

6.2.3 Kudos (2018)

The final volume in the trilogy, *Kudos*, sees narrator Faye at a literary festival in a foreign city by the sea where the writers are housed in a prize-winning hotel, formerly a water tower, that lies about 30 minutes from the city in an extensive area of dockyards and 'mile after mile of warehouses and silos and giant stacks of shipping containers' (Cusk 2018, 123). A party has been organized in the city centre which requires participants to follow a guide to the venue which operates a coupon system for food; they are bussed every day to and from a restaurant for their meals where they have a set menu at a long table away from the other members of the public whose culinary choices seem to be much more extensive and more interesting. There is a symmetry in the novel with the opening of *Outline* insofar as Faye meets a man on a plane who tells her his story; the difference is that she does not see him again in the course of her stay, unlike in *Outline*. Rather, *Kudos* centres on the world of literature and its producers and mediators, including publishers, translators, journalists and opinion-makers. Faye even meets Ryan, the writer and fellow teacher of Creative Writing from *Outline*, now much changed in terms of his appearance and indeed his literary career which has blossomed thanks to a partnership or collaboration with a student of his. While the novel follows the same basic structure in terms of Faye's reporting of conversations she has with those she meets, the reader begins to get more of a sense of who she is refracted in the conversations of others and the selection of topics for report. The reader also learns what has changed in her situation: we know, for example, that she has remarried in the interim. Indeed, in conversation at a restaurant with Paola and Felícia, her publisher and translator, she is asked why she has married again, 'when you know what you know' (Cusk 2018, 225), to which she replies that she hoped to 'get the better of those laws [...] by living within them'. Paola replies that she prefers to live outside the law, to be an outlaw.

Throughout *Kudos* there is much discussion of the world of literature, its values and its future; there is also, threaded through the novel, a focus on male–female interactions, on the destruction of relationships post-divorce and on the way in which societies seem to perpetuate gender inequalities. The incident at the end of the book where a god-like man pisses into the sea where Faye has gone swimming all the time looking at her 'with black eyes full of malevolent delight' (Cusk 2018, 232) might be seen as the culmination of this increasingly bleak thread in the novel. It leaves the reader feeling that exercise of power is felt in its abuse; the destruction of a moment of a woman's 'pleasure and peace' (Prose 2018, 534) by a man who does it 'for no other reason than the fact that he can' (534) reflects the negative substance of the stories told to Faye by other women in the novel, including Paola and Felícia. There is an undercurrent of negativity and violence in the behaviour of men towards women once they no longer play by the rules. This is reminiscent of the dinner party scene at the end of *Transit* where Lawrence points out to Faye that the male code of honour towards women no longer applies once they have opted for independence. As Prose

(2018, 534) puts it, 'Cusk isn't telling us any comforting lies about how the world works'. Rather, as throughout her work, she is disabusing the reader of any illusions they may have.

For critic and reviewer Lara Feigel (2018, 10), Cusk is not alone in reflecting on what it means to be a woman in a man's world and in reflecting on and rejecting the invisibility usually accorded women of a certain age. Rather she sees it as part of a larger move by a number of middle-aged female writers who are 'questioning ideas of femininity' and looking for a 'way to act with integrity' (10). She points to the fact that Cusk's work has always been driven by 'an urge towards a life lived in good faith, which is what all of Cusk's characters are struggling in their different ways to do' (Feigel 2018, 10). So while at one level Cusk's new trilogy represents a departure in terms of its narrative structure and the persona of the 'occluded' narrator (Feigel 2018, 9), at another level and at the same time, Cusk is doing what she has always done in terms of pushing the boundaries both thematic and formal. What is different is the manner in which her formal innovations and narrative stance in the trilogy compel a re-evaluation of genre and gender. The seeming invisibility of the narrator or more properly the ways in which she distances herself from the narrative through a one-sided conversational and reporting structure serves to interrogate taken-for-granted narrative techniques and confronts the reader with a series of questions about the world of storytelling and its connection to reality. There is a kind of distributed authority in a work that appears to report what others have said while keeping interventions to a minimum. At the same time, however, in choosing across the trilogy an intentional structure that highlights the power of intent listening over self-absorbed speaking, while ultimately authoring the design of the whole, what comes across is the shaping force of silence and of restraint, the power of acute observation and of skilful interrogation in generating insights and creating new forms. In calling attention to narrative structures even as she reinvents them, Cusk may be suggesting the need for radical change in the way in which literature functions today if it is to survive being displaced by other arts.

6.3 Concluding Remarks

What this chapter has highlighted in relation to Cusk's work through a focus on her well-received 'Outline' trilogy is the fact that there is continuity as well as change in her literary production. As a writer, Cusk has always mined terrain close to that of her own experience, even if the guise in which she has presented her concerns has changed and her work has been given different generic classifications. For example, *Aftermath* started life as an essay before being published as a memoir; part of it has since been republished in Cusk's most recent books of essays *Coventry: Essays*. Cusk's evolution as a writer can be attributed to her search for new forms in response to what she perceives as the limitations of existing modes of writing and assumptions about genre that she contests.

Insofar as her work is concerned with questions of voice, authority and freedom, she continues to explore and interrogate female experience from the perspective of a white, middle-class woman, and to challenge structures and institutions that appear to position women and female writers in particular ways, whether that be in terms of what it is permissible to say or in terms of reading their behaviours and modes of thought in ways that favour the status quo. In this sense, *Aftermath* should be read, according to Cusk herself in collected archival notes at the Harry Ransom Center, Austin, Texas, as a series of questions on the nature of authority and on what it means to have a duty of care to oneself and to one's family: 'Is authority male?'; 'Is female authority a re-enacting of the male version?'; 'Is the nature of duty caring of [sic] others or yourself?'. Her concern is also with the female body, with family life and with the consequences of a breakdown in family life.

The period following *Aftermath*, as indicated, was one in which Cusk re-examined the potentials of the novel form for responding to the kind of questions she wished to ask. In essence, she moves out from aspects of the material world to broader philosophical questions. The 'Outline' trilogy was both a reaction to the response to *Aftermath* and an action in its own right; together the three volumes constitute a journey through family life and gender. She wanted, she says in interview at The Library Foundation of Los Angeles, 'to correct the relationship between narrative and truth; language and truth' (Cusk and Friedman 2019), which I take to refer to her commitment to disentangle societal scripts from personal experience. Like Knausgaard in *My Struggle*, who turns his back on fabrication and invention in the novel and determines to use the facts of his own life as a means of getting closer to the reality of experience, Cusk wanted to find a novelistic form that would allow her to continue her investigations into female experience at particular stages of the life course in a way that would reflect truthfully on voice, authority and freedom. Given that 'you are made most real to yourself by what you notice' (Cusk and Friedman), her narrator Faye, who is close to Cusk's own persona, creates an image of herself by what she sees and hears. Even though she would not describe her work as autofiction, she sees herself as bringing to the novel form the sensibility of autofiction, whereby the self (or a version thereof) is used to verify what is presented.

Chapter 7

CONCLUSION

This book has been concerned with a number of inter-related phenomena: a seeming rejection, on the part of some writers, of fiction, fabrication, and conventional forms of the novel in favour of a turn towards the auto/biographical and/or work with a closer connection to the lived experience and existential realities of its authors. From the radical realism of Karl Ove Knausgaard's *My Struggle* series with its thick description and detailed representation of everyday life alongside the thoughts, feelings and reflections of narrator-protagonist Karl Ove, as he navigates the world around him, and seeks to realize his vocation as a writer, to the reinvention of the novel form actualized by Rachel Cusk in her 'Outline' trilogy following the malfunctioning, as she saw it, of her life-writing, there has been a rethinking of the affordances and rationale of the novel and its relationship to fact and fiction.

The seeming conflation of novel and fiction has been interrogated anew as writers such as Knausgaard and Cusk use and stretch the form to enable their investigations into the kind of links that may pertain between literature and life, and art and reality, addressing issues such as self-definition and the function of writing in the face of loss and trauma. After his father's death, Knausgaard recalibrates his relationship to the world and to those around him. He is both liberated by the process and at the same time forced to re-assess his conception of self, in the wake of the removal of the person who stood for many years in opposition to him, and whose presence helped define him both as a young boy and as an adult. Volume 1, *A Death in the Family*, has been described as a narrative of filiation (Meekings 2019, 420), in which '[t]he microscopic gaze [...] is a symptom of the self-concept trying to understand (and so renegotiate) its altered relationality to the world around it' (420). But the series as a whole reflects Knausgaard's desire to use the material facts of his own existence, inevitably filtered through memory, to pose questions about the role of experience in shaping us as individuals within particular societies and contexts and to explore what it means to write from life when writing is both a compulsion and a compensation insofar as it permits the author-narrator to bring to mind and to re-member what might otherwise be lost to the passage of time. In this sense writing brings to appearance and makes present what is otherwise ephemeral and intersubjectively unavailable. Knausgaard's writing method – to write fast and apparently without fear of the consequences – was a tool in his armoury to try and bypass the more critical and shaping voice of consciousness.

Cusk, too, is in a sense dealing in her work with loss and what is no longer there, as she navigates a period of silence and invisibility after *Aftermath*. For her, it is a question of finding a new form to accommodate her exploration of this new phase of life and a sense that a person is defined by what is outside them – by institutions, social structures and scripts – rather than by what exists within. Reacting against the author as an egotistical force in the novel, which might itself be considered an implied critique of works like *My Struggle*, she explores what it means to inhabit a world where the female narrator is defined by what she notices rather than what she is. Cusk wanted to represent the collapse of a belief in reality or rather to show what it means for Faye, her protagonist and alter ego, to have lost faith in her own reality. For Cusk, fiction had become a cultural commodity concerned with plot and imagination to the detriment of an interrogation of reality, moral questions and the freedom to be abstract. To a certain extent, for both Knausgaard and Cusk, writing became a mode of survival.

Writing as a mode of survival can also be seen to characterize the work of Winterson and Guo. While in their semi-autobiographical fiction they depict autofictional protagonists with a strong sense of difference and alienation, it is in their memoirs that they investigate and try to explicate their trauma. Yet in both cases, these so-called memoirs retrace paths familiar to the reader of their fictions and are consistent with a worldview already established by their autofictional narrators. Indeed, Winterson refers to *Oranges* on her website as an early example of what came to be called autofiction in English (https://www.jeanettewinterson.com/author). Like Winterson whose novels have always had a strong metafictional bias, Guo's so-called fictional works have engaged with larger political and cultural themes against the backdrop of the struggle of a generally female protagonist to realize her ambition as an artist. I say 'so-called' fictional works, since for Guo herself categorization of her work into fiction and non-fiction goes against the grain of what she sees herself as trying to do. Coming from a different cultural tradition and moving between writing and documentary filmmaking, Guo's work is characterized by border-crossing of all kinds (linguistic, cultural and generic); she remains somewhat sceptical about an Anglo-American preference for certain types of narrative, preferring in her own work to present a mix of fragments, essayistic passages, aphorisms and stretches of dialogue, alongside a somewhat sketchy narrative outline. It is not that her work is devoid of story – it usually has an overarching storyline – but the focus is not so much on change over time on the part of the protagonist but rather on an interrogation of different intellectual positions and cultural perceptions that the protagonist encounters and engages with as she inhabits a particular social and cultural milieu.

Guo prefers terms such as documentary novel to describe her memoir and like Cusk and Knausgaard, she is suspicious of the narrative drive which demands that novels concede to plot and to a sense of change over time. Like her literary touchstones such as Marguerite Duras and Roland Barthes before her, she is much more interested in the affordances of language as it changes its material base across cultures and media to generate images, scenes and fragments of discourse that convey through a mix of dialogue, essay and story a portrait of the artist at a particular point in time. The freedom to be abstract, which is something important to Cusk, is also a recognizable feature of Guo's work. Indeed, *A Lover's Discourse*, her riposte to Barthes, displays all the qualities for which Guo is known: her focus on language, on cultural difference, on intercultural communication and on the nature of art and the role of the artist in society. Guo's work, regardless of its library classification or marketing categorization, reveals certain writerly concerns and traits: it might best be described as an intellectual project concerned with the nature of art and its relationship to reality, with art and transformation, with notions of creative authority, and the struggle to become an artist, and with questions of genre and gender. Indeed, like Winterson, though of a different generation, a different culture and a different sexual orientation, Guo can be considered anti-realist insofar as her protagonists display romantic tendencies and have faith in the power of art and of the imagination to change perceptions of the world around them. This tendency is also relayed in Guo's memoir in terms of presentation of her reaction as a young girl to the group of artists who visit Shitang and paint the setting sun in colours that transform 'the brown water to blue and the cloudy sky to a half-orange, half-red sunset' (Gordon 2017). From her youthful perspective, art has a power that transforms the sometimes sordid, sometimes mean, facts of existence. Yet, even as an adult, it is to her life as an artist that Guo clings as a way of making sense of life.

While there are points of contact between and among all four writers, there are also some differences. Winterson has never actively turned her back on the novel, though she claims in *Art Objects*, her 1995 book of essays, not to write novels (Winterson 1995, 191), at least of the nineteenth-century variety and has, from the very beginning of her career, tried to steer her work away from modes of realism towards the creation of alternative universes where the laws of physics do not apply. She works against the grain of a conventional reproduction of an existing reality towards a search for a form that will hold her interest in narrative experimentation and the breaching of boundaries, whether they relate to ideas about space and time, or whether they relate to narrative and generic conventions. Winterson tends to include in her work a mix of fairy-tale-like elements and philosophical and speculative reflections alongside narrative elements. While a consummate storyteller, she is less concerned with narrative drive and plot and is more interested in finding forms that will do justice to her narrative experimentation, whether that be with the gender of the narrator, as in *Written on the Body*, or with concepts of time and travel through time and space, as in *Sexing the Cherry*. Indeed, it might be said that *Oranges*, while in some ways experimental, is one of her more traditional works. Winterson's lineage as a (post)-modernist writer is such that she expects the reader to follow the various lines of enquiry she embeds in her narratives by connecting juxtaposed blocks of text, making meaning at the level of recurring imagery rather than in a necessarily linear fashion. In this recursiveness, her work has points of contact with that of Knausgaard who constantly returns to themes and images across the various volumes of the *My Struggle* series, even if in other ways, their work is very different.

In sum, reacting against the commodification of the novel and narrativization of self, these writers (Knausgaard, Winterson, Guo and Cusk) have responded in slightly different but complementary ways to the challenge of creating works of philosophical and existential enquiry in forms appropriate to their aims at the time of writing. All four writers are concerned with the types of relationship that pertain between life and art, the person or persona who writes and the one who experiences life in all its diversity and intensity. They are all sceptical about conventionalized narrative forms and creating 'mere' fictions; rather, they are interested in the complexities and contradictions that permeate human existence and in creating works that respond at a deep, rather than superficial, level to questions of how to live meaningfully and with integrity, how to engage critically and creatively with the world around them without reproducing unnecessary fictions and lies, and how to make intersubjectively available aspects of the lives of 'real' subjects.

Yet their relationship to concepts of realism is variable, with Knausgaard a proponent of 'radical' realism, in the sense in which I have employed it, while Cusk's work is bound up with showing the 'realities' of societal structures (e.g. marriage, divorce, publishing) which impact differentially on individual subjects in accordance with the laws of gender and genre. Winterson would certainly recognize the kind of gender bias that distinguishes the 'metafictional' works of male writers from their 'confessional' or 'autobiographical' female counterparts, and across the years she has kept pushing the novelistic envelope to show the close entanglement of art and life, of poetry and prose, of the personal and the political. Hailing from a different culture and writing in a second language, Guo's authorial concerns have always been 'unapologetically intellectual', as one reviewer puts it in relation to *A Lover's Discourse* (Edemariam 2020) with the impact of French and American literature in translation already a feature of Guo's early works alongside a tendency to draw from life in her fiction. Indeed, all four writers can be seen in different ways and to differing extents to have produced serial portraits and multiple selves, as they present different and sometimes distributed versions of aspects of self across their work as a whole.

Insofar as the autofictional as a mode takes account of this kind of serial production (Menn and Schuh, 2022) and is attentive both to the referential ground of the 'I' (James 2022, 56) and its autofictionalization (Effe and Gibbons 2022), as well as permitting a degree of self-reflexivity or 'metanarrativity' (Meretoja 2022, 121), it may be said that all four writers have produced autofictional works and/or produced autofictional effects such as in the case of Cusk's 'Outline' trilogy (James 2022, 51). In this sense, recognition of an autofictional impulse in much contemporary work (Effe and Lawlor 2022) is justified. However, the question of the relationship of the autofictional to both the novel form and to autobiography remains, given the diversity of writerly aims and motivations that propel it and the range of readerly responses to the 'same' literary work, as has been shown in relation to Knausgaard's *My Struggle*. Perhaps ultimately what has been taking place is a revaluation of the novel as writers seek to divest it of its adequation with 'mere' fiction and a set of more or less 'naturalized' storytelling conventions with a view to reinvesting it with contemporary relevance and power.

Such contemporary relevance and power derive from treating issues and ideas of writerly (and readerly) import such as the extent to which it is possible to unfold or reveal a 'true' self over time; the role of culture, including narrative culture, in producing a sense of self; and the extent to which literature is able to compete with other media today by virtue of its immersive and world-building powers. The four writers I have considered are concerned to bring into realignment the novel's capacity for philosophical and existential enquiry and critique as well as formal invention. Their challenges to 'conventional genre-boxing', (Winterson 1995, 71) reflect a rejection of the commodification of the novel and a desire to return literature to the forefront of intellectual life through a reappraisal of its matter and of its relationship to life and to lived experience.

What seems to have been happening, in a sense from different directions, is a kind of assault on the boundaries separating fact and fiction, not as a nod to those who see no difference between them, but rather as an acknowledgement of fictionality as a mode in writing which can coexist with factuality in different proportions, perhaps, and to differing extents depending on what the author is trying to achieve within the confines of their work at particular moments. This is a view that depends on extra-textual factors and a sense of context in making determinations about text and one which acknowledges the novel as a form that changes over time. Adequation of fiction with the novel form is belied by a history of the novel which shows it to have been shaped by different forces at different times. Depending on where one sees the novel beginning, it is a form that has been shaped by romances and by fantasy, as well as by concerns with what is understood at various historical moments to constitute reality. Dickens is a good example of a novelist whose work has been treated both in terms of its critique of nineteenth-century social institutions and its particular blend of fantasy or romance and modes of realism.

The shape the novel has assumed since the eighteenth century has been a function of changing notions both of what the novel is for and of how best to realize that goal: whether it be a vehicle for the exploration of alternative or possible worlds or a means of social critique, the novel has been shaped by techniques that have evolved in relation to the novelist's intentional or fortuitous design, as well as in response to reader expectations and the views of critics and cultural gatekeepers. Writers today, it would seem, or at least a subset of them, are concerned with the direction that the novel has taken and wish to renew its critical and existential force by bringing it closer to the world of what constitutes reality for them and to deploy it in the service of an interrogation of self and of how we humans come to know both self and world. Rather than maintain boundaries that they see as contingent and changing as opposed to given and fixed, they bring to their work an interrogation of story and truth, drawing from real life rather than seeking to invent or fabricate character and plot; they break open and/or dissolve taken-for-granted boundaries between worlds. Insofar as autofiction occupies a liminal space between fiction and non-fiction, it is surely not surprising that it has become for many writers today an area of interest. Even if Cusk rejects the label of autofiction in respect of her 'Outline' trilogy, there is no doubt that many critics read it in such terms and readers familiar with Cusk's biography will see parallels between narrator Faye and author Cusk in her work. Cusk's admission that she brings an autofictional sensibility to the novel form confirms her understanding of what is at stake here: post-*Aftermath*, she has found a form that allows her to continue her interrogation of the female experience by creating a structure and a perspective that promote consideration of 'how, to what degree, and to what end, readers may share in the experiences of others' (Valihora 2019, 19–20). The path taken by

Knausgaard, while different in its insistent focus on Karl Ove's experience and thoughts, nevertheless pushes against assumptions of what the novel can or should do by crossing a threshold and producing what he calls a non-fictional novel.

The contemporary context, then, is such that both 'memoir and autofiction alike provide the writer with the possibility of blurring the distinctions between the real and the imaginary, between life and storytelling, and thus *hint that the self might also be a blend of fact and fiction*' (Meekings 2019, 422; the italics are mine). Far from being a continuation of a postmodernist sensibility, this is, rather, a return to a search for integrity and honesty, given the acknowledgement that not only is our vision of the world mediated, so too is the very language in which we seek to deliver it. Notions of what it is to be truthful and to get to the heart of the matter, whether that be a concept of self, or to an understanding of one's place in the world, therefore necessarily incorporate reflection on the ways in which language and certain forms of storytelling shape literary production. The questions of what reality is and how we know it to be so have come back into the frame but from a perspective of sincerity and authenticity rather than parody or playfulness. Terms such as metamodernism and post-postmodernism (Alber and Bell 2019; Gibbons, Vermeulen and van den Akker 2019) are being employed to reflect this writerly change in focus. Publication of *The Autofictional* (Effe and Lawlor 2022) is further evidence of critical interest in a series of phenomena grouped under the umbrella label autofiction or better the autofictional, given that for many of the contributors to the volume, it is a mode and/or an impulse rather than a genre *per se*.

In examining the trajectories of four contemporary writers, each of whom has consistently been pushing boundaries and interrogating literary and narrative norms, I have demonstrated the extent to which all four writers have in the course of their varied trajectories created forms designed to take forward their own intellectual projects, whether those projects relate to constructions of self, explorations of the connections that pertain between literature and life, art and reality and/or to questions of gender and genre. All have experienced and been shaped by the struggle to become an artist, though the specifics of their circumstances have not been the same. Winterson and Guo have come from working-class backgrounds and have had to overcome obstacles of class and culture as well as gender; in Winterson's case, her sexuality and religious upbringing have also positioned her as an outsider. Knausgaard and Cusk may not have been born outsiders, in terms of class; however, their literary aspirations and uncompromising approach to literature and art have put them on a collision course with their families and with some critics and readers.

Having said that, since working on this monograph, both Cusk and Knausgaard have published new books, the most recent of which, in different ways, and to differing extents, look like a re-investment in some aspects of the novel that they had previously rejected. In Cusk's case, *Second Place* (2021) is a novel that somewhat melodramatically paints a picture of a woman's mid-life crisis and her decision to invite a male artist whose work she has admired to occupy a cabin in the grounds of the home she shares with her husband, Tony. Cusk has 'taken the template for much of this story from Mabel Dodge Luhan's memoir *Lorenzo in Taos* (1932)' (Thomas-Corr 2021) and transposed the story to a place that is 'strikingly similar to Cusk's Norfolk eco-house overlooking the North Sea' (Thomas-Corr 2021). While this mixing of fact and fiction is very much in line with Cusk's method, what is different is her style in *Second Place*: 'a tone of breathless melodrama and frequent exclamation marks […] highly reminiscent of Dodge's writing' (Thomas-Corr 2021). It is as if the rather guarded, articulate but spare Cuskian sentences have been released or let loose and Cusk is exploring the consequences of the arrival of a stranger and the aftermath of the destruction he wreaks on the household, destruction and creative rebirth being themes close to the locus of Cusk's interest.

Knausgaard, likewise, has returned to a fictional novelistic universe, though readers of *My Struggle* may recognize that he nevertheless draws on his own life experience in investing his characters with backstories. Aspects of his own life experiences (e.g. having lived with a partner who suffers from a bipolar disorder; working as a helper in a psychiatric ward) are distributed among the nine characters in this multi-perspectival, biblically infused story entitled *The Morning Star* (2021) which outlines what happens over a couple of days in the lives of the characters, all of whom are aware of the appearance in the sky of a particularly bright star and of other phenomena that seem to suggest that the world is out of joint. For Knausgaard, this book, while different from *My Struggle* insofar as it is not focussed on himself and deals with an outside threat from the perspective of different characters, nevertheless shares with his previous work interest in how to deal with the big questions: Why are we here? What is death? What is life? (NPR's Book of the Day, 2021). In interview with J. P. O'Malley (2021) in Ireland's *Independent* he says: 'I want to explore ideas and see how they look in the inner life: within, say, a setting, or within a family, or within a relation'. In this sense, he continues to explore the kind of connections people make to the world outside them from their various locations but in *The Morning Star* he creates a choir of people (the term is Knausgaard's) and sets their necessarily restricted individual views against each other. Like Cusk, Knausgaard explores philosophical and current questions in his work, in this case: 'What happens if death and nature start to move'?

Interestingly both Cusk and Knausgaard discuss their new work – Cusk's *Second Place* and Knausgaard's *The Morning Star* – in terms of a chorus or choir, different voices that may overlap, complement one another and/or present alternative perspectives. And they both include in their new work the idea of threat and the possibility of destruction, even if the worlds they present are different: Cusk's is rooted in domesticity but is woven around ideas of suffering and freedom. As one reviewer puts it: It's 'a domestic novel combined with a novel of ideas in which Cusk continues her cerebral exploration of issues of freedom, how art can both save and destroy us, the rub between self-sacrifice and self-definition in motherhood, and the possibilities of domestic happiness' (McAlpin 2021). Knausgaard's *The Morning Star* has been seen as moving in the direction of genre fiction – a kind of Stephen King-like horror with undertones of apocalypse – yet it retains the Knausgaardian concern with daily life from the perspective of the characters in question. Knausgaard has indicated that this, like his other works, is one of a series. So just where Knausgaard plans to take it remains to be seen but some of his trademark features are already in evidence: a focus on mundanity and the everyday, even if in this case there is an underlying sense of dread and a conviction that we humans do not know it all.

What unites all four writers considered here is their investment in writing as a form of philosophical enquiry as well as a form of self-definition. For all of them, narrative conventions are there to be breached in accordance with their artistic mission and intellectual project at any given moment. Yet while singular individuals with their own histories, both cultural and biographic, they also belong to a particular *Zeitgeist*, one aware of the dangers for literature of failing to engage in the big questions, both personal and societal. In basing their work on their own experience and presenting it in different forms, they are raising questions about the value of literature not as cultural commodity but as an expressive and existential mode of enquiry capable of engagement beyond the distinctiveness and singularity of its roots in personal experience. In questioning the novel's ties to fabrication, invention and illusion, at the expense of the realities of lived experience and a search for meaning, they are attempting to rebalance the links between story and truth, representation and reality. If the novel, as an expression of the new and a story of now, is to survive, and it must, then it will maintain its Janus-faced position along a variable spectrum from fact to fiction. The border between art and life, between one person and another is a constantly shifting thing, as are ideas about what constitutes reality. It is the search for meaning that remains constant.

REFERENCES

Alber, Jan & Alice Bell. 2019. 'The Importance of Being Earnest Again: Fact and Fiction in Contemporary Narratives across Media', *European Journal of English Studies* 23, no. 2: 121–135. DOI: 10.1080/13825577.2019.1640414.

Ali, Monica. 2017. 'Monica Ali on Rachel Cusk's Risky, Revolutionary New Novel'. *The New York Times*, 23 January 2017. https://www.nytimes.com/2017/01/23/books/review/rachel-cusk-transit.html (accessed 18 July 2018).

Andersen, Claus Elholm. 2018. 'Narratives of a life: Karl Ove Knausgård's *My Struggle* as a literary centaur'. *The Critical Quarterly* 60, no. 2: 24–38.

Anthony, Andrew. 2015. 'Interview: Karl Ove Knausgaard: "Writing Is a Way of Getting Rid of Shame"'. *The Observer*, 1 March 2015.

Arts Week 2020: Online, 'In conversation: Deborah Levy'. Birkbeck, University of London, 18 May 2021. https://www.bbk.ac.uk/annual-events/arts-week/arts-week-2020 (accessed 6 December 2021).

Asia Society New York. 2017. 'ChinaFile Presents: "Nine Continents" – A Conversation with Memoirist Xiaolu Guo'. https://asiasociety.org/new-york/events/chinafile-presents-nine-continents-conversation-memoirist-xiaolu-guo.

Auerbach, Erich. 2003. *Mimesis: The Representation of Reality in Western Literature*. Princeton: Princeton University Press. https://hdl-handle-net.libezproxy.open.ac.uk/2027/heb.09353.

Backus, Margot Gayle. 2001. '"I Am Your Mother; She Was a Carrying Case": Adoption, Class, and Sexual Orientation in Jeanette Winterson's *Oranges Are Not the Only Fruit*'. In *Imagining Adoption: Essays on Literature and Culture*, edited by Marianne Novy, 133–149. Ann Arbor: University of Michigan Press.

Bal, Mieke. 1997. *Narratology: Introduction to the Theory of Narrative*, 2nd edition. Toronto: University of Toronto Press.

Barthes, Roland. 1968. L'effet de réel. *Communications*, 11, 1968. Recherches sémiologiques le vraisemblable. pp. 84–89; DOI: https://doi.org/10.3406/comm.1968.1158https://www.persee.fr/doc/comm_0588-8018_1968_num_11_1_115.

BBC Radio 4. 2020. *Front Row*, 'Xiaolu Guo, Belarus Free Theatre, Blindness, The Leach Pottery'. 10 August 2020. https://www.bbc.co.uk/programmes/m000lmtd.

Beyond Borders, Scotland. 2013. Rachel Cusk *Outline*, Interview with Dr. Meg Jensen, 3 September 2013. https://www.youtube.com/watch?v=1yyU4ZPTur0.

Blair, Elaine. 2015. 'All Told: Rachel Cusk's autobiographical fictions.' *The New Yorker* 90, no. 42: 70–71. http://libezproxy.open.ac.uk/login?url=https://www.proquest.com/magazines/all-told/docview/1645637666/se-2?accountid=14697.

Blake, Matt. 2020. 'Books that shaped the 1980s'. 22 October 2020. https://www.penguin.co.uk/articles/2020/october/books-that-shaped-1980s.html (accessed 7 December 2021).

Bloom, Myra. 'Sources of the Self(ie): An Introduction to the Study of Autofiction in English'. *English Studies in Canada* 45, no. 1–2 (March–June 2019), 1–18.

Booker Prizes. 2021. 'Rachel Cusk Q+A'. https://thebookerprizes.com/rachel-cusk-qa.
Boxall, Peter. 2015. *The Value of the Novel*. Cambridge: Cambridge University Press.
Boxall, Peter, & Cheyette, Bryan. 2016. 'The Life and Death of the Post-War Novel', *The Oxford History of the Novel in English*. Oxford: Oxford University Press. Available at Oxford Scholarship Online at https://oxford-universitypressscholarship-com.libezproxy.open.ac.uk/view/10.1093/oso/9780198749394.001.0001/oso-9780198749394 (accessed 20 July 2021).
Brown, Stephen & Anthony Patterson. 2021. 'Me-search? Search Me! A New Twist in the Tale of Introspection', *Journal of Marketing Management*. DOI: 10.1080/0267257X.2021.1928268.
Burgelin, Claude. 2010. 'Pour l'autofiction'. In *Autofiction(s)*, edited by Claude Burgelin, Isabelle Grell, and Roger-Yves Roche, 5–21. Lyon: Presses Universitaires de Lyon.
Burns, Shannon. 2015. 'The Rings of Saturn: A Lasting Chronicle of Mourning'. *Sydney Review of Books*, 11 December 2015. https://sydneyreviewofbooks.com/review/the-rings-of-saturn-a-lasting-chronicle-of-mourning/ (accessed 7 October 2021).
Camp, James. 'A Man in Full: Karl Ove Knausgaard Concludes His Autofiction Epic'. *Bookforum*; New York 25, no. 3 (September–November 2018). https://www-proquest-com.libezproxy.open.ac.uk/docview/2097999947?pq-origsite=primo&https://search_proquest_com/pq1lit= (accessed 13 August 2021).
CBC Radio. 2018. 'Xiaolu Guo Traces Her Life's Unlikely Journey from East to West'. https://www.cbc.ca/radio/writersandcompany/xiaolu-guo-traces-her-life-s-unlikely-journey-from-east-to-west-1.4494894.
Célestin, Roger. 1997. 'Interview with Serge Doubrovsky Autoficton and Beyond', *Contemporary French and Francophone Studies* 1, no. 2: 397–405. Published online 25 April 2008. https://doi.org/10.1080/10260219708455900.
Clark, Alex. 2018. 'Drawn from Life: Why Have Novelists Stopped Making Things up?'. *The Guardian*, 23 June 2018. https://www.theguardian.com/books/2018/jun/23/drawn-from-life-why-have-novelists-stopped-making-things-up.
Cummins, Anthony. 2020. '*A Lover's Discourse* by Xiaolu Guo, Review: Free-Floating Reflections on Art, Politics and Nationhood'. https://inews.co.uk/culture/books/a-lovers-discourse-xiaolu-guo-review-583813 (accessed 25 November 2021).
Cusk, Rachel. 2008. *A Life's Work*. London: Faber & Faber.
Cusk, Rachel. 2011. 'Preface'. *Literature Compass* 8, no. 12: 873–874. DOI: 10.1111/j.1741-4113.2011.00848.x.
Cusk, Rachel. 2012. *Aftermath*. London: Faber & Faber.
Cusk, Rachel. 2013. 'A Man in Love by Karl Ove Knausgaard – Review'. *The Guardian*, 12 April 2013. https://www.theguardian.com/books/2013/apr/12/man-in-love-knausgaard-review.
Cusk, Rachel. 2013. 'The Mirror and the Self'. *The New Statesman*, 26 July–8 August 2013, pp. 32–37.
Cusk, Rachel. 2014. *Outline*. London: Vintage.
Cusk, Rachel. 2016a. *Transit*. London: Jonathan Cape.
Cusk, Rachel. 2016b. 'Rachel Cusk, *Outline*'. In *Diacritik*, 6 March 2016. https://www.youtube.com/watch?v=b08bwoCSSFY (accessed 17 July 2018).
Cusk, Rachel. 2018. *Kudos*. London: Faber & Faber.
Cusk, Rachel. 2021. *Second Place*. London: Faber & Faber.
Cusk papers, Box 1.4, Harry Ransom Humanities Research Center, The University of Texas at Austin, PO Box 7219, Austin, Texas 78713. www.hrc.utexas.edu.

Cusset, Catherine. 2010. 'Je'. In *Autofiction(s)*, edited by Claude Burgelin, Isabelle Grell and Roger-Yves Roche, 35–41. Lyon: Presses universitaires de Lyon.

Dagnino, Arianna. 2015. *Transcultural Writers and Novels in the Age of Global Mobility*. West Lafayette, IN: Purdue University Press. DOI:10.2307/j.ctv15wxqk8.

Dawson, Paul. 2016. 'From Digressions to Intrusions: Authorial Commentary in the Novel'. *Studies in the Novel* 48, no. 2: 145–167. DOI:10.1353/sdn.2016.0025.

Deresiewicz, William. 2014. 'Why Has "My Struggle" Been Anointed a Literary Masterpiece?'. *The Nation*, 13 May 2014. https://www.thenation.com/article/archive/why-has-my-struggle-been-anointed-literary-masterpiece/ (accessed 16 August 2021).

Dewey, Donald. 2013. 'The Fiction of Non-Fiction'. *Scandinavian Review* 100, no. 2: 46–52.

Dix, Hywel. 2017. 'Autofiction: The Forgotten Face of French Theory'. *Word and Text: A Journal of Literary Studies and Linguistics* VII, no. 2017: 69–85.

Doloughan, Fiona. 2016. *English as a Literature in Translation*. New York: Bloomsbury. ISBN:987-1-62892-509-8.

Doloughan, Fiona. 2019. 'The Problematics and Performance of Self-Translation: The Case of Xiaolu Guo'. In *Hybrid Englishes and the Challenges of and for Translation: Identity, Mobility and Language Change*, edited by Karen Bennett and Rita Queiroz de Barros, 21–36. Routledge Advances in Translation and Interpreting Studies, ISBN 978-1-138-30740-7.

Doloughan, Fiona and Xiaolu Guo. 2019. 'Writing the Self'. Podcast in 'Life Stories' series produced by Open University *Contemporary Cultures of Writing Research Group*, 15 January 2019. https://www.open.ac.uk/arts/research/contemporary-cultures-of-writing/events/life-stories-0 (accessed 25 November 2021).

Doloughan, Fiona. 2015. 'The Construction of Space in Contemporary Narrative'. *Journal of Narrative Theory* 45, no. 1: 1+, https://link.gale.com/apps/doc/A458644245/AONE?u=tou&sid=bookmark-AONE&xid=0714220a (accessed 25 November 2021).

Doll, Jen. 2020. 'No Place Like Home: Xiaolu Guo Continues Her Examination of the Search for Authenticity with Her Latest Novel.' *Publishers Weekly* 267, no. 33: 46+. Gale Literature Resource Center, link.gale.com/apps/doc/A635353508/LitRC?u=tou&sid=bookmark-LitRC&xid=0c848192 (accessed 9 June 2021).

Dunmore, Helen. 2016. '*Transit* by Rachel Cusk Review – A Woman's Struggle to Rebuild Her Life'. *The Observer*, Sunday. https://www.theguardian.com/books/2016/aug/28/transit-by-rachel-cusk-review-complex-brilliant-prose (accessed 24 July 2018).

Eagleton, Mary. 2013. 'Why Be Happy When You Could Be Normal?', *Women: A Cultural Review*, 24, no. 2–3: 248–249. DOI: 10.1080/09574042.2013.805528.

Edemariam, Aida. 2020. 'Cross-Cultural Echoes: The Story of a Chinese Woman in London Becomes a Meditation on Language and Desire'. *The Guardian*, 10 October 2020.

Effe, Alexandra & Hannie Lawlor. 2022. *The Autofictional: Approaches, Affordances, Forms*. London: Palgrave Macmillan. https://doi.org/10.1007/978-3-030-78440-9.

Faber, Michel. 'Review: Fiction: Too Close to Home: Michel Faber Struggles with an Autobiographical Epic That Is a National Obsession in Norway: A Death in the Family by Karl Ove Knausgaard, translated by Don Bartlett 393pp, Harvill Secker, pounds 17.99.' *Guardian* [London, England], 28 April 2012, p. 10. Gale Academic OneFile, link.gale.com/apps/doc/A287947173/AONE?u=tou&sid=bookmark-AONE&xid=1d515b42 (accessed 15 September 2021).

Feigel, Lara. 2017. 'Once Upon a Time in the East by Xiaolu Guo – Between Two Worlds', *The Financial Times*, January 2017. https://www.ft.com/content/58c76ba8-d414-11e6-b06b-680c49b4b4c0 (accessed 22 November 2021).

Feigel, Lara. 2018. 'Which Way Next?', *The Guardian Review*, Saturday, 11 August 2018, no. 30: 6–11.

Finch, Charles. 'Autofiction for the Twitter Era'. *The New York Times Book Review*, 1 December 2019, p. 17. Gale Literature Resource Center, link.gale.com/apps/doc/A607140787/LitRC?u=tou&sid=bookmark-LitRC&xid=ea063dc5 (accessed 20 August 2021).

Frank, Joseph. 2012. *Responses to Modernity: Essays in the Politics of Culture*. New York: Fordham University Press. Available from ProQuest Ebook Central (18 August 2021).

Franklin, Ruth. 1993. 'Knausgaard Devours Himself'. *The Atlantic Monthly* 322, no. 4, 2018: 106–119.

Franklin, Ruth. "How Writing 'My Struggle' Undid Knausgaard". *The Atlantic*, November 2018 Issue. https://www.theatlantic.com/magazine/archive/2018/11/knausgaard-devours-himself/570847/.

Franklin, Ruth. 2017. 'The Uncoupling'. *The Atlantic Monthly* 319, no. 1, (Boston; January/February 2017): 37–39.

Garner, Dwight. 2021. 'In Karl Ove Knausgaard's Horror-Tinged New Novel, a Mesmerizing Star Appears in the Sky'. *The New York Times*, 20 September 2021. https://www.nytimes.com/2021/09/20/books/review-morning-star-karl-ove-knausgaard.html.

Garner, Dwight. 2018. 'Review: Rachel Cusk's "Transit" Offers Transcendent Reflections'. *The New York Times*, 17 January 2017. https://www.nytimes.com/2017/01/17/books/review-rachel-cusk-transit.html.

Garrido Sánchez, Violeta. 2018. 'Proust y La Superación Del Realismo.' *Castilla, Estudios de Literatura*, no. 9: 204–236. DOI: https://doi.org/10.24197/cel.9.2018.204-236.

Gasparini, Philippe. 2011. 'Autofiction vs autobiographie'. *Tangence*, no. 97: 11–24. https://doi.org/10.7202/1009126ar.

George, Rose. 2017. 'Cinderella in China'. *The Spectator* 333, no. 9845. https://www.spectator.co.uk/article/cinderella-in-china (accessed 22 November 2021).

Gibbons, Alison, Timotheus Vermeulen & Robin van den Akker. 2019. 'Reality Beckons: Metamodernist Depthiness beyond Panfictionality', *European Journal of English Studies* 23, no. 2: 172–189. DOI: 10.1080/13825577.2019.1640426.

Glancy, Josh. 2018. 'Why Men Should Take a Leaf Out of Karl Ove Knausgaard's Book and Own up to Sexual Shame'. *The Sunday Times*, 2 September 2018.

Gordon, Peter. 2017. 'Once Upon a Time in the East: A Story of Growing Up by Guo Xiaolu', *Asian Review of Books*, 3 January 2017. https://asianreviewofbooks.com/content/once-upon-a-time-in-the-east-a-story-of-growing-up-by-guo-xiaolu/ (accessed 10 November 2021).

Guo, Xiaolu. 2020. *A Lover's Discourse*. London: Chatto & Windus.

Guo, Xiaolu. 2019. 'Writing the Self". Podcast from *Contemporary Cultures of Writing Research Group* series on 'Life Stories'. With Fiona Doloughan and Xiaolu Guo. https://www.open.ac.uk/arts/research/contemporary-cultures-of-writing/events/life-stories-0.

Guo, Xiaolu. 2017. *Once Upon a Time in the East*. London: Chatto & Windus.

Guo, Xiaolu. 2016. 'My Writing Day: Xiaolu Guo: "One Language Is Not Enough – I Write in Both Chinese and English"', *The Guardian*, 13 October 2016. https://www.theguardian.com/books/2016/oct/13/my-writing-day-xiaolu-guo (accessed 22 November 2021).

Guo, Xiaolu. 2015. *I Am China*. London: Chatto & Windus.

Guo, Xiaolu. 2009. *Twenty Fragments of a Ravenous Youth*. London: Vintage Books.

Guo, Xiaolu. 2005. *Village of Stone*. Trans. Cindy Carter. London: Vintage Books.
Hampel, Regine. 2001. *I Write, therefore I am: Fictional Autobiography and the Idea of Selfhood in the Postmodern Age*. Frankfurt: Peter Lang.
Higgins, Charlotte. 2021. 'War Brides, Spies and Burning Bookshops: Marina Warner on Writing Her Memoir'. *The Guardian*, Saturday, 6 March 2021. https://www.theguardian.com/books/2021/mar/06/war-brides-spies-and-burning-bookshops-marina-warner-on-writing-her-memoir.
Hughes, Sophie E. 2011. 'J. M. Coetzee's Scenes from Provincial Life', *Opticon*, no. 11. https://www.researchgate.net/publication/286131409_JM_Coetzee_Scenes_from_Provincial_Life.
Hutton, Margaret-Anne. 2018. 'Plato, New Media Technologies, and the Contemporary Novel'. *Mosaic: A Journal for the Interdisciplinary Study of Literature* 51, no. 1(3): 179–195. http://libezproxy.open.ac.uk/login?url=https://www.proquest.com/scholarly-journals/plato-new-media-technologies-contemporary-novel/docview/2010774937/se-2?accountid=14697.
Isaacs, Jeremy. 1994. 'Face to Face: Jeanette Winterson'. *The Late Show*. https://www.bbc.co.uk/iplayer/episode/p00nw1xh/the-late-show-face-to-face-jeanette-winterson (accessed 18 April 2020).
Iser, Wolfgang. 1981. *The Act of Reading: A Theory of Aesthetic Response*. Baltimore and London: The Johns Hopkins University Press.
Jahn, Manfred. 2017. *Narratology: A Guide to the Theory of Narrative*. http://www.uni-koeln.de/~ame02/pppn.htm#N3 (accessed 14 June 2020).
Jeffery, Ben. 'In Search of Excitement: Just How Dead Is the Novel as a Literary Form?' *TLS. Times Literary Supplement*, no. 5947 (2017): 7+. Gale Academic OneFile. https://link.gale.com/apps/doc/A634972501/AONE?u=tou&sid=bookmark-AONE&xid=2226bcb6 (accessed 6 December 2021).
Johnston, Taylor. 2018. 'The Corpse as Novelistic Form: Knausgaard's Deconstruction of Proustian Memory', *Critique: Studies in Contemporary Fiction* 59, no. 3: 368–382. DOI:10.1080/00111619.2017.1398711.
Joyce, James. 1979 [1916]. *A Portrait of the Artist as a Young Man*. Open Road Integrated Media, Inc., New York. Available from ProQuest Ebook Central (25 November 2021).
Koetse, Manya. 2018. 'Top 25 Best Fiction Books on China: Understanding Contemporary China through Modern Literary Fiction'. https://www.whatsonweibo.com/top-25-best-fiction-books-on-china-understanding-contemporary-china-through-modern-literary-fiction/.
Knausgaard, Karl Ove. 2014a. *A Death in the Family. My Struggle: Book 1*. Translated by Don Bartlett. London: Vintage Books.
Knausgaard, Karl Ove. 2014b. *A Man in Love. My Struggle: Book 2*. Translated by Don Bartlett. London: Vintage Books.
Knausgaard, Karl Ove. 2014c. *Boyhood Island. My Struggle: Book 3*. Translated by Don Bartlett. London: Vintage Books.
Knausgaard, Karl Ove. 2015. *Dancing in the Dark. My Struggle: Book 4*. Translated by Don Bartlett. London: Vintage Books.
Knausgaard, Karl Ove. 2016a. *Some Rain Must Fall. My Struggle: Book 5*. Translated by Don Bartlett. London: Harvill Secker.
Knausgaard, Karl Ove. 2016b. 'Karl Ove Knausgaard: the shame of writing about myself'. In *The Guardian*, Friday, 26 February 2016. https://www.theguardian.com/books/2016/feb/26/karl-ove-knausgaard-the-shame-of-writing-about-myself (accessed 10 August 2021).

Knausgaard, Karl Ove. 2018. *The End. My Struggle: Book 6*. Translated by Martin Aitken and Don Bartlett. London: Harvill Secker.

Knausgaard, Karl Ove. 2021. *The Morning Star*. Translated by Martin Aitken. London: Harvill Secker.

Kunzru, Hari. 2014. 'Karl Ove Knausgaard: The Latest Literary Sensation'. In *The Guardian*, Friday, 7 March 2014. https://www.theguardian.com/books/2014/mar/07/karl-ove-knausgaard-my-struggle-hari-kunzru (accessed 10 August 2021).

Lanser, Susan S. 2005. 'The "I" of the Beholder: Equivocal Attachments and the Limits of Structuralist Narratology.' In *A Companion to Narrative Theory*, 206–219. Oxford, UK: Blackwell Publishing Ltd.

Lavocat, Françoise. 2016. *Fait et Fiction: Pour une frontière*. Paris: Editions du Seuil.

Lejeune, Philippe. 1982. 'The Autobiographical Contract'. In *French Literary Theory Today: A Reader*, edited by Tzvetan Todorov, translated by R. Carter, 192–222. Cambridge: Cambridge University Press.

Lerner, Ben. 'Each Cornflake'. *London Review of Books* 36, no. 10, 22 May 2014. https://www.lrb.co.uk/the-paper/v36/n10/ben-lerner/each-cornflake (accessed 13 August 2021).

Levine, Caroline. 2000. 'Visual Labour: Ruskin's Radical Realism'. *Victorian Literature and Culture* 28, no. 1: 73–86.

Levy, Deborah. 2021. *Real Estate*. London: Hamish Hamilton.

Leypoldt, Günter. 2017. 'Knausgaard in America: Literary Prestige and Charismatic Trust', *Critical Quarterly* 59, no. 3: 55–69. DOI: 10.1111/criq.12357.

Li, Hua. 2011. *Contemporary Chinese Fiction by Su Tong and Yu Hua: Coming of Age in Troubled Times*, Brill, Leiden. Available from ProQuest Ebook Central (25 November 2021). https://ebookcentral.proquest.com/lib/open/detail.action?docID=717552.

Library Foundation of Los Angeles. 2019. Rachel Cusk in conversation with Ann Friedman. https://lfla.org/media-archive/rachel-cusk/.

Lim, Natalie. 2018. 'Arrhythmia by Natalie Lim'. Winning poem in *CBC Books* 2018. https://www.cbc.ca/books/literaryprizes/arrhythmia-by-natalie-lim-1.4876962.

Lim, Shirley Geok-lin. 2009. 'The Troubled and Troubling Genre Life On-Going Writing or On-Going Life Writing', *Prose Studies* 31, no. 3: 300–315. DOI: 10.1080/01440350903438245.

Live from the NYPL. 2019. 'Rachel Cusk with Jennie McPhee: The Outline Trilogy – The Novel Reinvented'. 2 April 2019. https://vimeo.com/327995507 (accessed 10 August 2021).

Lockwood, Patricia. 2018. 'Why Do I Have to Know What McDonald's Is?'. *London Review of Books* 40, no. 9: 11–12.

London Review Bookshop. 2021. 'Karl Ove Knausgaard: *The Morning Star*'. https://vimeo.com/624337457/85e83c7210 (accessed 7 October 2021).

Lorentzen, Christian. 2018. 'Rachel Cusk's *Kudos*: The Outline Trilogy Gets Its Third Masterpiece'. Vulture, 5 June 2018. https://www.vulture.com/2018/06/rachel-cusks-next-masterpiece.html.

Louisiana Channel. 2019. Rachel Cusk Interview: 'You Can Live the Wrong Life'. 7 November 2019. https://www.youtube.com/watch?v=kGg_6BGIHuM.

Lukács, Georg. 1989. *The Theory of the Novel*. Cambridge, MA: The MIT Press.

McAlpin, Heller. 2021. 'Compassion Is the True Test of a Person in "Second Place"'. *NPR*, 8 May 2021. https://www.npr.org/2021/05/08/994800053/compassion-is-the-true-test-of-a-person-in-second-place (accessed 11 November 2021).

McArdle, Niall. 2015. 'Telling Tales Untold'. In *Canadian Literature* 227, Winter 2015: 163–165.
McKenna, Emma. 2016. 'Double Melancholy: The (Class) Politics of Loss in Jeanette Winterson's *Why Be Happy When You Could Be Normal?*', *Women: A Cultural Review* 27, no. 3: 296–316. DOI: 10.1080/09574042.2016.1256558.
Maftei, Micaela. 2013. 'Me and Not-Me: Dismissing Unity in Autobiographical Writing'. In *The Fiction of Autobiography: Reading and Writing Identity*, edited by Micaela Maftei, 59–94. New York: Bloomsbury.
Magnússon, Gísli. 'The Aesthetics of Epiphany in Karl Ove Knausgård's *Min kamp*', *Scandinavian Studies* 92, no. 3, Fall 2020: 348–368.
Mah, Adeline Yen. 1997. *Falling Leaves*. London: Penguin Books.
Maris, Kathryn. 2019. 'Rachel Cusk and the Dangers of Honesty'. *The New Statesman*, 28 August 2019. https://www.newstatesman.com/culture/books/2019/08/rachel-cusk-and-dangers-honesty.
Mazzoni, Guido. 2017. *Theory of the Novel*. Translated by Zakiya Hanifa. Cambridge, MA: Harvard University Press.
Meekings, Sam. 2019. 'Writing through Loss: The Rise of Grief Narratives …'. *Life Writing* 16, no. 3: 413–427. https://doi.org/10.1080/14484528.2018.153704.
Menn, Ricarda & Melissa Shuh. 2022. 'The Autofictional in Serial, Literary Works'. In *The Autofictional*, edited by Alexandra Effe and Hannie Lawlor, 101–118. Palgrave Studies in Life Writing. Palgrave Macmillan, Cham. https://doi.org/10.1007/978-3-030-78440-9_6.
Moi, Toril. 2013. 'Shame and Openness', *Salmagundi*, Winter 2013, no.177: 205–210.
Morrison, Blake. 2016. 'Some Rain Must Fall: *My Struggle*, Volume 5 by Karl Ove Knausgaard Review – Merciless Self-exposure'. *The Guardian*, 9 March 2016. https://www.theguardian.com/books/2016/mar/09/some-rain-must-fall-my-struggle-volume-5-by-karl-ove-knausgaard-review.
Nielsen, Henrik Skov, James Phelan, & Richard Walsh. 2015. 'Ten Theses about Fictionality'. *Narrative* 23, no. 1: 61–73. http://www.jstor.org/stable/24615502.
Nixon, Rob. 2012. 'Non-Fiction Booms, North and South: A Transatlantic Perspective'. *Safundi* 13, no. 1–2: 29–49. DOI: 10.1080/17533171.2011.642587.
NPR's Book of the Day: 'Karl Ove Knausgaard Didn't Mean to Write a 666-page Book'. 21 October 2021. https://www.npr.org/2021/10/20/1047602161/karl-ove-knausgaard-didnt-mean-to-write-a-666-page-book (accessed 10 November 2021).
O'Malley, J. P. 2021. 'Karl Ove Knausgaard: "I Often Go to That Boundary between Life and Death"'. *Independent.ie* 2 October 2021. https://www.independent.ie/entertainment/books/karl-ove-knausgaard-i-often-go-to-that-boundary-between-life-and-death-40905127.html (accessed 10 November 2021).
O'Reilly, Elizabeth. 2007. 'Rachel Cusk'. *Literature Online*. https://literature.proquest.com/display/printView.do?area=ref.
Oates, Joyce Carol. 2012. 'In a Panic about Love'. *The New York Review*, 24 May 2012. https://www-nybooks-com.libezproxy.open.ac.uk/articles/2012/05/24/panic-about-love/.
Oyler, Lauren. 2020. 'After the Aftermath: The Reinvention of Rachel Cusk.' *The New Republic* 3, no. 53. http://libezproxy.open.ac.uk/login?url=https://www.proquest.com/magazines/after-aftermath-reinvention-rachel-cusk/docview/2365082998/se-2?accountid=14697.
Peters, Torrey. 2021. *Karl Ove Knausgaard in Conversation with Torrey Peters*. New York, 2021-08-30.

Peterson, Britt. 2015. 'Mommy Meanest'. *The New Republic*, 4 February 2015. https://newrepublic.com/article/120931/rachel-cusk-outline-review-can-british-novelist-redeem-herself (accessed 10 June 2018).

Power, Chris. 2018. 'Double Exposure', *The New Statesman*, 24–31 August 2018, 36–39.

Preda, Alina. 2019. 'Crossing the Boundaries between Modernist and Postmodernist Poetics: The Critical Reception of Jeanette Winterson's Novels'. *Metacritic Journal for Comparative Studies and Theory* 5, no. 2. https://doi.org/10.24193/mjcst.2019.8.02.

Prose, Francine. 2018. 'Real Talk: Rachel Cusk's Kudos'. *Sewanee Review* 126, no. 3: 520–534.

Rademacher, Anne. 2015. Responses to questionnaire re German translation of *I Am China*. Unpublished, personal correspondence with Fiona Doloughan.

Rachel Cusk papers box 1.4, *Aftermath* Notes, Harry Ransom Center, Austin, TX, USA.

Robinson, Anne. 2011. 'Jeanette Winterson Talks about Her Favourite Books'. https://www.youtube.com/watch?v=tTBAhJ1pPk0 (accessed 5 September 2022).

Rohter, Larry. 2012. 'He Says a Lot, for a Norwegian'. *New York Times*, 19 June 2012, p. C1(L). Gale OneFile: News, link.gale.com/apps/doc/A293577801/STND?u=tou&sid=bookmark-STND&xid=b04b4a90 (accessed 24 August 2021).

Rosen, Elisheva. 1995. 'Littérature, autofiction, histoire: l'Affaire Dreyfus dans *La Recherche du Temps Perdu*'. In *Littérature*, no. 100: 64–80. DOI: https://doi.org/10.3406/litt.1995.2385. https://www.persee.fr/doc/litt_0047-4800_1995_num_100_4_238.

Rusk, Lauren. 2002. 'The Refusal of Otherness: Winterson's *Oranges Are Not the Only Fruit*.' In *The Life Writing of Otherness: Woolf, Baldwin, Kingston, and Winterson*. New York: Routledge, pp. 105–132. Available from ProQuest Ebook Central (17 April 2020).

Sacks, Sam. 2017. 'Sam Sacks on the Best New Fiction; Rachel Cusk's "Transit" Captures the Feelings of Agitation and Powerlessness that Come with Change'. *Wall Street Journal* (Online), 13 January 2017.

Sala, Michael. 2018. 'Knausgaard's *My Struggle*: The Interplay of Authority, Structure, and Style in Autobiographical Writing', *Life Writing* 15, no. 2: 157–170. DOI: 10.1080/14484528.2016.118798.

Sattin, Anthony. 2021. 'Inventory of a Life Mislaid: An Unreliable Memoir by Marina Warner – review'. *The Spectator*, London (24 April 2021). https://search-proquest-com.libezproxy.open.ac.uk/docview/2516085420?https://search_proquest_com/pq1lit=&pq-origsite=primo (accessed 4 May 2021).

Schmitt, Arnaud. 2020. 'Avatars as the Raison d'Être of Autofiction'. In *Life Writing*, 27 April 2020. DOI: 10.1080/14484528.2020.1753486. https://www.tandfonline.com/doi/full/10.1080/14484528.2020.1753486 (accessed 23 July 2020).

Schmitt, Arnaud & Stefan Kjerkegaard. 2016. 'Karl Ove Knausgaard's *My Struggle*: A Real Life in a Novel'. *a/b: Auto/biography Studies* 31, no. 3: 553–579 http://dx.doi.org/10.1080/08989575.2016.118454.

Schwartz, Alexandra. 2018. 'I Don't Think Character Exists Anymore': A Conversation with Rachel Cusk. *The New Yorker*, 18 November 2018. https://www.newyorker.com/culture/the-new-yorker-interview/i-dont-think-character-exists-anymore-a-conversation-with-rachel-cusk.

Semeiks, Jonna G. 2012. 'My Struggle: Book One'. *Confrontation* Fall 2012: 233–236. ProQuest. Web. 23 August 2021.

Shattuck, Roger. 2001. 'Lost and Found: The Structure of Proust's Novel'. In *The Cambridge Companion to Proust*, Cambridge Companions to Literature, chapter, edited by Richard Bales, 74–84. Cambridge, Cambridge University Press.

Shea, Hannah. 2020. *Ploughshares Book Review*, 9 October 2020. https://blog.pshares.org/a-lovers-discourse-by-xiaolu-guo/ (accessed 4 November 2022).

Shields, David. 2011. *Reality Hunger*. London and New York: Penguin Books.

Shi, Flair Donglai. 2021. 'Reborn Translated: Xiaolu Guo as a World Author'. *Kritika Kultura* 36 (2021): 166–194.

Smith, Zadie. 2008. 'Two Paths for the Novel'. *The New York Review of Books* 55, no. 18: 89. https://www-nybooks-com.libezproxy.open.ac.uk/articles/2008/11/20/two-paths-for-the-novel/ (accessed 26 July 2021).

Spaeth, Ryu. 'The World Beyond Knausgaard'. *The New Republic*, 25 September 2018.

Srikanth, Siddharth. 2019. 'Fictionality and Autofiction'. In *Style* 53, no. 3: 344–363 (accessed 9 April 2021).

Streeter, Ben. 'Karl Ove Knausgaard: Literary Celebrity'. *The Honest Ulsterman*, October 2018. Available online at: https://humag.co/features/karl-ove-knausgaard (accessed 24 September 2021).

Sullivan, Eric. 2017. 'Karl Ove Knausgaard: Three Books that changed my life'. *Esquire*, 25 August 2017. https://www.esquire.com/entertainment/books/a56608/karl-ove-knausgaard-books-that-changed-my-life/.

Tew, Philip. 2001. '(Re)-acknowledging B.S. Johnson's Radical Realism, or Re-publishing *The Unfortunates*'. *Critical Survey* (Oxford, England) 13, no. 1: 37–61. DOI: 10.3167/001115701782483589.

Thomas-Corr, Johanna. 2021. 'Rachel Cusk and the Art of the Midlife Crisis'. *The New Statesman*, 5 May 2021. https://www.newstatesman.com/culture/books/2021/05/rachel-cusk-second-place-review (accessed 10 November 2021).

Turner, Barnard. 2011. Karl Ove Knaugaard's *Min Kamp*, vol. 6, A Commentary. http://www.academia.edu/11064383/Karl_Ove_Knausgaard_My_Struggle_Min_Kamp_Book_6_Karl_Ove_Knausg%C3%A5rd_Min_kamp_sjette_bok_An_introduction.

Valihora, Karen. 2019. 'She Got Up and Went Away: Rachel Cusk on Making an Exit', *ESC* 45, no. 1–2 (March/June 2019): 19–35.

Vilain, Philippe. 2010. 'Démon de la définition'. In *Autofiction(s)*, edited by Claude Burgelin, Isabelle Grell and Roger-Yves Roche, 461–482. Lyon: Presses universitaires de Lyon.

Wagner-Egelhaaf, Martina. 2022. 'Of Strange Loops and Real Effects: Five Theses on Autofiction/the Autofictional'. In *The Autofictional: Approaches, Affordances, Forms*, edited by Alexandra Effe and Hannie Lawlor, 21–39. London: Palgrave Macmillan.

Walsh, Megan. 2017. 'Rock in a Hard Place'. *The New Statesman* 146, no. 5351 (27 January to 2 February 2017): 51.

Walezak, Emilie. 2018. 'The Fictional Avatars of Mrs W: The Influence of the Adoptive Mother and the Birth of Jeanette Winterson as a Writer.' *Prague Journal of English Studies* 7, no. 1 (2018): 123–139.

Wang, Shouren. 2021. 'Introduction: Realism in the Post-truth Era'. *Orbis Litterarum* 76, no. 4: 155–157. https://onlinelibrary-wiley-com.libezproxy.open.ac.uk/doi/10.1111/oli.12301 (6 September 2022).

Ward, Wendy. 2011. 'Does Autobiography Matter?: Fictions of the Self in Aleksandar Hemon's The Lazarus Project'. *Brno Studies in English* 37, no. 2: 185–199.

Warner, Marina. 2021. *Inventory of a Life Mislaid: An Unreliable Memoir*. London: William Collins.

Warner, Marina. 2012. 'Report from the Memoir Club: Scenes from a Colonial Childhood'. In *Contradictory Woolf*, edited by D. Ryan and S. Bolaki, 57–65. Oxford: Liverpool University Press. Available from ProQuest Ebook Central (4 May 2021).

Watt, Ian. 1963. *The Rise of the Novel: Studies in Defoe, Richardson, and Fielding*. Harmondsworth: Penguin.

Wilson, Frances. 2021. 'Monsieur Plum and Mother Rat'. *Literary Review* 21 March 2021. Reproduced on Marina Warner's website: https://www.marinawarner.com/publications/recently-published/.

Winterson, Jeanette. 2014. *Oranges Are Not the Only Fruit*. London: Vintage Books.

Winterson, Jeanette. 2012. *Why Be Happy When You Could Be Normal?*. London: Vintage Books. https://www.penguin.co.uk/books/411404/why-be-happy-when-you-could-be-normal-by-jeanette-winterson/9780099556091.

Winterson, Jeanette. 2001 [1989]. *Sexing the Cherry*. London: Vintage.

Winterson, Jeanette. 1995. *Art Objects: Essays on Ecstasy and Effrontery*. London: Jonathan Cape.

Winterson, Jeanette. 1994. *Art and Lies*. London: Jonathan Cape.

Winterson, Jeanette. 1991. *Oranges Are Not the Only Fruit*. London: Vintage Books.

Wood, James. 2012. 'Total Recall'. *The New Yorker* 88, no. 24 (New York; 13–20 August 2012): 88. https://www.proquest.com/docview/1034376006?accountid=14697&parentSessionId=3W%2BgHWNn3VVlCvDV0oGOv2H04vlj30wzGW%2FVBjSpA5A%3D.

Wood, James & Karl Ove Knausgaard. 2014. 'Writing My Struggle: An Exchange'. *The Paris Review*, Winter 2014, no. 211. https://www.theparisreview.org/miscellaneous/6345/writing-my-struggle-an-exchange-james-wood-karl-ove-knausgaard.

World Book Club with Harriet Gilbert. BBC World Service, 1 August 2015. On *Oranges Are Not the Only Fruit* with Jeanette Winterson (first broadcast in 2012). https://www.bbc.co.uk/sounds/play/p02y0dj0.

Worthington, Marjorie. 2017. 'Fiction in the "Post-Truth" Era: The Ironic Effects of Autofiction'. In *Critique: Studies in Contemporary Fiction* 58, no. 5: 471–483.

Wu, Cheng'en. 2005. *Journey to the West*, translated by Arthur Whaley. London: Penguin Classics.

Wurmser, Léon. 2015. 'Primary Shame, Mortal Wound and Tragic Circularity: Some New Reflections on Shame and Shame Conflicts.' *International Journal of Psychoanalysis* 96, no. 6: 1615–1634.

Zetterberg Gjerlevsen, Simona. 2016. 'A Novel History of Fictionality'. *Narrative* 24, no. 2: 174–189. https://www.jstor.org/stable/26405328.

INDEX

Aitken, Martin 42
Andersen, Claus Elholm 9
Anglophone 39
Auerbach, Erich 6
authenticity 8, 13, 15, 54, 153
autobiographical contract 101
autobiographical enquiry 37
autobiography 30, 55
   factually-oriented 28
   fictional 30
   non-fictional 30
autofiction vii, 14, 25–30, 35, 36, 39, 43, 97, 98, 119, 130, 141, 146, 148, 152, 153
autofictional vii, 14–16, 20, 27, 28, 37–39, 41, 44, 141, 151, 153

Backus, Margot Gayle 75
Bal, Mieke 92
Barthes, Roland 102, 111, 116–118, 149
BBC Radio 4
   Front Row 102, 103
Beijing 113
Beijing Film Academy 103, 109, 113
Bildungsroman 116, 117
Bloom, Myra 26
Boxall, Peter
   The Value of the Novel 1
Buddhist monk 112

Carter, Cindy M. 107
Célestin, Roger 28
Cervantes, Miguel de
   Don Quixote 5
chengzhang xiaoshuo 116
China 4, 17, 40
Christ 85
Clark, Alex 119
Coetzee, J.M.
   Summertime 36
critical interrogation 27
cross-cultural communication 17
Cultural Revolution 103, 106
Cusk, Rachel 3, 4, 6, 9–12, 19, 43, 44
   Aftermath 10, 11, 125–129, 141, 142, 145, 146, 148
   Diacritik 133
   Kudos 10, 129, 143, 144
   A Life's Work: On Becoming A Mother 9, 10, 11, 125, 127
   Literature Compass 132
   The New Statesman 128
   Outline 10, 129, 130, 134, 138
   Second Place 125, 128, 154, 155
   Transit 10, 129, 138–140, 143, 144
   trilogy 133
Cusset, Catherine 36

Defoe, Daniel
   Robinson Crusoe 5
Deresiewicz, William 9
Dog Woman 109
Doppelgänger 121
Doubrovsky, Serge
   Fils 26, 29
Dunmore, Helen 139
Duras, Marguerite 112, 116, 149

Edemariam, Aida 119
Egelhaaf, Martina Wagner viii
Eileen Chang 116
Ellis, Brett Easton
   Lunar Park 93
Emin, Tracey 128
England vii, 17, 131, 135
Eugenides, Jeffrey 43
existential enquiry 37, 150, 151

fact 5, 32, 41, 93
Feigel, Lara 145
fiction viii, 1–8, 10–12, 14, 15, 18, 20, 23, 24, 27, 32, 33, 40, 41, 67, 69, 72, 89, 90, 93, 101, 107, 127
  autobiographical 28, 35, 55, 81
  semi-autobiographical 17, 77, 117, 148
Forlaget Oktober 42
France vii, 14
Frank, Joseph 21

Garrido Sánchez, Violeta 65, 66
Gasparini, Philippe 29
George, Rose
  The Spectator 101
Glancy, Josh 67
Gulliksen, Geir 42
Guo, Xiaolu 4, 5, 12, 15, 19, 40
  autofictional narratives 119–121
  A Concise Chinese-English Dictionary for Lovers 117, 118
  The Guardian 44, 102, 103
  I Am China 108, 109
  A Lover's Discourse 102, 116–119, 149, 151
  Once Upon a Time in the East 4, 17, 72, 92, 101–108, 110–112, 114, 116, 122
  Twenty Fragments of a Ravenous Youth 114
  Village of Stone 107

Ha Jin 116
Hemon, Aleksandar 121
Hildegarde 34
Hoffman, Eva
  Lost in Translation 112
homonymy 35

identity 7, 15, 17, 29, 31, 35, 62, 80, 85, 92–94, 98, 110–112, 118, 119, 121, 122, 133, 139
imaginary personae 32
inter-personal communication 17
intertextuality 112
Isaacs, Jeremy
  The Late Show 76

Jahn, Manfred 94
Jordan 109
Joyce, James
  A Portrait of the Artist as a Young Man 48, 112

Kindertransport 135
Kingston, Maxine Hong
  The Woman Warrior: Memoirs of a Girlhood Among Ghosts 31
Kjerkegaard, Stefan 23
Knausgaard, Karl Ove 3, 4, 6–12, 19
  Boyhood Island. My Struggle: Book 3, 60, 63–65
  A Death in the Family. My Struggle: Book 1 viii, 30, 42, 46, 49, 52, 56, 67, 147
  The End. My Struggle: Book 6 37
  A Man in Love. My Struggle: Book 2 57, 59
  Min Kamp (*My Struggle*) 7–9, 11, 25, 26, 30, 37, 41–44, 46, 48, 49, 51, 53, 56, 57, 60, 61, 65–69, 146–148, 150, 151, 154
  Morgenstjernen 68
  The Morning Star 24, 68, 69, 154, 155
knowledge 9, 15, 28, 34, 38, 47, 52, 53, 60, 117
  cultural 115
  linguistic 115
Kunzru, Hari 8

Lanser, Susan S. 31, 32, 68
Lawrence, D. H. 137, 139, 144
  "The Wintry Peacock" 136
Lejeune, Philippe 55
Lerner, Ben 7, 9, 45
  The London Review of Books 24
Levine, Caroline 21, 22
Levy, Deborah 120
  Real Estate 120, 121
Lim, Natalie 106
Lim, Shirley Geok-lin 121, 122
Lockwood, Patricia 134
London 114, 127, 131
Luhan, Mabel Dodge
  Lorenzo in Taos 154
Lukács, Georg 6, 20

Maftei, Micaela 81
  The Fiction of Autobiography: Reading and Writing Identity 80
Magnússon, Gísli 26
Mah, Adeline Yen
  Falling Leaves 104
Mazzoni, Guido 6

McKenna, Emma 74
memory 7, 28, 37, 53, 62–68, 81, 89, 106, 107, 119, 122, 147
mere fiction 90, 150, 151
metanarrativity 151
Morrison, Blake 45

Naipaul, V.S.
  The Enigma of Arrival 36
narrative(s)
  auto/biographical 2, 13
  autofictional 13, 18, 26, 46, 122
  construction 77, 81
  contemporary 14
  conventional 3
  cross-cultural 104
  documentary 66
  fabrication 4, 16
  fiction/fictional 2, 23, 121
  first-person 35, 80, 91, 114, 129
  invention 4
  non-fictional 121
  persona 94, 120
  voice 77
Nine Continents 105
non-fiction 2, 10, 15, 26, 36, 69, 101, 127
non-fictional novel 37
non-fictional turn 2
Northern Norway 47
Norway 7, 9, 16, 22, 25, 37, 42, 55, 61

Oates, Joyce Carol 73
Old Testament God 86
"Outline" trilogy viii, 9, 11, 16, 38, 39, 127–129, 146, 147, 151, 152

philosophical enquiry 24, 127, 150, 151, 155
philosophical reflection 150
Power, Chris 37
  The New Statesman 37
Preda, Alina 95
pure fiction 38, 41

Qingming Festival 108

radical vii, 18, 21
radical inclusiveness 7
realism vii, 5, 18, 20
  aesthetic 21
  lyrical 6
  radical 3, 6, 7, 21, 22, 68, 147, 150
reality 2, 6, 37, 43, 44, 54, 63, 65, 66, 68, 76, 83, 88, 90, 93, 102, 106, 117, 126, 133, 135, 145, 146, 149, 150, 152, 153, 155
representation 2, 3, 8, 21, 29, 34, 37, 55, 60, 66, 68, 147, 155
  fictional 128
  modes of 133
  narrative 40
  politics of 95
  semi-fictional 77
  virtual 1
Rosen, Elisheva 29
Rusk, Lauren 76, 78
  The Life Writing of Otherness: Woolf, Baldwin, Kingston, and Winterson 76

Sacks, Sam
  Wall Street Journal 140
Sala, Michael 54
Scandinavia 42, 68
Schmitt, Arnaud 23, 97, 98
Sebald, W.G.
  Austerlitz 130, 135
  The Rings of Saturn 24
self-knowledge 14, 28, 122
self-reflexive/self-reflexivity 3, 54, 120, 151
Shattuck, Roger 29
Shelley, Mary
  Frankenstein 13
Shields, David
  'reality hunger' viii
sincerity 15, 33, 54, 153
singularity 81
Smith, Zadie viii, 9, 43
  'Two Paths for the Novel' 6
social media 1, 18
speculative reflection 150
Srikanth, Siddharth 36
Su Tong 116
Sweden 48

Tew, Philip 23
  The Unfortunates. Critical Survey 22
The New Yorker 10, 31, 44
Tromøya 61, 63
Tromøya Church 65
truth 2, 5, 6, 8, 11–15, 20, 27, 30, 34, 37, 38, 40, 44, 54–56, 87, 89, 115, 119, 121, 126, 133, 139, 140, 143, 152, 155
truth-telling 10, 38, 81
Turner, Barnard 55

uncertainty 1, 36, 54, 62, 63, 74, 98

Valihora, Karen 39
Vilain, Philippe 27, 40
Virgin Mary 85

Wagner-Egelhaaf, Martina 27, 28
Walezak, Emilie 98
Walsh, Megan
  The New Statesman 101
Warner, Deborah 74
Warner, Marina
  Inventory of a Life Mislaid: An Unreliable Memoir 32
Watt, Ian 6, 20

Wilson, Frances 35
Winterson, Jeanette 4, 12, 13, 19, 24
  Art and Lies 96
  Art Objects: Essays on Ecstasy and Effrontery 95, 149
  Jane Eyre 76
  Oranges Are Not the Only Fruit 12, 13, 16, 35, 71–80, 82, 85–90, 92–99, 108, 121, 148, 150
  Sexing the Cherry 97–99, 109, 150
  Why Be Happy When You Could Be Normal? 13, 16, 35, 71–75, 77, 78, 86–88, 90, 93–95, 97–99, 101, 108, 121
Wood, James 9
Woolf, Virginia 4, 23, 35, 76, 81
Worthington, Marjorie
  'Fiction in the "Post-Truth" Era: The Ironic Effects of Autofiction' 141
Wu, Cheng'en
  Journey to the West 105, 106, 112–116
Wurmser, Léon 59

Zeitgeist 5, 37, 120, 155
Zetterberg Gjerlevsen, Simona 24, 25

www.ingramcontent.com/pod-product-compliance
Lightning Source LLC
Chambersburg PA
CBHW021143230426
43667CB00005B/230